Illusions of Progress

DDR-Studien/East German Studies

Richard A. Zipser
General Editor

Karl-Heinz Schoeps
Associate Editor

Vol. 13

PETER LANG
New York · Washington, D.C./Baltimore · Boston · Bern
Frankfurt am Main · Berlin · Brussels · Vienna · Oxford

Brigitte Rossbacher

Illusions of Progress

Christa Wolf and the Critique of Science in GDR Women's Literature

PETER LANG
New York · Washington, D.C./Baltimore · Boston · Bern
Frankfurt am Main · Berlin · Brussels · Vienna · Oxford

Library of Congress Cataloging-in-Publication Data

Rossbacher, Brigitte.
Illusions of progress: Christa Wolf and the critique of science
in GDR women's literature / Brigitte Rossbacher.
p. cm. — (DDR-Studien/East German studies; vol. 13)
Includes bibliographical references.
1. Wolf, Christa—Criticism and interpretation. 2. Science in
literature. 3. Literature and science—Germany (East). 4. German
literature—Women authors—History and criticism. 5. German
literature—Germany (East)—History and criticism. I. Title.
II. Series: East German studies; vol. 13.
PT2685.O36Z87   833'.914—dc21   99-037420
ISBN 0-8204-4471-5
ISSN 0882-7045

Die Deutsche Bibliothek-CIP-Einheitsaufnahme

Rossbacher, Brigitte:
Illusions of progress: Christa Wolf and the critique of science
in GDR women's literature / Brigitte Rossbacher.
–New York; Washington, D.C./Baltimore; Boston; Bern;
Frankfurt am Main; Berlin; Brussels; Vienna; Oxford: Lang.
(DDR-Studien; Vol. 13)
ISBN 0-8204-4471-5

The paper in this book meets the guidelines for permanence and durability
of the Committee on Production Guidelines for Book Longevity
of the Council of Library Resources.

© 2000 Peter Lang Publishing, Inc., New York

Printed in the United States of America

CONTENTS

ACKNOWLEDGMENTS

This book grew out of my dissertation, "Gender, Science, Technology: The 'Dialectic of Enlightenment' in GDR Women's Literature" (1992), written in the Department of German and Russian at the University of California at Davis. Its genesis thus precedes the dramatic collapse of the GDR. In the last decade, rapid political transformations have reshaped Germany's literary landscape in fundamental ways. To work on GDR literature at a time when the country itself became historical has meant to read and reread, to challenge previous assumptions, and to be surprised time and again by the vicissitudes of history and individual stories.

Preliminary research in Germany during the summer of 1990 was funded in part by a Graduate Research Award from the University of California at Davis. Two Faculty Research Grants from Washington University helped to finance research at the Deutsches Literaturarchiv in Marbach.

Parts of chapter five of the present work appeared in a different version in my article "The Status of State and Subject: Reading Monika Maron from *Flugasche* to *Animal Triste*," *Wendezeiten/Zeitenwenden. Posistionsbestimmungen zur deutschsprachigen Literatur 1945*–1995, edited by Robert Weninger and Brigitte Rossbacher (Tübingen: Stauffenburg, 1997) 193–214. I would like to thank Brigitte Narr for granting permission to reprint sections of the article.

I would like to acknowledge the assistance of the editors and production managers at Peter Lang Publishing, specifically Dr. Richard Zipser, Dr. Karl-Heinz Schoeps, Heidi Burns, Benjamin Hallman and Bernadette Alfaro.

In every phase of this project Dr. Anna K. Kuhn has been a superb mentor, mindful reader and valued friend. Colleagues at Washington University, foremost Lynne Tatlock and Robert Weninger, provided useful feedback on the manuscript. I owe thanks to Alyssa Lonner and Sarah McGaughey for their careful proofreading. Finally, I would like to express my sincere gratitude to my family and other friends for their support while I worked on this project. Among others, Friederike Emonds, Christa Johnson, Claire Baldwin, Susan Rava, Lisa Hock, Angela Gulielmetti, David Byrd and, last but not least, Charles Byrd, have provided encouragement, spirited friendship, and vital diversions.

ABBREVIATIONS

DA   *Dialektik der Aufklärung*
DiA1   *Die Dimension des Autors. Essays und Aufsätze, Reden und Gespräche 1959–1985.* Vol. 1
DiA2   *Die Dimension des Autors. Essays und Aufsätze, Reden und Gespräche 1959–1985.* Vol. 2
ES   *Ein sehr exakter Schein. Satiren und Geschichten aus dem Gebiet der Wissenschaften*
FA   *Flugasche*
GH   *Der geteilte Himmel*
K   *Kassandra*
KON   *Kein Ort. Nirgends*
LS   *Lesen und Schreiben. Neue Sammlung. Essays, Aufsätze, Reden*
MN   *Moskauer Novelle*
MT   *Meine ungehörigen Träume*
N   *Nachdenken über Christa T.*
NL   "Neue Lebensansichten eines Katers"
RU   *Respektoser Umgang*
S   *Störfall. Nachrichten eines Tages*
SV   "Selbstversuch"
ÜB   *Die Überläuferin*
UB   *Ungelegener Befund*
UdL   "Unter den Linden"
VK   *Voraussetzungen einer Erzählung. Kassandra*
WB   *Was bleibt*

INTRODUCTION

In his classic essay "The Two Cultures and the Scientific Revolution" (1959), C. P. Snow expressed the relationship of science and literature in terms of "two cultures" with distinct languages and worldviews. Snow, a novelist, essayist and established physicist, lamented the split of Western intellectuals into two polar groups: on the one side the scientists, on the other those engaged in literature, the self-proclaimed "intellectuals." Of these two groups Snow stated: "The non-scientists have a rooted impression that the scientists are shallowly optimistic, unaware of man's condition. On the other hand, the scientists believe that the literary intellectuals are totally lacking in foresight, peculiarly unconcerned with their brother men, in a deep sense anti-intellectual, anxious to restrict both art and thought to the existential moment."[1] Snow's "two cultures" thesis, formulated at a time when the horrors of the Second World War, nuclear proliferation and Cold War politics exacerbated fears of humankind's self-destruction, continues to find great resonance among the scientific community and its self-styled critics. While we may be quick to discredit his crass polarization of scientists and humanists, Snow sought to bridge the cultural divide between them. Pointing to the grave consequences brought by technology, he sought to convey the vital importance of communication for averting potential disasters and "fulfilling—what is waiting as a challenge to our conscience and goodwill—a definable social hope."[2]

In recent decades, writers and scholars have examined the interplay of scientific and literary discourses from a myriad of perspectives, ranging from inquiries into literature's relationship to medicine and natural history to examinations of specific aesthetic techniques such as the literary appropriation of scientific metaphors.[3] Stressing the encroachment of science onto all social and cultural realms, Teresa de Lauretis, Andreas Huyssen and Kathleen Woodward argue in *The Technological Imagination*, "that the pervasive technologization of everyday life [...] has shaped and transformed all cultural processes from the ways in which we communicate with each other to the ways in which we perceive ourselves and the world. Values, beliefs, and attitudes—both personal and social—are inextricably bound up with technical developments."[4]

Framed by post-Wall cultural debates, this study probes the enmeshment of the literary and scientific in women's prose of the former German Democratic Republic (GDR). It explores the relationship between the critique of scientific-technological progress and issues of gender as expressed in the works of Christa Wolf (1929–), widely considered the GDR's most prominent living author.

Through a diachronic examination of gender and science from Wolf's *Moskauer Novelle* (1961) to *Störfall* (1987), I map Wolf's transition from an early conformity to orthodox Marxism and its reliance on science/reason as the primary vehicle for political emancipation to her broad-based critique of this ideology of progress. This chronological organization embeds Wolf's texts culturally and positions them within broader discursive frameworks. I expand my perspective by reading Wolf's later works with and against thematically related narratives by Monika Maron (1941–) and Helga Königsdorf (1936–). These writers exhibit a wide range of political and aesthetic positions and, like Wolf, view the potentially destructive and dehumanizing character of modern science and technology through the lens of gender.

The cultural pessimism of Wolf, Maron and Königsdorf resonates with the critique of enlightenment articulated by Max Horkheimer and Theodor Adorno in *Dialektik der Aufklärung* (1947/1969). As Wolfgang Emmerich argues, the shift towards a critique of progress in GDR literature of the late 1970s and 1980s in many ways parallels the dialectic of enlightenment theorized by Horkheimer and Adorno in the 1940s. For these Frankfurt School critics, the rise of Stalinism after the Russian revolution, the ineffectiveness of left-wing workers' movements in Western Europe in the 1930s, and the spread of fascism and its atrocities exposed the fundamental inadequacy of orthodox Marxism to account for twentieth-century developments.[5] The GDR of the late 1970s, marked by disillusionment with Stalinist socialism, the irrationality of nuclear proliferation, environmental degradation, and the 1986 nuclear disaster at Chernobyl, presents an analogous paradigm that ultimately found expression in that country's critical literature. The authors discussed here, while they censure the privileged status of science within orthodox Marxism, also reflect the widespread cultural pessimism in the West and fundamental moral and ethical issues.

While Wolf, Königsdorf and Maron articulate central theses of the Frankfurt School, they go further in illuminating how the course of Western civilization is inflected by gender. From a feminist perspective, they represent the gender inequity that informs such seemingly neutral categories as science, reason, autonomy and emancipation, and show how gender interacts with and affects the production of knowledge. In addition to these thematic similarities, all three writers employ aesthetic techniques such as dreams, fantasy and myth to subvert the realist paradigm and rational discourse, creating an aesthetic realm that allows for the (free) play of possibilities for social change.

Numerous feminist scholars have noted the enmeshment of gender, science and epistemology in Wolf's oeuvre, most notably Anna Kuhn, *Christa Wolf's Utopian Vision: From Marxism to Feminism* (1988), Therese Hörnigk, *Christa Wolf* (1989), Myra Love, *Christa Wolf: Literature and the Conscience of History* (1991), Patricia Herminghouse, "Phantasie oder Fanatismus? Zur feministischen Wissenschaftskritik in der Literatur der DDR" (1992), and

Robert Sayre and Michael Löwy, "Romanticism as a Feminist Vision: The Quest of Christa Wolf" (1995). However, none of the book-length studies shares my specific focus or reads the theme of gender and science in Wolf's works in relation to other GDR women writers. Two recent studies call attention to the extensive critique of progress and modernity in German literature of the 1980s, Joseph Federico's *Confronting Modernity. Rationality, Science and Communication in German Literature of the 1980s* (1992) and Michael Schenkel's *Fortschritts- und Modernitätskritik in der DDR-Literatur. Prosatexte der achtziger Jahre* (1995). While Federico similarly examines literary representations of science within a German context, his study excludes texts from the GDR as well as issues of gender. Schenkel, by contrast, offers a detailed analysis of the critique of progress and modernity in GDR literature; it is not his purpose, however, to view this critique through the lens of gender.

The first chapter, "Collaboration and Critique: GDR Writers and the State," situates *Illusions of Progress* within the fundamental reassessment of GDR literature that followed that country's collapse. The officially prescribed role of literature was to support and further socialist development, a role regulated through censorship and other government-implemented controls. Yet the literary realm also constituted one of the few domains of the public sphere in which societal conflicts and contradictions could be voiced. The resulting double bind of collaboration and critique characterizes GDR literary production of the 1970s and 1980s, years in which the glaring disparity between the dream and reality of socialism became apparent. At the time of the GDR's demise, Christa Wolf was among those writers who expressed hope in forging a so-called "third way" divergent from Stalinist socialism *and* Western capitalism. This continued and expressed belief in at last developing "socialism with a human face" found little resonance among GDR citizens who, lacking the privileges of travel, hard currency, and status garnered by some established writers, were understandably weary of participating in any renewed socialist experiment. Many writers previously viewed as allied with the populace (their readers) consequently appeared to be affiliated more closely with the defunct regime—even though "real existing" socialism had little in common with the utopian socialist ideals to which those writers again appealed.

In East and West, Christa Wolf's reception both during and after the Cold War reflects ideological battles that have tended to appropriate author and text to satisfy specific political and cultural agendas. It thus comes as no surprise that the reassessment of GDR intellectuals and their literary works targeted Christa Wolf, whose ill-timed publication of *Was bleibt* in June 1990 ushered in critical debates that recast Wolf in the public eye as a "state poet" ("*Staatsdichterin*") and collaborator with the repressive regime. These debates, engaged in primarily by West German critics whose agendas extended far beyond their views of Wolf, also fostered a reexamination of literary critiques of scientific-technological progress. Richard Herzinger and Heinz-Peter Preußer assert, for example, that the *Zivilisationskritik* expressed by GDR writers was directed primarily at Western capitalism and thus functioned to exculpate the GDR and uphold the status quo.[6] They contend that values such as the "sisterliness" Wolf advocates could only be cultivated in the GDR, where modernization occurred less efficiently and consequently less rapidly than in the West. From this perspective, underdevelopment comes to represent a distinct advantage for the strengthening of "feminine" values, and the critique of progress appears further to legitimize the communist regime. Allying GDR critiques of modernity (and of the *Dialektik der Aufklärung*) with a German *Zivilisationskritik* that romanticized pre-modern, pre-scientific times and found its expression in fascism, Herzinger and Preußer perpetuate the opposition between "liberal" and "conservative" that marks all recourses to Romanticism as regressive. In so doing, they preclude the progressiveness of any revolutionary utopian vision, of any subversive *Zivilisationskritik* such as that expressed by Wolf, Maron, Königsdorf and much of feminism. In contrast to Herzinger and Preußer, I argue that these writers seek to integrate those "feminine" values that have been repressed and devalued in the process of enlightenment since in their view the masculine line of one-dimensional thought has led society to the brink of destruction. Far from depicting the GDR as a country in which "sisterly" values flourish, their critiques of enlightenment explicitly point to the GDR's convergence with the capitalist West.

In Chapter 2, "Science and the 'Dialectic of Enlightenment,'" I continue to lay the theoretical groundwork for the subsequent chapters of literary analysis. I begin by delineating the preeminent status of science within orthodox Marxism. As encapsulated in the term "scientific-technological revolution" (STR), the GDR posited science and technology as revolutionary forces that would unequivocally bring about Marx's vision of a truly human society. Official ideology attributed all negative consequences of progress to advanced capitalism, where the STR was seen further to subordinate man to machine. A rejection of this mechanistic worldview comprises one of the central tenets of the critical Marxism of Horkheimer and Adorno, who consider why society, rather than progressing toward a "truly human condition," has regressed to a new type of barbarism. They argue that the concepts of progress and reason (as an instrument of domination) advanced in the Enlightenment contain within themselves the seeds of their own destruction. This recognition leads these Frankfurt School critics to underscore the need for reflexivity, for a "dialectic" of enlightenment.

In the preface to the 1969 edition of *Dialektik der Aufklärung*, Horkheimer and Adorno explicitly subsume the development of socialism within the Enlightenment tradition and its positivist legacy: lacking reflexivity, socialism had become a reified theory divorced from praxis. By examining the GDR's official, party-line reception of *Dialektik der Aufklärung* in the 1970s, I show how the Frankfurt School's "modern" Marxism was discredited as a "third way" since it drew attention to the discrepancies between Marxism's emancipatory aims and its Stalinist manifestations. The shift to a practical reassessment of Critical Theory in the late 1980s illuminates the growing recognition of the gross inadequacies of "real existing socialism" as well as the influence of *glasnost*. Predating this reappraisal by approximately twenty years is the positive literary reception of the Frankfurt School.

The orthodoxy of Wolf's early texts offers a point of contrast for her emerging opposition. *Moskauer Novelle* (1961), Wolf's first literary work, reflects her fervent commitment to socialist ideals at that time and her conviction that literature plays a central role in realizing these ideals. The writing and publication of *Moskauer Novelle* falls within the period in which Wolf, as came to light in 1993, collaborated with the *Stasi* (1959–1962). Though not surprising within the context of Wolf's early dogmatism, revelations of this collaboration further fueled the raging debate about Wolf's status vis-à-vis the regime. Wolf's disenchantment with GDR cultural politics was already apparent in her contribution to the II. Bitterfelder Konferenz (1964), and her confidence was further shaken by the events at the 11. Plenum of the Central Committee of the SED in 1965. At least up to that time, however, she remained a "faithful comrade." In *Moskauer Novelle*, Wolf adheres closely to the normative aesthetic of Socialist Realism and its demand for the "objective" mirroring of reality, positive, typical heroes, and a clear didactic message. A mere two years later in *Der geteilte Himmel* (1963), she calls this idealized representation into question. Particularly through the character of Manfred, a scientist, pragmatist and skeptical outsider of Wolf's generation, her apprehensions regarding the GDR's mechanistic view of progress emerge.

Chapter 3, "Gender and the 'Dialectic of Enlightenment,'" centers on how GDR writers express the dialectic of enlightenment in gendered terms. I first sketch the divergent development of women's literature in West and East Germany, focusing on the relation of women's literary production to feminism. Since orthodox Marxism subordinates questions of gender to those of class, reducing the "woman question" to the economic aspect of women's integration into the realm of production, it is important to point out that the description of GDR women writers as "feminists" often counters their self-descriptions as Marxists. Despite their trenchant critiques of patriarchy, the writers I discuss distance themselves from those branches of Western feminism that disregard the socio-historic contexts that produce gender differences. Yet they also show how an exclusive focus on the productive realm excludes many dimensions of women's experience. Not only do they censure the privileged status of the realm of production, but also the valorization of the "masculine" values of reason, objectivity and rationalism attributed to it over the "feminine" values of caring, subjectivity and sensitivity associated with the realm of reproduction.

In *The Man of Reason*, philosopher Genevieve Lloyd convincingly argues that the "maleness" of reason represents much more than a simple metaphor, as the symbolic content of maleness and femaleness interacts with socially constructed gender to have very real effects. In *Dialektik der Aufklärung*, for example, Horkheimer and Adorno illuminate that reason as an instrument of domination functions through man's suppression and mastery of myth, nature, magic, the body and woman—all elements of the symbolic feminine. Grounded in the Western philosophical tradition which, steeped in sexual metaphor, defines reason symbolically through its "maleness" and consequently constitutes the "feminine" through exclusion, Horkheimer and Adorno cast woman as reason's Other. However, their statements on woman's position within the dialectic of enlightenment must be situated within their fundamental critique of patriarchal society and the domination of nature—of precisely those mechanisms that have led to the domination of woman, nature, and ultimately, of man himself. Accentuating symbolic and structural gender ("woman") rather than individual gender (attributed to specific "women"), they ground woman's subjugation in the gendered division of human activity attributed to biological difference, as do feminist standpoint theorists such as Nancy Hartsock and Sandra Harding. Unlike their Frankfurt School counterparts, however, feminist standpoint theorists articulate their theory from the perspective of women's lives, contending that the sexual division of labor affords women a unique vantage point from which to view the mechanisms of those in power and from which to effect change. Hartsock explains how feminists can use the epistemological perspective Marx attributed to the proletariat, yet broaden and enhance Marx's account to include all human activity, reproduction as well as production. This theory of marginality and vision, as well as the more multifaceted theoretical perspective of positionality, helps illuminate the interplay of gender and science in texts by Wolf, Maron, and Königsdorf.

The four chapters centering on literary texts begin with Chapter Four, "'Self-Experiments': *Nachdenken über Christa T.* and *Unter den Linden*." This chapter interprets Wolf's *Nachdenken über Christa T.* (1968) and her "improbable stories" *Unter den Linden* (1974) as reactions to the push to systematize socialist life. The new economic reforms of 1963 (NÖSPL) and growing emphasis on cybernetics accelerated the forced rationalization of all societal realms, effectively reducing the role of the individual to one of conformity and accommodation. In *Lesen und Schreiben* (1968) Wolf underscores that in a scientific age in which reality proves "more fantastic than every product of fantasy," literature's task is to represent that which lies beyond the world of fact: the world of emotions, feelings, and values. For Christa T., not science but fantasy and conscience are necessary for human progress. In a society that equates productivity solely with efficiency in the public sphere,

Wolf casts Christa T. as an "unproductive" anti-hero: rather than integrate into the realm of production and the collective, she turns inward and attempts to say "I." Wolf continues this subversion of one-dimensionality in *Unter den Linden*, a collection of three "improbable stories" that employ "unrealistic" narrative techniques to mediate and dialectically displace reified oppositions. "Neue Lebensansichten eines Katers" centers on a group of male scientists who attempt to create a cybernetic system informed by the separation of reason from human qualities they find useless and disruptive such as emotion and the "soul." Wolf also sets "Selbstversuch" in the scientific realm where objectivity dominates. Narrated from the perspective of a female scientist after she reverses her experimental sex change to again be a woman, "Selbstversuch" highlights gender construction and advocates a woman-centered ontology and epistemology.

Chapter 5 focuses on Monika Maron's novels *Flugasche* (1981) and *Die Überläuferin* (1986). Since none of Maron's literary works were granted publication in the GDR, Maron's status as a "GDR writer" differs significantly from Wolf's. Maron also represents a generation that came of age in socialist society and, unlike Wolf's generation, lacked an incipiently positive identification with the state. In *Flugasche*, Maron sounds a radical critique of literary and cultural censorship, women's continued subjugation and human instrumentalization, while she also accentuates East Germany's extreme environmental degradation. The attempts of *Flugasche*'s protagonist, the journalist Josefa Nadler, to document the environmental devastation and brutality of industrial labor are thwarted by government officials, by the majority of her colleagues, and by her own partner. Maron interweaves Josefa's efforts to offer a truthful journalistic account with Josefa's unsuccessful struggle for fulfillment and independence in her private life. Josefa's only routes of escape are dreams, fantasy, and surreal flight—"no place on Earth" is she able to transcend social restrictions and play out those desires and fantasies repressed by reason. *Die Überläuferin* begins where *Flugasche* left off, the female protagonist alone in her room and severed from all relationships. Maron's protagonist Rosalind wakes up to find herself paralyzed, a physical condition she welcomes since it allows her completely to retreat into the world of the imagination. There, in the surrealist theater of her mind, the repressed aspects of her self take center stage.

The sixth chapter, "Beyond the 'Dialectic of Enlightenment': *Kein Ort. Nirgends, Kassandra* and *Störfall*," looks at three works in which Wolf turns to the past in search for the turning points that set society on its self-destructive course. In *Kein Ort. Nirgends* (1979), Wolf parallels the transition from the historical Enlightenment to Romanticism and the reification of Marxism in her own time, revealing as empty the utopian promises of humanity, freedom and brotherliness that inform the Enlightenment and Marxist projects. *Kein Ort.*

Nirgends centers on a fictive meeting in 1804 of the early Romantic writers Karoline von Günderrode and Heinrich von Kleist. By contrasting these two marginalized figures, Wolf addresses the suppression of the "feminine" in the process of the Enlightenment. In her complementary essays on Günderrode and Bettine von Arnim, she further identifies and advocates an alternate and radical feminine/feminist epistemology based on sensuality, fantasy and humanity.

Kassandra (1983) invokes myth and matriarchy to critique the course of patriarchal Western civilization. In response to the acute global nuclear crisis of the early 1980s, *Kassandra* offers a feminist perspective on militarism and environmental destruction that reflects and responds to Western cultural feminism. Through her feminist reinterpretation of the mythological Cassandra figure and the reflections on the present offered in her accompanying lectures, Wolf creatively weaves together the threads of literary representation, techno-logical progress, utilitarian thinking, and women's subordination to reveal previously unseen patterns and connections.

Störfall. Nachrichten eines Tages (1987), a highly autobiographical work that appeared in the wake of the Chernobyl nuclear disaster, expresses Wolf's harshest critique of instrumental reason and abstract thought. In *Störfall*, Wolf opposes the everyday life of women with the world of science and scientists. She suggests that the different life experiences into which women have been socialized result in different epistemologies. This recognition leads her ultimately to question the "brotherliness" at the heart of socialist ideology. In addition, Wolf juxtaposes scientific reason with the "unscientific" powers of psychic healing and insights gained through mysticism and hand reading, asserting a feminist way of knowing that transcends reason's limiting strictures and unifies the mind and the senses.

Chapter 7, "An Insider's View on Gender and Science: Helga Königsdorf's *Respektloser Umgang* and *Ungelegener Befund*," centers on works by the GDR writer Helga Königsdorf, herself a woman in science. Like *Störfall*, *Respektloser Umgang* (1986) appeared in the wake of the Chernobyl nuclear disaster. It also relies on aesthetic techniques, most notably the fantastic, to transcend the rational world of science and expand notions of reality. From an "insider's perspective," Königsdorf addresses aspects of gender and science that both converge with and deviate from Wolf's standpoint. Similar to Wolf, Königsdorf interweaves politics and the personal, and brings subjective and ethical concerns to bear on global issues. Casting a woman scientist, the physicist Lise Meitner, as instrumental in the discovery of nuclear fission, Königsdorf dismantles the notion of a unified female perspective on or outside of science. By highlighting women's complicity, she also breaks down the traditional opposition of victims and perpetrators. Yet ultimately Königsdorf also attributes to women a particular role in changing society's course, in carrying out what she terms the "mission." In *Ungelegener Befund* (1989), Königsdorf's reweaves the themes of her earlier work within the context of *Vergangenheitsbewältigung* and highlights the repercussions of a conformist ideology.

In the conclusion I expand on the theme of gender, science and progress by casting a glance at select post-Wall texts by Wolf (*Medea. Stimmen*, 1996), Maron (*Animal triste*, 1996), and Königsdorf (*Die unverzügliche Rettung der Welt*, 1994). My focus is the extent to which the significant social and cultural changes of unification enter into these works. It appears that the toppling of the Berlin Wall and the demise of socialism have not radically altered the expression of a feminist dialectic of enlightenment. These works suggest that the "illusions of progress" continue to animate the narratives of women writers.

Notes

1 The article is a reprint of a lecture with the same name Snow held at Cambridge in 1959. C. P. Snow, "The Two Cultures and the Scientific Revolution," *Public Affairs* (New York: Charles Scribner's Sons, 1971) 15–16.

2 C. P. Snow, "The Two Cultures: A Second Look," *Public Affairs* 76. This article was first printed in 1963 in the *Times Literary Supplement*.

3 See for example Stuart Peterfreund, ed., *Literature and Science* (Boston: Northeastern University Press, 1990).

4 Teresa de Lauretis, Andreas Huyssen, Kathleen M. Woodward, ed., "Preface," *The Technological Imagination* (Milwaukee/Madison: University of Wisconsin Press, 1980) viii.

5 See in particular Wolfgang Emmerich, "'Dialektik der Aufklärung' in der jüngeren DDR-Literatur," *Die Literatur der DDR. 1976–1986. Akten der internationalen Konferenz. Pisa. Mai 1987*, ed. Anna Chiarloni, Gemma Sartori and Fabrizio Cambi (Pisa: Giardini, 1988) 407–422.

6 See Richard Herzinger and Heinz-Peter Preußer, "Vom Äußersten zum Ersten. DDR-Literatur in der Tradition deutscher Zivilisationskritik," *Text und Kritik. Literatur der DDR. Rückblicke* (München: text + kritik, 1991) 195–209. Christian Joppke draws on Herzinger and Preußer's argument to support his thesis that there was no real dissidence in East Germany. See *East German Dissidents and the Revolution in 1989. Social Movement in a Leninist Regime* (New York: New York University Press, 1995) 210–221.

CHAPTER ONE

Collaboration and Critique: GDR Writers and the State

Die enge Verbundenheit unserer Partei und der Schriftsteller und Kunstschaffenden ist ein kostbares Gut und Grundlage für die erfolgreiche Weiterentwicklung unserer sozialistischen Nationalkultur.

Erich Honecker, 1981

Seit Jahren hatte die bewußt in Opposition stehende Literatur *sich bestimmte Aufgaben gestellt: Durch Benennen von Widersprüchen, die lange Zeit nirgendwo sonst artikuliert wurden, bei ihren Lesern kritisches Bewußtsein zu erzeugen oder zu stärken, sie zum Widerstand gegen Lüge, Heuchelei und Selbstaufgabe zu ermutigen* [...] *nicht zuletzt, moralische Werte zu verteidigen, die der zynischen Demagogie der herrschenden Ideologie geopfert werden sollten.*

Christa Wolf, 1989

The juxtaposition of Erich Honecker's affirmation of literature's central role in developing and strengthening socialist national culture and Christa Wolf's insistence that literature illuminate contradictions, raise critical consciousness and counter the demagoguery of the ruling ideology lays bare the incongruity that came to characterize literature's status in the GDR. Particularly in the 1970s and 1980s, as the disparity between the utopian dream and the quotidian reality of socialism increased, literature's position in the socialist public sphere was as vital as it was precarious. For while censorship and other government-implemented controls reinforced literature's officially-sanctioned function to uphold the status quo, the realm of literature constituted one of the few arenas of the public sphere in which societal conflicts could be addressed. In this regard GDR writer Helga Königsdorf reflects: "Je schmerzhafter die Differenz zwischen Traum und Realität wurde, um so stärker die Verpflichtung, sich einzumischen. [...] Nicht allein die Ersatzfunktion, die Literatur hatte, erklärt ihre Rolle in diesem Land, sondern genau diese Verbundenheit."[1] With the GDR's demise in the fall of 1989, the role of writers in the "revolution" became a matter of public debate, which triggered a more fundamental reexamination of the relation of GDR authors and intellectuals to socialism in both its lived and utopian forms.

A quick look back at events directly preceding the GDR's collapse reveals an initial image of harmony between the writers and the populace. It bears remembering that demonstration at East Berlin's Alexanderplatz on November 4, 1989, with 500,000 participants the largest government-sanctioned demonstration in GDR history, was organized by the Writer's and Artist's Union. As Christa Wolf recounts, "Es war der Kulminations- und Höhepunkt einer Vorgeschichte, in der Literaten, Theaterleute, Friedens- und andere Gruppen unter dem Dach der Kirche miteinander in Kontakte und Gespräche gekommen waren, bei denen jeder vom anderen Impulse, Gedanken, Sprache und Ermutigung zu Aktionen erfuhr."[2] The November 4 speeches by prominent GDR authors, among them Christoph Hein, Stefan Heym, and Christa Wolf, evince the seeming contradiction of at once criticizing Stalinist socialism and upholding the idea of socialism as the only viable alternative to capitalism. Hein underscored the historical conditions that contributed to the difficult birth of GDR socialism: "Es war keine gute Chance, denn der besiegte Faschismus und der übermächtige Stalinismus waren dabei die Geburtshelfer. Es entstand eine Gesellschaft, die wenig mit Sozialismus zu tun hatte. Von Bürokratie, Demagogie, Bespitzelung, Machtmißbrauch, Entmündigung und auch Verbrechen war und ist diese Gesellschaft gezeichnet."[3] Despite his ominous depiction of the present, Hein contends that more favorable conditions would have allowed a genuinely socialist society to emerge, namely "eine Gesellschaft, die dem Menschen angemessen ist und ihn nicht der Struktur unterordnet" (73). In a similar vein, Heym draws out his vision of "Sozialismus—nicht der Stalinsche, der Richtige—, den wir endlich erbauen wollen."[4] In consonance with her colleagues, Wolf calls on her fellow citizens to remain in the GDR and work together to build a new socialist society. With a play on Bertolt Brecht's statement "Stell dir vor es gibt Krieg und keiner geht hin," Wolf hypothesizes: "Stell dir vor, es ist Sozialismus, und keiner geht weg!"[5] She thus hones in on a factor that accelerated the GDR's rapid collapse: the mass exodus to the West of the country's citizens.

While shared disillusionment with the system initially united the intellectuals and the masses, crass differences in the type of future envisioned soon came to light. Many intellectuals sought the route of dialogue and internal reform, the masses the complete abolishment of the system. Symbolic of this critical division is the shift from East German citizens' demand for recognition—"*Wir* sind *das* Volk"—to the post-Wall call for unification with

West Germany—"*Wir* sind *ein* Volk." While the term "*das* Volk" referred to those who brought about the peaceful revolution, "*ein* Volk" marked the end of East Germany, and of socialism, through unification.

The strong push for German unification prompted leading GDR intellectuals, among them Wolf, Heym, and Volker Braun, to formulate the call "Für unser Land" (28 November 1989). In the midst of what they saw as their country's "deep crisis" after the fall of the Wall, they articulated two possible alternatives for the GDR's future:

> Entweder können wir auf der Eigenständigkeit der DDR bestehen und versuchen, [...] in unserem Land eine solidarische Gesellschaft zu entwickeln, in der Frieden und soziale Gerechtigkeit, Freiheit des einzelnen, Freizügigkeit aller und die Bewahrung der Umwelt gewährleistet sind.
>
> Oder wir müssen dulden, daß, veranlaßt durch starke ökonomische Zwänge und durch unzumutbare Bedingungen, an die einflußreiche Kreise aus Wirtschaft und Politik in der Bundesrepublik ihre Hilfe für die DDR knüpfen, ein Ausverkauf unserer materiellen und moralischen Werte beginnt und über kurz oder lang die Deutsche Demokratische Republik durch die Bundesrepublik vereinnahmt wird.[6]

While the subsequent vote for unification in March 1990 precluded the possibility of a "third way," the perceptions inscribed in the plea for a sovereign GDR lend insight into the hopes and fears that arose from the sudden shift in events. Most striking is the continued definition of socialism as the "other" of capitalism. Solidarity, peace, justice, freedom and specific material and moral values are attributed to socialism, while capitalism, in other words unification, signifies a complete sell-out of these values.

"Für unser Land" goes on to illuminate the options that were deemed desirable at that time. The plea continues: "Noch haben wir die Chance, [...] eine sozialistische Alternative zur Bundesrepublik zu entwickeln. Noch können wir uns besinnen auf die anti-faschistischen und humanistischen Ideale, von denen wir einst ausgegangen sind" (171). This invocation of anti-fascist, humanist ideals reasserts the GDR's foundational narrative, the heritage stressed throughout the country's forty year existence and the cornerstone of the state's legitimacy. Particularly for writers of Wolf's generation, those who came of age under fascism, the moral vision of anti-fascism effected a basic loyalty to the regime and subordination to its authority. Yet for many GDR citizens, the recourse to the anti-fascist master narrative signaled a renewed attempt at the "socialist" experiment, albeit under vastly different conditions. When Egon Krenz, already discredited by his long-standing affiliation with the party machinery, added his signature to the "Für unser Land" petition, popular belief that the so-called "third way" would not diverge too radically from the past course of GDR socialism became solidified. Furthermore, the timing of the plea coincided with Helmut Kohl's 10-Point Plan for German unification. With its guarantee of rapid unification with the prosperous West and a swift end to economic hardship, it is easy to see why Kohl's plan held greater credence and promise than yet another seemingly utopian project. Reflecting on "Für unser Land" in February 1990, Christa Wolf had to concede:

> Die Kritiker hatten recht: Für viele war das Wort "sozialistisch" zerschlissen, nach stundenlanger Diskussion hatten wir es, natürlich neu definiert, ein einziges Mal in unseren Text aufgenommen, als "sozialistische Alternative"; es machte viele wütend und aggressiv, sie fürchteten wohl auch, ein einziges solches Wort könnte die dringend notwendige Finanzhilfe der Bundesrepublik verzögern. Sie wollten selbst nicht noch einmal an einem Experiment teilnehmen, lieber offensichtlich Bewährtes übernehmen.[7]

History has shown that in formulating their appeal, GDR authors severely miscalculated not only their own influence but also the strength of the ideological ties binding their county's citizens to socialism. After all, communism, in its anti-fascist cloak, was the GDR's raison d'être. Without it the rationale for a separate German state disappeared.

In "Die Revolution entläßt ihre Schriftsteller," Lothar Probst suggests that critical GDR authors' continued belief in the "utopia" of socialism had long separated them from the masses. He asserts:

> Die kritische Literatur hat die 'gute' Utopie gegen die 'schlechte' Realität eingeklagt, aber sie hat diese Utopie selbst nicht in Frage gestellt. In diesem Sinne hatte sie schon vor der politischen Wende in der DDR den Kontakt zur gesellschaftlichen Realität verloren, in der der Vorrat an sozialistischer Utopie angesichts der Tristesse des Alltags längst aufgebraucht war.[8]

As Probst points out, socialism was not questioned as a desirable goal. Yet at the same time it is important to underscore the increasingly dystopic nature of GDR literature. The "really existing socialism" proclaimed by Honecker in 1971 had very little to do with the ideals of socialism to which many writers continued to hold. In fact, Honecker's official proclamation only served to highlight the disparity between the original socialist dream and GDR reality. To be sure, critical authors attempted to keep the dream of socialism alive. Yet they distanced that dream from GDR reality. Helga Königsdorf expresses this incongruity:

Wir akzeptierten es nicht, das System, das uns umgab, aber wir liebten die Utopie, die es einst auf seine Fahnen geschrieben hatte. Und wir hatten immer noch die Hoffnung, wir könnten irgendwie dahin gelangen. Dafür schrieben wir, waren wir listig, verbündeten uns zeitweilig sogar mit den Gegnern unserer Hoffnung.[9]

While she holds to socialist ideals, then, Königsdorf divorces these from the system and its leaders. Indeed, the regime came to present more an obstacle than a guidepost en route to utopia.

Socialism, moreover, was not only the utopia of intellectuals and writers of the East, but also of many leftist intellectuals in the West. Andreas Huyssen rightly draws attention to the significant role the socialist GDR played for the intellectual left in the Federal Republic, arguing that "the abstract need for a potentially utopian space, an 'other' of capitalist Germany, led to the continued hold of the official GDR on the West German left's imagination, however subliminal it may have been."[10] Huyssen consequently stresses that "the falling of the wall and the March elections in the GDR implied the collapse of a whole set of long-held leftist assumptions and projections" (117). The collapse of the East bloc fostered a fundamental reassessment of socialism's future and raised the question whether the death of communism in Eastern Europe necessarily bought with it the end of the dream of socialism, the end of utopia. As a 1990 inquiry by *Die Zeit* on the question "Ist der Sozialismus am Ende?" concluded: "Die Geschichte des Sozialismus ist auch die Geschichte der Intellektuellen, ihrer Visionen und ihrer Träume, ihrer Kämpfe und ihrer kritischen Energie. Darauf verzichtet man nicht so leicht."[11]

By invoking the end of utopia, post-*Wende* discussions echo Ernst Bloch's attempt to save the concept of utopia for Marxism. Bloch, a Marxist philosopher forced in 1957 to leave his university post in Leipzig because of his explicit critique of Marxist-Leninism, argued for a more differentiated understanding of utopia based not on "wishful thinking" but on tendencies and potentialities ascertainable within society, a "concrete utopia" closely connected to everyday life. For Bloch, utopian thinking had subversive potential. In contrast to ideologies, which he defined as groups of ideas that reflect and defend the status quo, he attributed the idea of utopia to groups who attempt to undermine and rupture the status quo in the hope of a better society.[12] In his essay "Abschied von der Utopie?" (1974), Bloch responded to the notion of an end of utopia by reiterating the need for the utopia inherent in Marxist thinking which he underlined in his classic work, *Prinzip Hoffnung*. Bloch stresses: "Marxismus ist nicht keine Utopie, sondern konkrete Utopie, und der Abschied vom Marxismus ist deshalb nur eine Ideologie-Formel [...] für Abschied von jeder ernsthaften sozialen Bewegung überhaupt."[13] In Bloch's view, the concept of utopia continued to be misunderstood rather than be seen as an essential element of social progress.

In *Der zerstörte Traum. Vom Ende des utopischen Zeitalters* (1991), a text written in the aftermath of the GDR's collapse, German historian Joachim Fest characterizes Ernst Bloch as "ein fremder, monströser Anachronismus in der Gegenwart."[14] Echoing the dominant post-Wall tenor, Fest implies that the Blochian insistence on the need for utopia upheld the status quo in the former socialist societies: "Durch ihn [Bloch] erst hat das Totale und Totalitäre eine Art zweiter Unschuld zurückgewonnen und ist, unabhängig von seinem Vorzeichen, wie ein verlorener Sohn in das deutsche Denken zurückgekehrt" (77). In contrast to Bloch, Fest defines utopia narrowly as a totalizing system with a fixed vision of the future. Given the suffering wrought by Nazism and Stalinism, which he characterizes as the dominant "System-Utopien" of the twentieth century, Fest asserts: "Der schrittweisen Verwirklichung einer humaneren Ordnung steht das utopische Erlangen geradezu im Wege, weil es alle Ordnung entweder überhaupt beseitigen oder aber von oben dekretieren will" (98). The link between the concept of utopia, totalizing theories and totalitarian regimes leads Fest to conclude, "daß ein Leben ohne Utopie zum Preis der Modernität gehört" (98). Fest, then, rejects the notion that socialism can have a "human face" and highlights the difficulty of moving beyond the equation of the GDR's "real existing socialism" with socialism per se.

In a similar vein, Monika Maron adamantly denies that there was anything about the GDR, about socialism, worth saving. Maron argues that those who draw on a particular "GDR identity" such as the signers of the "Für unser Land" petition and Western leftist intellectuals, fail sufficiently to recognize "daß die Voraussetzung für das idyllische Detail die geschlossene Gesellschaft war."[15] For Maron, those qualities worth retaining can be at home anywhere, namely "die Hoffnung auf die Stärke der Vernunft und der Kampf für die soziale Gerechtigkeit und Demokratie, was manche Menschen noch Sozialismus nennen können" (99). Maron concludes, "Die Utopie lebt in den Köpfen. Mit der Macht gepaart, wird sie zur Diktatur. Sie ist das Maß für die Wirklichkeit, aber sie kann die Wirklichkeit nicht sein" (99).

With the GDR's rapid disintegration and the populace's turn to the West, both with their feet and their vote, polemic headlines in the Western press, such as "Bleibt die Avantgarde zurück?"[16] (*Der Spiegel*) and "Wunschbilder statt Erkenntnis: Warum die DDR-Revolution ohne Intellektuelle stattfand: Heimatlos im Supermarkt"[17] (*Die Welt*), drew attention to the seemingly anachronistic utopianism and anti-capitalism of GDR intellectuals. Issues that came to the fore during this time provide an interpretive framework for post-Wall studies of GDR literature. In the following, I sketch out specific conditions of literary production that influence post-Wall interpretations of GDR literature and, more specifically, are brought to bear on literary critiques of progress.

Although Western scholars and critics had long addressed the conditions of literary production in the GDR, open discussion in the East did not take place until the Tenth Writers' Congress in 1987. At that congress Christoph Hein delivered a powerful speech that signaled the impact *glasnost* was beginning to have on the GDR's cultural sphere. Hein bluntly proclaimed: "Die Zensur ist überlebt, nutzlos, paradox, menschenfeindlich, volksfeindlich, ungesetzlich und strafbar."[18] Explaining his claim that censorship was "outdated," Hein asserts that while censorship perhaps served a purpose in the GDR's early years, it should have disappeared by 1956 with the official advent of de-Stalinization. Moreover, he remarks that because censorship of a text generally led only to a delay in production, it had the paradoxical effect of drawing attention toward controversial works. "Das zensierte Objekt verschwindet nicht, sondern wird unübersehbar, wird selbst dann zum Politikum aufgeblasen, wenn Buch und Autor dafür untauglich sind und alles andere zu erwarten und zu erhoffen hatten" (82), Hein states. Literary texts that were eventually granted publication did not necessarily toe the party line: despite censorship, literature provided a space for—though perhaps subtle and indirect—criticism of the system. This circumstance elevated the status of writers and allied them with their readers. Günter de Bruyn claims, for example, "daß unter Zensurbedingungen jedes kritisches Wort gegen die Unterdrücker als das eines Verbündeten gilt."[19] While de Bruyn addresses readership in the GDR, Maron makes a similar point about the effect censorship had on GDR literature's reception in the West. Maron, a writer never granted publication in the East, contends: "Selbst wer der Zensur anheimfiel, wußte sich im anderen Deutschland um so aufmerksamer gelesen und auch im eigenen Land genossen als verbotene Frucht."[20] The marketability of literary texts in the Federal Republic precisely because of their censored status thus played a critical role in shaping the GDR's literary landscape.

Censorship, in conjunction with other punitive measures such as sanctions, arrest, expulsion from the Writers' Union and expatriation, impelled the continuous exodus of writers to the West. The option of "exit," whether forced or chosen, contributed to the lack of strong internal opposition in East Germany.[21] On the one hand, the regime thwarted the growth of radical opposition by forcing dissidents into exile, on the other hand dissidents, particularly those censored and otherwise rebuked, were driven to apply for exit visas. The continuous exodus of the country's intellectuals presented a critical problem for GDR literary culture and seriously undermined the regime's legitimacy. After the *Wende*, however, the exit option was invoked to support the belief that those GDR writers who remained in the country and published there were essentially in collusion with the regime—despite their varied attempts to reform the system from the inside.

Because censorship fostered self-censorship, the contradictory situation also emerged in which the author became both perpetrator and victim. Hein argues: "Er wird Selbstzensur üben und den Text verraten oder gegen die Zensur anschreiben und auch dann Verrat an dem Text begehen, da er seine Wahrheit unwillentlich und möglicherweise unwissentlich polemisch verändert" (82). The demise of their country has led many GDR writers to grapple with the consequences of self-censorship and evaluate the extent of their collaboration with the defunct regime. Königsdorf elaborates on the notion of inner-censorship as follows: "Wenn man später wissen will, wie es gewesen ist, in dieser DDR, wird man es vor allem aus der Literatur erfahren. Oder besser, man wird erfahren, wie es auch gewesen ist. Man erfährt nur die halbe Wahrheit, die zur Halbwahrheit verkäme, unterstellt man ihr den Anspruch eines Gesamt-berichts."[22] Distinguishing between "half the truth" and a "half-truth," Königsdorf accentuates the crucial difference between accurate yet partial accounts and those that mingle truth and falsehood. In so doing, she calls on readers to evaluate their own expectations of literary texts and draw their own conclusions about what constitutes realism in literature.

The press's official function as a government mouthpiece no doubt enhanced the status of literature. As Hein stressed:

> Eine einseitig vermittelnde Presse, eine Presse, die nur eine erwünschte Realität vermittelt, die aus der vorhandenen Meinungsvielfalt und von den vorhandenen Lösungsvorschlägen zu gesellschaftlichen Fragen und Problemen allein die ihr opportunen heraussucht und öffentlich macht, beraubt sich selbst der Wirkung, macht Agitation und Propaganda unglaubwürdig. (88)

Hein also points to the misleading use of the term "Lesegesellshaft" to describe the GDR reading public. Since the significance of literature must be seen in relation to other written media, Hein finds it more appropriate to speak of a "Buchlesegesellschaft" (87). Literature, as GDR critic Rüdiger Bernhardt emphasizes, to a great extent substituted for a public sphere: "Aus der Literatur [...] erfahren wir mehr über die tatsächlichen Verhältnisse, Widersprüche und Entwicklungstendenzen in unserem Alltag als aus den gesamten Massen-medien."[23] This status not only affected literary style, but also heightened readers' expectations, leading them to depend all too facilely on the author as mentor. In this way literature came to fulfill functions that would perhaps be better served by other media.

In her open letter exchange with West German critic and writer Joseph von Westphalen, *Trotzdem herzliche Grüße. Ein deutsch-deutscher Briefwechsel*, Maron addressed this much touted "Ersatzfunktion," stating "daß die Schrift-steller in der DDR im ohnehin schlecht besetzten Chor der öffentlichen Meinung den Part der Journalisten mitsingen müssen, weil die entweder in falschen Tönen trällern oder ganz und gar schweigen."[24] Maron stresses journalism's propagandistic role within a society where ideological proclamations were divorced from lived experience. As a consequence there was immense pressure on literature, a genre subject to less stringent control than other written media, to document public opinion and address societal contradictions.

The mechanisms of control and censorship also contributed to the socialist public sphere's markedly didactic character. Writing in 1979, the GDR scholar Robert Weimann defines the public sphere as follows[25]: "Öffentlichkeit ist [...] eine Agentur der Sozialisation, ein Moment der Organisation sozialistischer Lebens- und Denkprozesse. Als eine von Wirklichkeitserfahrung und Lebenspraxis gespeiste Form gesellschaftlichen Verkehrs ist also Öffentlichkeit [...] ein hochgradig bewußtseinsbildender Grund von Kommunikation und Wertsetzung ...."[26] Weimann depicts the public sphere as a place for fostering a socialist consciousness and worldview. He goes on to argue against official notions that the socialist public sphere should be a "konfliktfreier Ausdruck einer Menschengemeinschaft" (221), underscoring the need publicly to address the gap between the socialist ideal and its real existing variant. Such an open examination of the discrepancy between ideology and individual experience, the establishment of a genuine dialogue between readers and writers unfettered by state control and intervention, never became possible in the GDR. In 1990, Weimann remarked on his public sphere essay: "Zum Zeitpunkt, als ich den Aufsatz über Öffentlichkeit schrieb, war im Lande, wie auch später 'Glasnost', 'Öffentlichkeit' noch keine gesellschaftliche Realität."[27]

Established writers held a privileged position in the GDR not only by virtue of their professional standing but also because of their ability to travel and earn hard currency. These privileges in turn proved highly problematic since they stood in opposition to one of the most fundamental precepts of socialism, the classless society. Hein emphatically makes this point:

> Privilegien sind Krebsgeschwüre einer sozialistischen Gesellschaft, denn sie schaffen Klassen, die sich durch Vorrechte unterscheiden, die durch Ausnahmen voneinander getrennt sind, denen durch Sonderrechte eine Verständigung erschwert wird. Privelegien vernichten eben damit jene Öffentlichkeit, die Vorraussetzung der Arbeit aller Künstler ist. Sie vernichten damit die Wirkung ihrer Arbeit, und mit der Wirkung zerstören sie letztendlich die Künstler selbst. (101)

The disjunction between writers and the masses stemming in part from the privileged position of the former came to the fore after the *Wende*. Writers were certainly granted numerous liberties, yet one must also consider how their status shaped their relationships to the regime and to their GDR readers.

Maron addresses this question in her pointed criticism of those GDR authors who, like Wolf, condemned the mass call for unification and expressed their continued commitment to the GDR and its democratic socialist ideals.

Maron's perspective from the outside the official canon of GDR literature sheds additional light on the writers' status. Maron illuminates the writers' privileged position in the public sphere:

> Die Schriftsteller in der DDR waren eine besonders verwöhnte Gruppe ihres Berufstandes. Damit meine ich weniger die von der Obrigkeit gewährten Privilegien als eine allgemeine Verehrung, die ihnen zuteil wurde. [...] Es brauchte nicht viel Mut, besonders nicht für die durch die Öffentlichkeit geschützten Autoren, um den Schein des Heldentums um sich zu entfachen. Und oft genügte eine halbe Wahrheit, um ihrem Verkünder in einer Umgebung dummer und dreister Verlogenheit den Ruf des Propheten zu verleihen.[28]

Maron understandably questions the right of GDR writers privileged through travel and access to hard currency to condemn those who fled to the West or jubilantly celebrated the fall of the Wall. In particular, Maron assails Heym's negative portrayal of the masses' rush to consume—the flight to the glitzy West Berlin Kurfürstendamm—as "die Arroganz des Satten, der sich vor den Tischmanieren eines Ausgehungerten ekelt" (98). In an article published in *Spiegel*, Heym had written:

> Aus dem Volk, das nach Jahrzehnten Unterwürfigkeit und Flucht sich aufgerafft und sein Schicksal in die eigenen Hände genommen hatte und das soeben noch edlen Blicks einer verheißungsvollen Zukunft zuzustreben schien, wurde eine Horde von Wütigen, die, Rücken an Bauch gedrängt, Hertie und Bilka zustrebten auf der Jagd nach dem glitzernden Tinnef. Welche Gesichter, da sie mit kannibalischer Lust in den Grabbeltischen, von westlichen Krämern ihnen absichtsvoll in den Weg plaziert, wülten.[29]

Heym's concession that economic failures attributable to the GDR government makes the reaction of the masses "understandable" hardly justifies his crude portrayal of those citizens whom he had previously heralded as the heroes of the revolution.

The issue of privilege again came under the limelight in the polemic debate sparked by the publication of Christa Wolf's *Was bleibt* in June 1990. Written in June–July 1979 but revised and submitted for publication nearly a decade later in November 1989, *Was bleibt* depicts a day on which the first-person narrator, a writer who closely resembles Wolf, is under direct surveillance by the secret police, the *Stasi*. Situated in the late 1970s, Wolf's narrative expresses the personal ramifications of the increasingly dogmatic and repressive cultural politics exemplified and compounded by the expatriation of Wolf Biermann:

reprimands, expulsions and other punitive measures sent a clear message regarding the limits of dissention and the consequences for breaching those limits. In its representation of the poet's marginalized position in society, of literature's potential to activate change, and in its skepticism of language's representational ability, *Was bleibt* reflects many themes informing Wolf's *Kein Ort. Nirgends*, which was published the year she first penned *Was bleibt*. Yet in the historical context of the early 1990s Western critics such as Ulrich Greiner and Frank Schirrmacher framed *Was bleibt* as Wolf's attempt to stylize herself as a victim of the GDR regime and thereby to undercut her privileged status.[30]

Greiner reads the text as indicative of "die real existierende Bedrohlichkeit, die Christa Wolf ebenso virtuos wie verlogen immerzu verwertet," and criticizes Wolf's "Mangel an Feingefühl gegenüber jenen, deren Leben der SED-Staat zerstört hat."[31] Disregarding the key distinction between *Was bleibt*'s narrator, its author and the GDR regime, critics were quick to mount an attack on Wolf herself, judging her a coward for not publishing the text earlier, an opportunist, a collaborator and a privileged state poet of the toppled regime. Greiner depicts Wolf as a writer protected and coddled by the state, a sentimental painter of private idylls that blossom against a somber background of doom. For Greiner, she exemplifies "die altbekannte machtgestützte Innerlichkeit, die sich literarische Fluchtbürgen baut." His harsh attack on Wolf, then, extends well beyond Wolf alone. Through the writer, Greiner launches an affront on "Gesinnungsästhetik," the coupling of aesthetics and morality that characterizes Wolf's "subjective authenticity" in particular and postwar German literature in general. Schirrmacher similarly depicts Wolf as an authoritarian personality and a timid, servile and motherly opportunist.[32] Like Greiner, he infuses his personal attack with a broader political agenda—the dismissal of a generation of postwar writers burdened by history. For Schirrmacher, self-denial, guilt and martyrdom characterize those authors who resisted with words rather than actions. In Schirrmacher's view, grabbing for the pen in protest of Biermann's expatriation or couching one's criticism in words palpable to state censors seems inconsequential and downright cowardly in light of the significant abuses of the GDR regime.

Was bleibt explores precisely the question of actions and culpability targeted by Wolf's critics, yet offers no simple answers. In a self-explorative process, Wolf's narrator attempts to fill in memory gaps and to understand her part in maintaining the regime. Rather than work within oppositional categories such as victim/perpetrator, the narrative examines and disrupts simple binaries. In "Lesen und Schreiben" (1968), Wolf uses the term "Medaillons" to refer to the creation in our memories of one-dimensional, encapsulated and ossified pieces of life, miniatures which we fit with neat captions such as "the end of childhood" and classify as beautiful or ugly, as good or bad (LS 24). In the process of forgetting, we polish, recast and reframe these miniatures. Prose, in

Wolf's view, must work against this deceptive process; like memory, it must swim against the strong current of forgetting.

The first page of *Was bleibt* lays bare Wolf's continuation of this memory project, as the first-person narrator contemplates, "wie ich in zehn, zwanzig Jahren an diesen noch frischen, noch nicht abgelebten Tag zurückdenken würde" (WB 7). What marks this particular day is the narrator's surveillance by the *Stasi*: from morning to evening men in trench coats hover outside her window; her phone is tapped; she suspects *Stasi* informants within her close circle of friends; at an evening reading her audience is comprised primarily of government officials. The text resonates with tension, insecurity and paranoia, the narrator's psychological state one of "heller Angst," "panischer Angst," "Unruhe," "Schlaflosigkeit," and "Schmerz." Feeling controlled from above like a marionette, she repeatedly invokes the "Herrn, [...] der unangefochten meine Stadt beherrschte" (WB 35). At the same time, she remains painfully aware of the privileges she has garnered because of her own complicity.

Struggling to find her own voice among those competing within her, the narrator attempts to make whole a self fragmented by the simultaneous endeavor for self-knowledge, self-protection and conformity: "Ich selbst. [...] Wer war das. Welches der multiplen Wesen, aus denen 'ich selbst' mich zusammensetzte. Das, das sich kennen wollte? Das, das sich schonen wollte? Oder jenes dritte, das immer noch versucht war, nach derselben Pfeife zu tanzen wie die jungen Herren da draußen vor meiner Tür?" (WB 57) In an interview with Hans Kaufmann in 1973, Wolf warned of censorship begetting self-censorship, of writers internalizing the demands of the state and consequently becoming unable to pose to their readers, or even to themselves, the burning questions of the day: "Wenn man über längere Zeit daran gehindert wird, es öffentlich zu tun, kann man überhaupt verlernen, die—verdammten oder nicht verdammten, jedenfalls bedeutsamen—Fragen ... zu stellen, und sei es zunächst nur sich selbst. Das betrifft nicht nur die Literatur, aber sie trifft es im Kern" (DiA2 790). In the progressive flow of unpunctuated questions *Was bleibt*'s narrator poses to herself and to the reader, we see Wolf's continuing battle with censorship and self-censorship. The narrator, aware of her inability to free herself from her third, acquiescent voice and to find an uncensored "new language," admits that her present language consists of "Wörter aus dem äußeren Kreis, sie trafen zu, aber sie trafen nicht, sie griffen die Tatsachen auf, um das Tatsächliche zu vertuschen" (WB 17).

As mentioned earlier, Wolf belongs to a generation of writers whose historical experiences and socialization first in the Third Reich and then in the GDR led them to hold fast to their belief in the "better Germany" and, ultimately, to acquiesce to authority.[33] In her complicity and language, the narrator stands in stark contrast to a younger writer who pays her a visit on the day depicted in the text. Unlike the cautious, accommodating and privileged narrator, the young female writer has suffered at the hands of the state. Refusing to let herself be blackmailed into denunciation, she was expelled from the university; because of her involvement in protests surrounding Biermann's expatriation, she was incarcerated in a cold and damp prison cell. In contrast to the narrator, this writer has no third, self-censoring voice; she writes the uncloaked truth. "Es ist soweit. Die Jungen schreiben es auf" (WB 76) the narrator comments. She recognizes that the young woman does not ask "what remains": "Das Mädchen fragte nicht krämerisch: Was bleibt. Es fragte auch nicht danach, woran es sich erinnern würde, wenn es einst alt wäre" (WB 79). Despite her admiration, the narrator nonetheless advises the writer against making her manuscript public, assured of the bitter consequences that would follow.

Commenting on what came to be known as the "Christa Wolf Debate," Günter de Bruyn stated: "Wer heute entdeckt und vorwurfsvoll anmerkt, daß Christa Wolfs Denken und das anderer Autoren sozialistische Prägungen aufweist, gibt damit zu, sie vorher nicht richtig gelesen zu haben oder aber in ihnen, nachdem ihre oppositionelle Rolle gegenstandslos wurde, nur noch politische Gegner zu sehen."[34] The failure of many Western critics to acknowledge the complexities of literary production in the GDR contributed to one-sided readings of texts published in that country. This tendency became even more evident in the full-blown "deutsch-deutscher Literaturstreit" that developed out of the debate surrounding *Was bleibt*. Huyssen likens the *Literaturstreit* to a second *Historikerstreit*, stating that its immediate purpose was "a selective and self-serving apportioning of guilt, as well as the erasure of the past, this time that of the predominant culture of the two German states from 1949 to the present" (125–126). Its purpose, Huyssen stresses, is "Abwicklung," is closure. Greiner makes a similar claim in his "Zwischenbilanz" to the debate: "Es geht um die Deutung der literarischen Vergangenheit und um die Durchsetzung einer Lesart. [...] Wer bestimmt, was gewesen ist, der bestimmt auch, was sein wird. Der Streit um die Vergangenheit ist ein Streit um die Zukunft" (139). Before 1989 most Western critics focused on the oppositional function of GDR literature, after 1989 those writers who had chosen to remain in the GDR and succeeded at getting published within the system were often framed in hindsight as colluding with the regime and its repressive politics.

This post-Wall interpretive paradigm also brought about a re-reading of representations of science and technology in GDR literature. Richard Herzinger and Heinz-Peter Preußer explicitly reject previous scholarship that interprets the literary *Zivilisationskritik* of prominent authors such as Christa Wolf, Heiner Müller, Volker Braun and Christoph Hein as a counter-discourse to the dominant ideology.[35] Herzinger and Preußer argue instead,

daß die literarische Zivilisationskritik einen Legitimationsdiskurs absichert, der den sozialistischen Utopiekern vor seiner Beschädigung

durch den Bankrott des Realsozialismus zu retten versucht und zudem
eine   Rechtfertigungsargumentation   für   das   Fortbestehen   des
sozialistischen Staates bereitstellt, die dessen offizielle Ideologie nicht
mehr zu leisten vermag. (195)

Herzinger and Preußer acknowledge *Zivilisationskritik* as a characteristic of later
GDR literature, yet contend that this critique signaled a consensus with the state.
Fundamental to their thesis is the premise that this critique served to warn
against the alienation and instrumentalization associated with Western
capitalism. In this light, the slowness of scientific-technological progress in the
East comes to be seen as a distinct advantage for resisting the negative
consequences of modernity against which these authors write. The
interpretations that follow will reveal the extent to which Herzinger and
Preußer's thesis can be upheld.

Notes

1 Helga Königsdorf, "Der Schmerz über das eigene Versagen," *Die Zeit* 1
   June 1990.
2 Christa Wolf, "Schreiben im Zeitbezug," *Im Dialog* 159.
3 Christoph Hein, "Die Vernunft der Straße," *TAZ: DDR Journal zur
   Novemberrevolution* (1990): 73.
4 Stefan Heym, "Nach den Jahren der Dumpfheit," *TAZ: DDR Journal zur
   Novemberrevolution* (1990): 74.
5 Christa Wolf, "Befreite Sprache und Gefühlswörter," *TAZ: DDR Journal
   zur Novemberrevolution* (1990): 75.
6 Christa Wolf et al., "Für unser Land," *Im Dialog* 170–171.
7 Christa Wolf, "Nachtrag zu einem Herbst," *Im Dialog* 13–14.
8 Lothar Probst, "Die Revolution entläßt ihre Schriftsteller," *Deutschland
   Archiv* 23.6 (1990): 923.
9 Königsdorf, "Der Schmerz über das eigene Versagen."
10 Andreas Huyssen, "After the Wall: The Failure of German Intellectuals,"
   New German Critique 52 (Winter 1991): 117.
11 "Ist der Sozialismus am Ende?" *Die Zeit* 19 January 1990.
12 Ernst Bloch, "Topos utopia," *Abschied von der Utopie*, ed. Hanna Gekle
   (Frankfurt a. M.: Suhrkamp, 1980) 69.
13 Ernst Bloch, "Abschied von der Utopie?," *Abschied von der Utopie* 79–80.
14 Joachim Fest, *Der zerstörte Traum. Vom Ende des utopischen Zeitalters.*
   (Berlin: Corso bei Siedler, 1991) 78.

15 Monika Maron, "Das neue Elend der Intellektuellen," *Nach Maßgabe meiner Begreifungskraft* (Frankfurt a. M.: Fischer) 90. First published in *TAZ. Journal No. 2: Die Wende der Wende* (1990): 96–98.

16 "Bleibt die Avant-Garde zurück?" *Der Spiegel* 49 (4 December 1989): 230–233.

17 Gerd Ueding, "Wunschbilder statt Erkenntnis: Warum die DDR-Revolution ohne Intellektuelle stattfand. Heimatlos im Supermarkt," *Die Welt* 28 July 1990.

18 Christoph Hein, "Die Zensur ist überlebt, nutzlos, paradox, menschenfeindlich, volksfeindlich, ungesetzlich und strafbar," *Als Kind habe ich Stalin gesehen.* (Berlin/Weimar: Aufbau, 1990) 77–104.

19 Günter De Bruyn, "Jubelschreie, Trauergesänge," *Die Zeit* 14 September 1990.

20 Monika Maron, "Die Schriftsteller und das Volk," *Der Spiegel* 7 (12 February 1990): 68–70.

21 Christian Joppke explores the exit/voice option in *East German Dissidents and the Revolution of 1989. Social Movement in a Leninist Regime* (New York: New York University Press, 1995). See in particular pages 185–187.

22 Königsdorf, "Der Schmerz über das eigene Versagen."

23 Klaus Jarmatz et al., "40 Jahre DDR Literatur. Rundtischgespräch," *Weimarer Beiträge* 35.9 (1989): 1454.

24 Monika Maron and Joseph von Westphalen, *Trotzdem herzliche Grüße. Ein deutsch-deutscher Briefwechsel* (Frankfurt a. M.: Fischer, 1991) 59.

25 For a discussion of the GDR public sphere, see: David Bathrick, "Kultur und Öffentlichkeit in der DDR," *Literatur der DDR in den siebziger Jahren*, ed. Peter Uwe Hohendahl and Patricia Herminghouse, 53–81.

26 Robert Weimann, "Kunst und Öffentlichkeit in der sozialistischen Gesellschaft. Zum Stand der Vergesellschaftung künstlerischer Verkehrsformen," *Sinn und Form* 31.2 (1979): 221.

27 Colin B. Grant, "Öffentlichkeit—Diskurs—Kommunikation. Ein Interview mit Robert Weimann," *Weimarer Beiträge* 37.8 (1991): 1154. The interview was held on June 28, 1990.

28 Maron, "Das neue Elend der Intellektuellen," 98.

29 Heym, "Nach den Jahren der Dumpfheit," quoted in Maron, "Das neue Elend der Intellektuellen," 82.

30 For documentation of the debate see Thomas Anz, ed. *Es geht nicht um Christa Wolf. Der Literaturstreit im vereinten Deutschland. Erweiterte Neuausgabe* (Frankfurt a. M.: Fischer, 1995). See also the analyses and materials collected in *Der deutsch-deutsche Literaturstreit oder "Freund, es spricht sich schlecht mit gebundener Zunge,"* ed. Karl Deiritz and Johannes

Krauss (Hamburg: Luchterhand, 1991).

31 Ulrich Greiner, "Mangel an Feingefühl. Eine *ZEIT*kontroverse über Christa Wolf und ihre neue Erzählung," *Die Zeit* 1 June 1990. Reprinted in Anz, *Es geht nicht um Christa Wolf* 66–70.

32 Frank Schirrmacher, "'Dem Druck des härteren, strengeren Lebens standhalten'. Auch eine Studie über einen authoritären Charakter: Christa Wolfs Aufsätze, Reden und ihre jüngste Erzählung *Was bleibt*," *Frankfurter Allgemeine Zeitung* 2 June 1990. Reprinted in Anz, *Es geht nicht um Christa Wolf* 77–89.

33 The vast majority of those fleeing the country in the summer of 1989 were of the younger generation. 80 percent were under 40 years of age. See Joppke, 138.

34 De Bruyn, "Jubelgeschreie, Trauergesänge."

35 Richard Herzinger and Heinz-Peter Preußer, "Vom Äußersten zum Ersten. DDR-Literatur in der Tradition deutscher Zivilisationskritik," *Text und Kritik. Literatur der DDR. Rückblicke* (München: text + kritik, 1991) 195–209.

CHAPTER TWO

Science and the "Dialectic of Enlightenment"

> *Die Vernunft—wir nennen es Sozialismus—ist in den Alltag einge-drungen. Sie ist das Maß, nach dem hier gemessen, das Ideal, in dessen Namen hier gelobt und getadelt wird.*
>
> Christa Wolf, 1964

As outlined in the previous chapter, the GDR's demise raised a myriad of questions regarding the extent to which the country's writers had helped to support and solidify the status quo. A central argument of this study is that with the semi-magical power attributed to science in Marxist ideology, a critique of scientific-technological progress became a significant means to question the status quo and the regime's legitimacy. Profound concern over nuclear proliferation in the Cold War and mounting ecological degradation engendered extreme skepticism in science's role in developing a truly socialist society and fostering the "new human being." As GDR author Günter Kunert poignantly expressed in 1966: "Am Anfang des technischen Zeitalters steht Auschwitz, steht Hiroshima, die ich nur in bezug auf gesellschaftlich organisiert verwendete Technik hier in einem Atemzug nenne. Ich glaube, nur große Naivität setzt Technik mit gesellschaftlich-humanitären Fortschreiten gleich."[1] Kunert's dissociation of scientific-technolgogical progress and social progress, as we shall see, prefigures the fundamental critique of progressive GDR literature in the 1970s and 1980s. Before turning more specifically to literary representations in the following chapters, this chapter first contextualizes the theme of science and technology, establishing a framework that reveals how the emerging critique of progress evinces many parallels to the "dialectic of enlightenment."

The revolutionary role attributed to science and technology constitutes a cornerstone of literary critiques. Marxism itself claimed the status of a science, an autonomous and objective truth, and also elevated scientific-technological progress to a quasi-religious ideal. James Schmitt and James Miller highlight the positive teleology of Marxist theory by pointing to three key aspects: the Promethean ideal of the "full development of human control over the forces of

nature—those of his own nature as well as those of so-called 'nature;'" the
perceived neutrality of technology; and the revolutionary aspect of
industrialization, i.e., the belief that progress functions in an unequivocally
positive sense for the worker.[2] Contrasting Marx's position within the
Enlightenment tradition with Jean Jacques Rousseaus's anti-Enlightenment
stance, Schmitt and Miller bring to the fore divergent conceptualizations of the
relationship between technological and economic development on the one hand
and human freedom on the other (87). For Marx, technological progress and
economic development provided the very basis for true emancipation. Rousseau,
by contrast, viewed men as blind to the disproportionate relationship between
the benefits of progress and the devastation it has wrought. Postulating that
humankind must make a moral choice, Rousseau argued for the limitation of
wants in exchange for "the possibilities for virtue and happiness afforded by
autonomy, altruism and harmonious coexistence" (86). Rousseau, then, viewed
human progress in terms of choices between material wealth and personal
autonomy.

The widespread use of the term "scientific-technological revolution" in the
GDR reflects the status of science and technology as the driving forces of
history. The pervasiveness of this phrase in the East bloc calls for a more
detailed definition. In their examination of the relationship between "Mensch—
Technik—Wissenschaft," M. Buhr and G. Kröber provide an orthodox Marxist
interpretation of the "scientific-technological revolution" (hereafter STR) that
reflects the GDR's ideology of progress.[3] Situating the term STR squarely
within socialism, they assert its vital role in the development of communism:

> Die sozial-ökonomischen Voraussetzungen der gegenwärtigen
> wissenschaftlich-technischen Revolution sind eng verwoben mit den
> Besonderheiten der historischen Epoche, die mit dem Sieg der Großen
> Sozialistischen Oktoberrevolution in Rußland eröffnet wurde und die
> eine neue Ära in der Geschichte der Menschheit darstellt, die Ära des
> Übergangs vom Kapitalismus zum Sozialismus und Kommunismus im
> Weltmaßstab. (13)

The STR ascribes to science and technology a fundamental role in the transition
to communism. It also signals a qualitative transformation of the relationship
between science and technology in which the development of new technologies
follows the discovery of new laws of nature. Buhr and Kröber describe the
current situation as one in which "die Wissenschaft gegenüber der Technik und
Produktion als führender Faktor in Erscheinung tritt, der ihrer weiteren
Entwicklung den Weg bahnt" (27). This shift transforms the question of human
capability to the question of the limits of knowledge or scientific inquiry; as
Roger Shattuck recently put it, it raises the ethical question of "forbidden

knowledge."[4] In particular with the discovery of nuclear energy, the situation has emerged in which humankind's self-annihilation has become thinkable. Alfons Auer expresses how these moral and ethical concerns bear on notions of progress: "die Menschheit [ist] durch die Wissenschaft instand gesetzt worden, sich selbst zu vernichten. Damit ist die These, daß das wissenschaftlich Erkennbare und technische Machbare auch das Gute ist, falsifiziert; sie hat ihre Legitimation verloren."[5]

Although contradictions and negative consequences are seen to arise in both Cold War systems, the STR accentuates the "human face" of progress under socialism and attributes to capitalism all facets of an "anti-human" relationship between individuals, science and technology. In this vein, Buhr and Kröber state: "Ein [...] entstelltes Verhältnis kann jedoch nur in einer antagonistischen Gesellschaft aufkommen, die auf der Ausbeutung des Menschen durch den Menschen beruht und in der Wissenschaft und Technik als Werkzeuge dieser Ausbeutung dienen" (20). In capitalist societies, science and technology are seen to serve the interests of monopolies and thereby to solidify the economic and political position of the bourgeoisie, confirming "[die] Unvereinbarkeit einer freien Entwicklung der Produktivkräfte mit dem kapitalistischen Produktions-system" (31). By contrast, technology's role in socialist society is presented as follows: "In einer Gesellschaft dagegen, die keinerlei Ausbeutung des Menschen durch den Menschen kennt, wird die Technik zu einem der wichtigsten Mittel, den Menschen aus der spontanen Gewalt der blinden Naturkräfte zu befreien, zu einem wesentlichen Faktor des allseitigen Fortschritts" (20). While Marx theorized class conflict as the motor of history, the concept of STR is predicated on a society free of class antagonism. Positing in effect that "really existing socialism" conforms to Marx's notion of a classless society, science and technology come to replace class conflict as the driving forces of human emancipation. The socialist struggle shifts from a struggle against a bourgeois class structure to one against the "blind forces of nature" to be brought under control through the STR. In contrast to Kant's maxim of enlightenment as "der Ausgang des Menschen aus seiner selbstverschuldeten Unmündigkeit," where "Unmündigkeit" is to understood as "das Unvermögen, sich seines Verstandes ohne Leitung eines anderen zu bedienen,"[6] the concept of STR excludes the factor of human agency vital to Kant's notion of emancipation.

Bracketing negative consequences of scientific-technological progress within socialist society, the notion of "scientific-technological revolution" reveals the positivist legacy of Marxism in the GDR, the tendency to receive Marxist doctrines as an objective body of truths and accordingly to view the development toward communism as inevitable. In this mechanistic view, negative consequences are seen as mere aberrations rather than as serious threats to socialism's advancement toward the "realm of freedom." The latent positivism of Marx's "objective" concepts, Albrecht Wellmer argues, conceals

the differences between "der unvermeidlichen und der praktisch notwendigen
Transformation der kapitalistischen Gesellschaft und lassen daher den Übergang
zur klassenlosen Gesellschaft als zwangsläufiges Resultat der Lösung der
kapitalistischen Systemprobleme erscheinen."[7]

Unlike later GDR literature, GDR literature of the 1950s and 1960s can be
characterized as "Literatur der Aufklärung *unter Ausschluß* von deren
immanenten Dialektik" (Emmerich 407). Wolfgang Emmerich explains:

> Ganz im Sinne der historischen Aufklärung, etwa eines Condorcet,
> meinte man, die Fortschritte des Menschengeschlechts (auf dem Boden
> der DDR zumindest) vorraussehen, lenken und beschleunigen zu
> können, da man in der bisherigen Geschichte aller Fortschritte den
> rechten Leitfaden gefunden habe, sprich: den wissenschaftlichen
> Sozialismus. (407)

Accordingly, a belief in "scientific socialism" informs Christa Wolf's early
texts. In her first published fictional work, *Moskauer Novelle* (1961), Wolf
figures science and technology as unequivocally progressive forces in the
humanistic development of socialist society. Adhering closely to the normative
aesthetic of Socialist Realism, *Moskauer Novelle* "objectively" mirrors reality,
represents positive and typical heroes, and sounds a clear didactic message. The
work's orthodoxy reflects Wolf's fervent commitment to socialist ideals at that
time and her firm belief in literature's central role in fostering those ideals. The
writing and publication of *Moskauer Novelle* coincides with the years in which
Wolf, as came to light in 1993, passed on information to the Stasi (1959–1962).
While this collaboration is not surprising when one considers Wolf's early
dogmatism, its disclosure after the GDR's collapse further fueled the debate
about Wolf's status vis-à-vis the regime that had been raging since the
publication of *Was bleibt* in 1990. At least up to the time of the 11th Plenum of
the SED in 1965, whose events significantly rattled Wolf's confidence in her
country's cultural politics, Wolf was "sehr parteiverbunden."[8] Although this
study focuses primarily on the critical literature that emerged in the 1970s and
1980s, Wolf's early works present an important point of contrast.

Set in 1959 against the backdrop of postwar Soviet/East German relations,
Moskauer Novelle relates a rekindled romance between a German doctor, Vera
Brauer, and her Russian translator, Pawel Koschkin. Fourteen years after Vera,
like Wolf approximately sixteen at the time, and Pawel, a former Soviet army
officer, first met in the Mecklenburg village of Fanselow, the two coincidentally
meet again when Vera visits Moscow as part of an East German medical delegation for whom Pawel acts as interpreter. Wolf interweaves this love story with
Vera's feelings of guilt about the past. Here the national narrative coincides with
Vera's personal story, from Germany's wartime atrocities to her own ideological

zealousness in the Third Reich and personal failure to act morally in the past. More specifically, the reader learns that Vera could have possibly prevented an act of arson committed upon the arrival of the Soviet occupation forces. The resulting fire permanently damaged Pawel's eyesight and put an end to his dream of becoming a surgeon.

Despite Vera's guilt, the novella's underlying tenor is overwhelmingly optimistic. The narrative illuminates Vera's successful ideological conversion from fascism to socialism: she acts ethically, works for the collective good and, with the guidance of her older colleagues, musters the strength to resist the temptation of a romantic liaison with Pawel. Vera not only makes the socially and morally acceptable choice, she also educates Pawel about the prudence of exercising restraint and leads him to find renewed satisfaction in his marriage. In *Moskauer Novelle*, Wolf couples the development of the "new human being," exemplified by Vera, with the conviction that science and technology will bring about Marx's vision of a society of fully actualized human beings. As Gisela, a member of the German delegation, proclaims about the teleology of socialism: "Eines Tages wachen wir auf [...] und die Welt ist sozialistisch. Die Atombomben sind im Meer versenkt, und der letzte Kapitalist hat freiwillig auf sein Aktienpaket verzichtet" (MN 51). Although the others mock Gisela's grand illusion, it by and large coincides with Pawel's widely accepted view of the "human being of the future." Pawel hypothesizes:

> Er wird das Problem der Raumschiffahrt ebensogut gelöst haben wie das der Verkehrsdichte auf der Erde. Er wird es fertigbringen, die doppelte Menge von Menschen zu ernähren. Er wird Leben erzeugen und es—vielleicht—auf anderen Planeten entdecken. [...] Bei alldem aber wird er—und das wird seine größte Leistung sein—kein Roboter werden, kein perfektioniertes Ungetüm, sondern endlich: Mensch. (MN 52)

Gisela's and Pawel's future projections echo the belief that technological progress, from space exploration to the reduction of traffic density, can be had without cost. This idealistic perspective also colors Wolf's representation of Moscow as a wonderfully modern and vibrant city. In Pawel's statement, the positive gains attributed to technological progress are inextricably linked to, indeed a prerequisite for, "Menschwerden." For him, the most important characteristic of the future human being is (socialist) "brotherliness," in other words: "Mit offenem Visier leben können. Dem anderen nicht mißtrauen müssen. Ihm den Erfolg nicht neiden, den Mißerfolg tragen helfen. Seine Schwächen nicht verstecken müssen. Die Wahrheit sagen können" (MN 53). Although Pawel projects these qualities into the future, Wolf's narrator, in accordance with the dictates of Socialist Realism, ascribes the very same characteristics to Pawel and Vera in the present when she states: "Sie lebten mit 'offenem Visier,' arglos, ohne Hinterhalt" (MN 54). Far from challenging the progress of socialism, then, she figures Pawel and Vera in a fashion typical for *Ankunftsliteratur*: they already embody the socialist ideal and live in near to perfect conditions under the 'favorable sky' (MN 54) of socialist brotherhood.

With its conformity to cultural politics and reflection of the morality of a new generation, its comes as no surprise that *Moskauer Novelle* garnered Wolf the "Kunstpreis der Stadt Halle." As Gerda Schultz underlines in *Neue Deutsche Literatur*: "Die tragende Idee der Erzählung ist die tief im Gesellschaftlichen wurzelnde Ethik der sozialistischen Intelligenz."[9] Even the private story of the love affair, Schultz stresses, becomes resolved through the collective and through the character's firm grounding in socialist ethics.

A little over a decade later, Wolf reflected on her "Erstlingswerk" with considerably less favor. In her 1973 essay "Über Sinn und Unsinn der Naivität," she labels the novella "traktathaft," viewing it in retrospect as a pious text resembling a formal, moral treatise (DiA1 47). She goes on to criticize its narrative closure, formal rigidity, mechanical and predictable plot and lack of differentiated character portrayal—all factors that in her view distance it from a "realistic" style or worldview. In short, she directly targets her prior adherence to a doctrinaire Socialist Realist aesthetic, a break with which she had in the meantime articulated theoretically in "Lesen und Schreiben" (1968) and aesthetically in *Nachdenken über Christa T.* (1968).

In "Über Sinn und Unsinn," Wolf also illuminates how the immense pressure to conform fostered an "inner censorship" that led her to exclude from her text certain politically unacceptable topics such as *Vergangenheitsbewältigung*, the coming to terms with Germany's Nazi past. To be sure, in *Moskauer Novelle* Wolf disavows the continuity between past and present and instead supports the GDR's foundational master narrative of anti-fascism by depicting how the establishment of socialism erased all traces of Germany's fascist, capitalist past. In retrospect Wolf sees that while the ideological shift from fascism to socialism had led to a radically different worldview, it had not brought about dramatic changes in the way of thinking (DiA1 51). The new ideology, in other words, did not necessarily reflect the thoughts and actions of its citizens. According to Wolf, what remained was "die Gewohnheit der Gläubigkeit gegen übergeordnete Instanzen, der Zwang, Personen anzubeten oder sich noch ihrer Autorität zu unterwerfen, der Hang zu Realitätsverleugnung und eifervoller Intoleranz" (DiA1 51). Despite this overt comparison between the authoritarian structures of fascism and socialism, Wolf emphasizes that at the time she penned *Moskauer Novelle*, she firmly believed what she wrote, namely that the ideological transformation of her generation was complete (DiA1 50).

Wolf had begun to call this smooth transformation into question in her next literary work, *Der geteilte Himmel*. Published in 1963, Wolf based this novel in part on her own experience from 1960–1961 in the VEB Waggonwerk Ammendorf, Wolf's response to the demand of the "Bitterfelder Weg" that writers enter into the factories and set their texts in the realm of production. Like *Moskauer Novelle*, *Der geteilte Himmel* is a love story in which collective duty triumphs over personal inclination and reason reigns over emotion. Yet Wolf no longer adheres as closely to the prescriptive tenets of Socialist Realism: the novel's narration is non-linear, its style more reflexive, the character portrayal more differentiated, and its political message more ambiguous.

Der geteilte Himmel traces the socialist development of its protagonist, Rita Seidel, and her successful integration into the socialist collective. Rita shares with Vera of *Moskauer Novelle* the conviction that individuals have the ability to change, a deeply held belief in the socialist ideal, and a willingness to realize that ideal in the GDR. As Wolf states, "Sie hat [...] ein großes ursprüngliches Bedürfnis nach menschlicher Sauberkeit, nach Ehrlichkeit, nach Güte. [...] Rita hat das Gefühl: Dieses Leben hier verlangt von ihr die Anspannung aller Kräfte. Es lohnt sich."[10] In *Der geteilte Himmel*, Rita faces the choice of remaining in the GDR or joining her partner Manfred, a disillusioned scientist who defects to West Berlin. Rita's choice to stay in East Berlin coincides temporally with the construction of the Berlin Wall, an historical event that renders her separation from Manfred final. Initially plagued by severe doubt that she had made the best decision, Rita attempts suicide by throwing herself in front of an oncoming train. Rita's suicide attempt on August 13, 1961 at first remains implicit. The exact nature of her "accident" becomes clear late in the novel, and the reader must reconstruct its precise date. Rita's mental and physical rehabilitation in a sanatorium frames the narrative and provides the context through which the other events must ultimately be viewed. Rita's story, narrated primarily from her perspective in the third person, unfolds as she reflects on her relationship with Manfred and her past actions and choices. Through this process she convinces herself—and the reader—that her (irrevocable) decision to stay in the East was sensible after all.

Wolf opens *Der geteilte Himmel* with a description of the city of Halle that, with our present knowledge of the vast environmental destruction in the former GDR, in retrospect appears quite ominous. Thick factory smoke clouds the air, the water supply is polluted: "Die Luft legte sich schwer auf sie, und das Wasser—dieses verfluchte Wasser, das nach Chemie stank, seit sie denken konnten—schmeckte ihnen bitter" (GH 7). The "günstiger Himmel" of *Moskauer Novelle* has become veiled and hard to endure, a feeling of restlessness prevails: "Die Leute, seit langem an diesen verschleierten Himmel gewöhnt, fanden ihn auf einmal ungewöhnlich und schwer zu ertragen, wie sie überhaupt ihre plötzliche Unrast zuerst und den entlegensten Dingen ausließen" (GH 7). Despite this decidedly negative description, the narrative continues with a sense of optimism: "Aber die Erde trug sie [die Leute] noch und würde sie tragen, solange es sie gab" (GH 7). Everyday life goes on despite "sehr naher Gefahren, die alle tödlich sind in dieser Zeit" (GH 7). Both the novel's opening and closing frames end with the positive expression of life and its endless possibilities: "Wir gewöhnen uns wieder, ruhig zu schlafen. Wir leben uns dem vollen, als gäbe es übergenug von diesem seltsamen Stoff Leben, als könnte es nie zu Ende gehen" (GH 7).

The depiction of the river running through Halle similarly juxtaposes environmental degradation with a positive expression of life's pleasures and possibilities:

> Der [Fluß] war, seit Manfred ihn als Kind verlassen hatte, nützlicher und unfreundlicher geworden: er führte watteweißen Schaum mit sich, der übel roch und vom Chemiewerk bis weit hinter die Stadt den Fisch vergiftete. Die Kinder von heute konnten nicht daran denken, hier schwimmen zu lernen, obwohl die Ufer flach und von Gras und Weiden gesäumt waren. (GH 28)

By relating the descriptions "more useful" and "less friendly," Wolf counters the negative image with its positive, social benefit: the river's usefulness for industry and, ultimately, for GDR citizens. She thereby illuminates that the ends justify the means, and leaves the reader with a picture of the river valley as a life-bringing source where the approaching spring gathers its forces and prepares for the powerful blossoming of color. The river, moreover, continues to provide a source of pleasure: "Auch hatte der Fluß nicht verlernt, Menschengesichter zu spiegeln, wenn sie sich an einer ruhigen Stelle weit genug über ihn beugten, den Atem anhielten und in das fließende Wasser blickten, lange" (GH 28-29).

One finds a similar justification of ends and means in Wolf's description of the Soviet Union's manned space mission in April 1961. In *Der geteilte Himmel*, Wolf offsets *"Die Nachricht"* of Juri Gagarin's successful space mission through italics and heightens the anticipation of the news by repeating it seven times in the twenty-third chapter. Though the extraordinary event provided a concrete symbol for the heralded progress in socialist countries, Wolf goes on to undercut its significance by simultaneously depicting obvious shortcomings of scientific-technological progress in the GDR. The group receives "Die Nachricht" precisely at the moment that the brakes of the new railway coach they are test-riding malfunction. This technological setback compounds with other obstacles to progress. Wolf highlights the shortage of essential raw materials, the defection of skilled labor to the West, the government's rejection of innovative projects, such as Manfred's innovative design for a spinning jenny, and the hardships resulting from primitive farming conditions. Combined, these factors shape and in many ways justify Manfred's skepticism. Whereas the others applaud "the news," Manfred responds soberly: "Was jetzt kommt, das weiß ich schon. Eine Propagandaschlacht größten Stils um den ersten Kosmonauten. Sirrende, glühende Telegrafendrähte. Eine Sturmflut von bedrucktem Papier, unter der die Menschheit weiterleben wird wie eh und je" (GH 145-146). Emphasizing the discrepancy between means and ends, Manfred argues that the space race will not alleviate the hardships of everyday life:

> Der Bauer da, [...] der wird auch morgen sein Pferdchen anspannen. Und unsere ausgediente Lokomotive, dieses Vehikel des vorigen Jahrhunderts, läßt uns wie zum Hohn schon heute im Stich. Welch ein Haufen von unnötiger Alltagsmühsal! Die wird kein bißchen leichter durch die glanzvollen Extravaganzen in der Stratosphäre. (GH 146)

Manfred's pessimism and individuality set him apart from the collective. The others respond to Manfred's diatribe with silence and view his cynical resignation as a sign of weakness.

Unlike the collective Manfred acknowledges and addresses societal contradictions. He admits: "Vielleicht fehlt mir die glasharte Nüchternheit des wissenschaftlichen Denkens. Aber der Sinn für die Pikanterie gewisser Widersprüche fehlt mir nicht.—Zum Beispiel: Für den Widerspruch zwischen Mittel und Zweck" (GH 147). Himself a chemist, Manfred directs his critique at the political instrumentalization of science and technology. A pragmatist, he seeks to realize the positive impact of science and technology on everyday life and recognizes that in this regard the East lags far behind the West. In Manfred's view, scientists should not seek to launch man into space, but instead contribute to "ein Dasein ohne Leerlauf durch technische Unvollkommenheiten, Lebensverlängerung durch Intensivierung..." (GH 100). Rather than bold explorations of the universe, he envisions: "Ein Haus, das funktioniert wie eine gut geölte Maschine [...]. Städte, in welchen ein genau geplanter Kreislauf menschlichen Lebens sich ohne Reibung und Stockung vollzieht..." (GH 100).

Manfred's skepticism stems in part from his recognition of socialism's dogmatism and contradictions, the mechanistic and facile claims that rapid advances in science and technology will necessarily usher in a new morality. In this regard, he exclaims: "Ich bedaure nur die Unmasse von Illusion und Energie, die an Unmögliches verschwendet wird. Moral in diese Welt bringen!" (GH 147) Born in 1929, the same year as Wolf and ten years before Rita, Manfred in some ways typifies his generation. His parents' fascistic attitudes and the hypocrisy he encounters in his professional life have profoundly affected his worldview, and have left him unconvinced that the ideological shift from fascism to socialism has transformed attitudes and behaviors. Expressing his lack of conviction, he states: "Ich spreche von Erfahrungen. Von Erfahrungen mit—Menschlichkeit. Wenn's drauf ankommt, blättert die doch zuerst ab. Ja:

Habsucht, Eigenliebe, Mißtrauen, Neid—darauf kann man sich immer verlassen. Gute alte Gewohnheiten aus unserer Halbtierzeit. Aber Menschlichkeit?" (GH 148)

In casting Manfred, Wolf prefigures many of the qualities of the positive, female figures we find in her later works: he weighs means and ends, recognizes the lack of *Vergangenheitsbewältigung* in the GDR and upholds the importance of the individual. It would be going too far to claim that Wolf wants her readers to identify with Manfred rather than with Rita, yet these shared traits indicate that Wolf at the very least wants her readers to understand him.

In the 1960s, literature's function in the GDR was political and didactic: it was to support and strengthen the country's socialist goals by presenting "typical" and exemplary heroes whom readers would strive to emulate. While numerous reviewers in the East praised such aspects of *Der geteilte Himmel* as Rita's socialist development, the differentiated character portrayal and blending of subjectivity and objectivity, orthodox critics were quick to claim that Wolf's "mixed" and "untypical" characters rendered the novel's ideological message overly ambiguous. Since the majority of reviewers read the text for authorial intention rather than for its aesthetic merits, Wolf's own ideological stance became suspect. Interpretations that conflate the perspectives of the author, the narrator and fictional characters draw attention to the marked tendency, not only on the part of GDR critics, to read GDR literature foremost for its political tenor and ideological content. This predeliction came to characterize the debate surrounding *Was bleibt*. With regard to *Der geteilte Himmel*, negative appraisals equated Manfred's pessimism with the seeming shakiness of Wolf's own ideological stance. Among GDR critics, Dietrich Allert and Hubert Wetzelt articulate the most scathing criticism. In their opinion, Wolf's prime concern is the "Manfreds," those who lack faith in socialist progress.[11] Despite the counter example offered by Rita, Manfred's failure to change and become a "good socialist" along with his decision for life in the West lead Allert und Wetzelt to maintain: "von der alles verändernden Kraft unserer Gesellschaft ist in der Erzählung zuwenig spürbar" (81). With the character of Manfred, they argue, Wolf attempts to connect two incompatible ideologies and thereby weaves "den Faden dekadenter Lebensauffassung" (83) into the development of socialism.

This accusation of "decadence" is based on Manfred's pessimism about scientific-technological progress. In a similar vein, GDR critic Günter Wirth emphasizes: "Dieser Nihilismus, diese Menschenverachtung, die sich bei Manfred mit einer Vergötzung der Technik verbindet [...] diese kleinbürgerlichen weltanschaulichen Elemente sind der Kontrapunkt zu dem neuen Lebensgefühl...."[12] By setting nihilism, contempt for others, and the demonization of technology in opposition to the "new feeling for life," Wirth reflects the unwavering optimism in scientific-technological progress inscribed in socialist ideology.

While *Der geteilte Himmel* provoked a major literary debate upon publication,[13] positive assessments prevailed. Wolf even received the 1963 Heinrich Mann Prize from the GDR Academy of Arts for the work, an unequivocal indication of its ultimate acceptance by cultural officials. In awarding Wolf this prize, Alfred Kurella praised the novel for fulfilling "die Mission der sozialistischen Kunst, die Gedanken- und Empfindungswelt der Werktätigen wiederzugeben, den Erlebnisreichtum unserer Zeit zu erschließen und die Verstandes- wie die Gefühlskräfte des Volkes zu bilden."[14] For Kurella, Wolf's novel paradigmatically represents the expectations for literature announced at the VI. Party Congress of the SED in 1963. The following excerpt from the program of the Party Congress highlights the close conformity of Wolf's text to official cultural policy:

> Die im Kunstwerk gestalteten Erkenntnisse und Gefühle dienen der moralischen Veränderung der Menschen im Geiste des Sozialismus. [...] Da unsere Epoche der großen gesellschaftlichen Umwälzungen, der kühnen Vorstöße in den Weltraum, der Herausbildung wahrhaft menschlicher Beziehungen reich an großen und starken Gefühlen ist, sind unsere Künstler und Schriftsteller vor die Aufgabe gestellt, in ihren Werken dieses neue Lebensgefühl zu gestalten. (Kurella 29)

According to Kurella, then, *Der geteilte Himmel* successfully conveyed the new "feeling for life" brought about by the grand social changes of the epoch. While Kurella stresses the instrumental role of scientific-technological progress in creating this new feeling, he stresses that the socialist writer's task is to express this crucial nexus of the public and the private. By showing how Rita's fundamental belief in socialism weighed in her decision to remain in the GDR and become fully integrated into the collective, *Der geteilte Himmel* succeeds at doing just that.

As rapid, forced industrialization led to the emergence of an industrial culture similar to that of the West, "mit ihren fetischen Wachstum, Sicherheit und Effektivität, aber auch mit Konsumismus und Entfremdung" (Emmerich 409), literary representations came to constitute part of a fundamental *Zivilisationskritik*. Wolf makes her growing disenchantment with cultural politics readily apparent in her contribution to the *II. Bitterfelder Konferenz* in 1964. In her conference speech, Wolf openly rejects the exceedingly optimistic and objective representations characteristic of Socialist Realism and the *Bitterfelder Weg*. Attempting to broaden the definition of socialist writing while simultaneously underscoring her support for socialism, a rhetorical strategy she again employs in her essay collection *Lesen und Schreiben*, she argues that prevailing representations are far from "realistic" or "truthful." To support her position, Wolf draws on reader reception and asks: "Was ist denn Wahrheit? ...

Und was ist die Wahrheit der Kunst, die statistische, die soziologische, die agitorische? Und was kann man Lesern an Problematik und Konflikten zumuten?" (DiA1 390) In expanding the concept of "truth," Wolf seeks to create a space in literature both for the "atypical" and for the subjectivity of the author. The representation of conflicts and contradictions, she argues, should not be seen as reflecting negatively on the GDR, but rather as comprising a natural aspect of socialist development.

With her revision of the concept of "realism," Wolf challenges the dominant aesthetic doctine that, strongly influenced by Georg Lukács, long the authoritative voice in matters of socialist aesthetics, demands that literature mirror reality. Wolf contends that this mode of representation fails to "mirror" reality, but reflects an ameliorative picture thereof—one consonant with an objective and mechanical worldview. A literature that addressed societal contradictions would give Western readers a better understanding of the GDR. In addition, GDR readers would benefit from seeing their lives, which diverge from the "typical," depicted. To substantiate her view Wolf relates an anecdote about a writer sent to interview a reputable brigade commander who had recently become a party member. Told to offer a true-to-life account, the author's portrayal naturally differs from the socialist ideal: the worker is divorced, joined the party for purely pragmatic reasons rather than out of conviction, and, to top it off, his son has been jailed for attempting to flee the country. One by one, the writer is forced to strike these details. Finally, he is informed that he was sent to the wrong brigade commander. His story goes unpublished. With this anecdote, Wolf accentuates that the writer's story is not a mere figment of his imagination: it is "realistic" and should be understood as such. Writers, in her view, must be allowed to represent such deviations as they neither oppose nor impede socialist development. In this way Wolf seeks to counter the prevalent interpretation of cultural officials that writing which is less than "objective" and "optimistic" necessarily weakens the position of socialism. Wolf grounds this mode of writing firmly in socialist society and presents it as consonant with its goals: "Für die Kunst bestehen die Vorzüge unserer Gesellschaft darin, daß ihr Wesen mit den objektiven Gesetzen der Entwicklung, mit den objektiven Interessen der Menschen übereinstimmt" (DiA1 389). In the GDR, she suggests, the foundation has been laid "zu einem vernünftigen Zusammenleben der Menschen" (DiA1 398). Thus, while she renounced normative cultural politics Wolf retained her belief that a truly socialist society could emerge in the GDR. In fact, between 1963 and 1967 (between the VI. and VII. Party Congress of the SED), she was a candidate for the Central Committee of the SED. In 1964, then, Wolf still expresses complete confidence in socialism, as accentuated by her claim: "Die Vernunft—wir nennen es Sozialismus—ist in den Alltag eingedrungen. Sie ist das Maß, nach dem hier gemessen, das Ideal, in dessen Namen hier gelobt und getadelt wird" (DiA1 398).

The "Dialetic of Enlightenment" in GDR Literature

Wolfgang Emmerich argues that the literary *Zivilisationskritik* of the late 1970s and 1980s evinces numerous parallels to the dialectic of enlightenment theorized by Horkheimer and Adorno in the 1940s. The rise of Stalinism after the Russian revolution, the failure of left-wing workers' movements in Western Europe in the 1930s, the spread of fascism and the atrocities of Nazism led Horkheimer and Adorno to question the adequacy of orthodox Marxism to account for twentieth-century developments. The GDR of the late 1970s and 1980s, Emmerich asserts, generated "analoge Traumata, Analysen und Gedanken" (411). This paradigm shift, brought about by the disillusionment over Stalinist socialism, the irrational nuclear buildup, environmental destruction, the Chernobyl disaster, and the failure of Marxist movements in the Third World, found expression in that country's critical literature (411).

An analysis on the scientific tendencies of orthodox Marxism is central to early Frankfurt School thought. The interdisciplinary Institute for Social Research was formed in Frankfurt in the 1920s in response to the diffusion of socialist goals after World War I. Its primary aim was to examine the scientific tendencies in Marxist theory, to ascertain Marxism's ""true' or 'pure' form."[15] With the rise of fascism and the advent of World War II, the Marxist Institute faced a precarious future. Its members were forced into exile and, in response to the mounting irrationality of their time, grew more skeptical in their appraisals of Marxism. Martin Jay notes that "although criticizing the adequacy of orthodox Marxism, they [Horkheimer and Adorno] had not rejected its ambitious project: the ultimate unity of Critical Theory and revolutionary practice. By the 1940s, however, the Frankfurt School began to have serious doubts about the feasibility of this synthesis" (253).

Addressing the development of "critical Marxism" after the Second World War, Albrecht Wellmer unifies the diverse critical Western Marxisms of Korsch, the Frankfurt School, Sartre, and Marcuse, as well as critical strains of East bloc Marxism insofar as

[kritischer Marxismus] als Ausdruck oppositioneller Strömungen genötigt ist, implizit oder explizit gegen die objektivistischen Züge der Marxschen Geschichtsphilosophie Stellung zu beziehen; daß er Partei ergreift für die Autonomie- und Glücksansprüchen der Individuen gegen die historisch wirksamen Tendenzen zur Totalisierung technischer und bürokratischer Rationalität; daß er—darin ganz unmarxistisch—Partei ergreift für die "Tugend" und gegen den "Weltlauf." (135–136)

In the following, I will concentrate on those aspects of Horkheimer and

Adorno's *Dialektik der Aufklärung* that developed in opposition to orthodox Marxist-Leninism and address scientific and technological progress.

Horkheimer and Adorno conceptualize fascism as the culmination of enlightenment progress, and retain little faith that the course of history can be changed, that a truly human society can emerge. They employ the term "enlightenment" not only in reference to the historical Enlightenment of the eighteenth century, but also in the broader sense of progressive thought whose goal it is, "von den Menschen die Furcht zu nehmen und sie als Herren einzusetzen."[16] They contend: "Das Programm der Aufklärung war die Entzauberung der Welt. Sie wollte die Mythen auflösen und Einbildung durch Wissen stürzen" (DA 9). The attempt to demythologize the world, they argue, led to the creation of a new myth: the myth of progress through reason and technology. Strongly criticizing the teleology of Western civilization, they argue that objectivity, man's domination of nature and the instrumentalization of reason have resulted in manipulation and, ultimately, in the negation of the individual: thought and reason have become reified, the object and subject world separated. Horkheimer and Adorno claim: "Die Aufklärung verhält sich zu den Dingen wie der Diktator zu den Menschen. Er kennt sie, insofern er sie manipulieren kann" (DA 15). In short, the Enlightenment's totalitarian and authoritarian nature threatens our individuality and, as history has proven, our very existence.

Horkheimer and Adorno pursue the question why society has regressed to "a new type of barbarism" rather than progressing toward the "truly human condition" postulated by Marx (DA 3). Reflecting on the course of Western civilization, they theorize that Enlightenment concepts of progress and reason (as an instrument of domination) contain within themselves the seeds of their own destruction, negatively coupling progress and regression, enlightenment and myth, emancipation and the annihilation of the self, reason and power:

> Wo die Entwicklung der Maschine in die der Herrschaftsmaschinerie schon umgeschlagen ist, so daß technische und gesellschaftliche Tendenz, von je verflochten, in der totalen Erfassung der Menschen konvergieren, vertreten die Zurückgebliebenen nicht bloß die Unwahrheit. Demgegenüber involviert Anpassung an die Macht des Fortschritts den Fortschritt der Macht [...] Der Fluch des unaufhaltsamen Fortschritts ist die unaufhaltsame Regression. (DA 42)

This leads Horkheimer and Adorno to underscore the need for reflexivity, for a dialectic of enlightenment. They state:

> Wir hegen keinen Zweifel [...] daß die Freiheit in der Gesellschaft vom aufklärenden Denken unabtrennbar ist. Jedoch glauben wir, [...] daß der Begriff eben dieses Denkens, nicht weniger als die konkreten his-

torischen Formen, die Institutionen der Gesellschaft, in die es verflochten ist, schon den Keim zu jenem Rückschritt enthalten, der heute überall sich ereignet. Nimmt Aufklärung die Reflexion auf dieses rückläufige Moment nicht in sich auf, so besiegelt sie ihr eigenes Schicksal. (DA 3)

As evinced by the above citation, Horkheimer and Adorno do not completely reject the Enlightenment project. Rather, they see "enlightenment" thought as integral for human freedom. This leads them to develop a concept of enlightenment, "der sie aus ihrer Verstrickung in blinder Herrschaft löst" (DA 6). Despite the positive aspects of an "enlightenment" of the Enlightenment, Jürgen Habermas characterizes Horkheimer and Adorno as cynical, "schwarze Schriftsteller." Habermas analyses Horkheimer and Adorno's indebtedness to Nietzsche, and asks: "Wie können die beiden Aufklärer, die sie immer noch sind, den vernünftigen Gehalt der kulturellen Moderne so unterschätzen, daß sie in allem nur eine Legierung von Vernunft und Herrschaft, Macht und Geltung wahrnehmen?"[17] The bleak circumstance under which Horkheimer and Adorno wrote helps to explain why they place so little faith in reason or human agency to alter the course of history.

Positivism, rapid technological progress and the domination of nature are key areas of Horkheimer and Adorno's critique of enlightenment. "Nicht bloß durch die Entfremdung der Menschen von den beherrschten Objekten wird für die Herrschaft bezahlt: mit der Versachlichung des Geistes wurden die Beziehungen der Menschen selber verhext, auch die jedes Einzelnen zu sich" (DA 34), they emphasize. In other words, the culmination of enlightenment reason has not only legitimated domination and power over others and over nature but also resulted in self-alienation. Unreflected scientific-technological progress goes hand in hand with the tenets of positivism: "Technik ist das Wesen dieses Wissens. Es zielt nicht auf Begriffe und Bilder, nicht auf das Glück der Einsicht, sondern auf Methode, Ausnutzung der Arbeit anderer, Kapital" (DA 10). Rather than learning from nature, man has employed technology to control both nature and others.

In the preface to the 1969 edition of *Dialektik der Aufklärung*, Horkheimer and Adorno stress the continued relevance of the major tenets of their text, completed in 1944 and first published in 1947. With the escalation of Cold War politics, increased technocracy and continued domination of man and nature, they argue: "In der Periode der politischen Spaltung in übergroße Blöcke, die objektiv dazu gedrängt werden, aufeinander zu prallen, hat das Grauen sich fortgesetzt" (DA ix). In the preface to *Kritische Theorie* (1968), Horkheimer similarly reflects on postwar developments, stating: "Jetzt ist der Faschismus zwar besiegt, doch keineswegs überwunden."[18] It must be underscored that despite their Marxist orientation Horkheimer and Adorno direct their critique not only at advanced capitalist society, but rather subsume Marxism, and with it socialist society, under the Enlightenment tradition and its positivist legacy. Lacking reflexivity, it has become a dogmatic and reified theory far removed from reality. By broadening their scope to include Western civilization in general, Horkheimer and Adorno reveal the convergence of liberal and totalitarian ideologies to which they count not only fascism, but also Stalinism. Indicting the teleology of progress, they state:

> In dem er [der Sozialismus, B.R.] für alle Zukunft die Notwendigkeit zur Basis erhob und den Geist auf gut idealistisch zur höchsten Spitze depravierte, hielt er das Erbe der bürgerlichen Philosophie allzu krampfhaft fest. So bliebe das Verhältnis der Notwendigkeit zum Reich der Freiheit bloß quantitativ; mechanisch, und Natur, als ganz fremd gesetzt, wie in der ersten Mythologie, wurde totalitär und absorbierte die Freiheit samt dem Sozialismus. (DA 47)

The idea of socialism, Horkheimer states in 1968, "wurde in den Ländern des Diamat [Dialektischen Materialismus] längst zum Instrument der Manipulation pervertiert."[19] This theory of convergence helps to explain the official dismissal of Frankfurt School theories in the GDR.

The Reception of the Frankfurt School in the GDR

The GDR's negative official reception of Horkheimer and Adorno's writings, more specifically of *Dialektik der Aufklärung*, until the late 1980s exposes how the Frankfurt School undermined the Marxist-Leninist critique of late-capitalist society. A closer look at the official GDR reception shows the extent to which it distinguished itself from critical Marxism's unofficial and positive reception in the literary realm.

Given stringent controls on publishing, the publication history of *Dialektik der Aufklärung* in the GDR lends insight into this work's official reception. The first edition of that text, only 500 hectograph copies, was published in the United States in 1944 under the title "Philosophische Fragmente."[20] The text as we commonly know it today was published in Amsterdam in 1947. As Waltraud Naumann-Beyer points out, the revisions Horkheimer and Adorno undertook between the 1944 and the 1947 editions document their shift from a narrow focus of late-capitalist society to an encompassing critique of Western civilization. Naumann-Beyer notes the following changes: "Ausdrücke, die sich auf den Kapitalismus und auf den Monopolkapitalismus beziehen, und solche, die an Marx oder sogar an Lenin erinnert hätten, sind ausgetauscht worden, als wäre nicht von einer bestimmten Gesellschaft die Rede, sondern von der

Gesellschaft im allgemeinen" (1222). Martin Jay attributes this subtle terminological shift in part to the precarious situation of the Institute members' at Columbia University during the time of growing anti-communist hysteria in the postwar United States (44). More generally, he views these changes as "a reflection of their fundamental aversion to the type of Marxism that the Institute equated with the orthodoxy of the Soviet camp" and a result of "a growing loss of that basic confidence, which Marxists had traditionally felt, in the revolutionary potential of the proletariat" (44). This obvious departure from orthodox Marxist-Leninism helps to explain why *Dialektik der Aufklärung* remained largely unavailable in the GDR: segments of the text were printed in the journal *Sinn und Form* in 1949, yet only in early 1989 was the complete work published in the GDR.

In the early 1970s, two Marxist works on the Frankfurt School appeared in the GDR: *Die "Frankfurter Schule" im Lichte des Marxismus* (1970/1974) and *Die Sünden der Frankfurter Schule* (1971). Both texts document the renewed reception of the Frankfurt School precipitated in the late 1960s by the left-wing student movement in the West, which again brought Marxist ideas into the limelight. In the Federal Republic, the resurgence of radicalism among the younger generation led to the republication of *Dialektik der Aufklärung*. In the GDR, however, the Frankfurt School's unorthodox interpretation of "Marxism" was harshly discredited as a significant threat to the party line.

The afterword of *Die "Frankfurter Schule" im Lichte des Marxismus* cites the following aspects of Horkheimer and Adorno's theory proved particularly contentious[21]: their loss of faith in the revolutionary potential of the proletariat, without which true political action is not seen as possible; the negative dialectic, which was thought to lead to an "abstrakt-negative, also weitgehend richtungs- und ziellose politische Praxis;" the conviction that the Frankfurt School's theories weaken the position of Marxism, creating prejudices and barriers against "eine unverfälschte Rezeption der Theorien von Marx, Engels und Lenin, gegen den realen Sozialismus und die revolutionäre Bewegung" (179–180). The following quote of Lenin prefaces *Die Sünden der Frankfurter Schule* and echoes the antagonistic tenor and ideological thrust of these works:

> [B]ürgerliche oder sozialistische Ideologie. Ein Mittelding gibt es hier nicht (denn eine 'dritte' Ideologie hat die Menschheit nicht geschaffen, weil es überhaupt ... niemals eine außerhalb der Klassen und über den Klassen stehende Ideologie geben kann). Darum bedeutet *jede* Herabminderung der sozialistischen Ideologie, jedes *Abschwenken* von ihr zugleich eine Stärkung der bürgerlichen Ideologie.[22]

The diametrical opposition of socialist and bourgeois ideologies precludes any differentiation. As a "modern" version of Marxism, Critical Theory is not only discredited as an unviable "third way," but seen to undermine the status of socialist ideology by laying bare its deficiencies.

Because the revolutionary role of the working class constitutes one of the basic tenets of Marxist theory, the failure of Frankfurt School theorists to regard class conflict as the motor of history in effect places them into the opposing bourgeois camp. Wellmer expounds on Horkheimer and Adorno's break with Marx's concepts of political economy and revolution, and details their move toward a critique of instrumental reason and technological society (139):

> Die Kritische Theorie bringt somit Marx gegenüber zur Geltung, daß der schicksalhafte Prozeß der "Rationalisierung" aller gesellschaft-lichen Lebensprozesse gerade nicht in einer emanzipierten Gesellschaft sein naturwüchsig vorgezeichnetes Ende hat, sondern seiner innersten Logik nach eher in das Gegenteil münden muß: in die Subsumption der Menschen unter die von ihnen selbst errungene Herrschaft über die Natur. Damit ist aber "Revolution" nicht mehr als bewußter und kollektiver Vollzug einer objektivierbaren historischen Notwendigkeit denkbar. "Revolution" im Sinne einer Emanzipation von der Naturgeschichte der Menschheit wäre vielmehr das aus sich selbst resultierende Durchbrechen jener Dialektik der Aufklärung, deren blinder Vollzug die bisherigen Revolutionen lediglich waren. (141)

Whereas Marx posited that class conflict would bring about emancipation through the revolution of the working class, for Horkheimer and Adorno the revolution of the proletariat no longer seemed possible in light of changed historical conditions. Rather than draw out a positive development toward emancipation and the full development of individual freedoms, they assert that increased rationalization and technologization would further domination and control over nature and others. As stressed earlier, emancipation in their view only becomes possible through reflection on the Enlightenment's dark side.

Relating Critical Theory and Marxist-Leninism, Walter Jopke, acting chair of sociology at the GDR Institute for Social Sciences at the time, focuses on the theoretical positions outlined in *Dialektik der Aufklärung* and Adorno's *Negative Dialektik*.[23] Jopke defines the two main tenets of Marxist-Leninism as the materialist analysis of bourgeois society and the dialectic, and argues that Critical Theory and scientific socialism are utterly incongruous as the former negates and denies these key aspects. In contrast to the orthodox view that historical progress is objectively definable, Frankfurt School critics account for perceptions and agency (51). Jopke argues:

> Das, was in Wahrheit die große Leistung der materialistischen Dialektik ausmacht—daß sie es ermöglicht, die notwendigen

objektiven Entwicklungsgesetztmäßigkeiten, die zu einer höheren Ordnung führen, zu erkennen, wird in der "kritischen Theorie" gerade beseitigt.[...] Aus der Überwindung des Kapitalismus wird die gedenkliche Negation jedes gesellschaftliche Systems überhaupt. (61)

Jopke draws on the purportedly successful development of socialism in Eastern Europe to support the thesis of communism's inevitability and uphold the central role of the working class. Because it fails to attribute a revolutionary role to the proletariat, Critial Theory is seen to lack a concrete historical subject and to foster resignation. Jopke summarizes:

Pessimistische Prognosen über die revolutionäre Perspektive der Arbeiterklasse und aller fortschrittlichen sozialen Kräfte, das ist hier unbedingt festzuhalten, folgen bei Horkheimer und Adorno aus einer falschen, liberal-kulturpessimistischen, subjektivistischen Geschichts-theorie, aus dem Ansatz einer kleinbürgerlichen Resignations-ideologie—aus einer antimarxistischen, spätbürgerlichen philo-sophischen Position! Es ist einfach Unsinn, diese antimaterialistische, antisozialistische philosophische Auffassung als 'modernen Marxis-mus' ausgeben zu wollen! (52)

Harsh attacks against Horkheimer and Adorno are typical of orthodox Marxists who view the search for alternate paths of social development, i.e., alternate interpretations of Marxism, as undermining Marxism's status in socialist countries.

In the early 1970s, orthodox GDR critics vehemently rejected the notion of a convergence of capitalism and socialism. In short, then, a theory pessimistic of the working class's revolutionary potential did not fall into the GDR's narrow definition of Marxism. Moreover, since Horkheimer and Adorno's critique of late capitalism encompasses developments in socialist societies, it also highlights the discrepancy between Marxism's emancipatory aims and its Stalinist manifestations. In his introduction to *Kritische Theorie* (1968), Horkheimer noted "[d]er scheinbar oppositionelle Anspruch, aggressive Begriffe wie Klassenherrschaft und Imperialismus auf kapitalistische Staaten allein und nicht ebensosehr auf angeblich kommunistische zu beziehen...."[24] Orthodox GDR critics counter the accusation that orthodox Marxist categories had proven inadequate to account for historical changes with the argument that the development of socialism in the East bloc consitutes an "optimaler Verwirklichung gemäß der immanenten Zwecken der sozialistischen Gesellschaftsordnung" (62). The inability to recognize and come to terms with the apparent contradictions of orthodox doctrine contributed significantly to the GDR's collapse in 1989.

The Frankfurt School's negative appraisal of technology constitutes one of the primary points of criticism on the part of GDR theorists. The Frankfurt School critique of technologization and the instrumentalization of reason is clearly incompatible with the notion of the STR's unique development in socialist countries discussed earlier. Wilhelm Raimund Beyer emphasizes:

> Technik als solche wird in der "Kritischen Theorie" eine an sich vorhandene, aus sich selbst erzeugte Produktivkraft, die politische Bindungen ablehnt. Ihre Klassenneutralität ist es gerade, die die selbständige Technik zu dem Ungeheuer anwachsen läßt, das wie ein Golem seinen Erzeuger unter sich zwingt. (89)

Regarding Horkheimer and Adorno's view of the self and nature as dominated by unreflected technological progress, Jopke likewise stresses their failure to situate these negative consequences within capitalism: "Es ist ihnen offensichtlich unmöglich, daß die Entwicklung der Produktivkräfte anderen Gesetzen als denen der kapitalistischen Produtionsverhältnissen gehorchen kann" (55–56). Without acknowledging conflicts or individual consequences, he triumphs socialism over capitalism and legitimates his position with recourse to the Marxist ideal that technological advances will free individuals from the toils of manual labor, allow more leisure time and help to develop the "allseitig entwickelte Persönlichkeit."

The underlying antagonism between orthodox Marxist-Leninism and Critical Theory with regard to the role of the proletariat and the relation of political praxis to "real existing socialism" reveals the tension between objective and subjective readings of Marx. As with the *Positivismusstreit*, the conflict between empirical analyses that constitute the legacy of positivism and social analyses that consider individualistic and speculative elements came to the fore in the GDR reception of the Frankfurt School. Martin Jay argues, however, that Critical Theory in many ways represents a return to Marx, in effect a reinvigoration of Marxist theory (42). "One of the essential characteristics of Critical Theory from its inception," states Jay, "had been its refusal to consider Marxism a closed body of received truths" (254). In the GDR of the late 1980s, the acute disillusionment with socialist orthodoxy signaled the dire need for a critical assessment of socialist society. This, in turn, rekindled interest in Frankfurt School theories. As Andras Gedö recognized in 1970, "Die 'kritische Theorie' ist zum Prototyp der vom Marxismus-Leninismus verschiedenen, ihm gegenüberstehenden, sich als 'westlicher Marxismus' bezeichnenden Ideologie des 'Dritten Weges' geworden."[25] Yet, while in the early 1970s the Frankfurt School's ideology of a "third way" posed a significant threat and was officially discredited, the late 1980s presented a radically different historical context.

The search for an alternative yet Marxist path characterizes Waltraud

Naumann-Beyer's interpretation of *Dialektik der Aufklärung* upon the text's publication in 1989 by the Leipzig Reclam publishing house. That the text was published at all attests to a renewed interest in Frankfurt School Marxism in the GDR. In her reading of *Dialektik der Aufklärung*, Naumann-Beyer underscores Horkheimer and Adorno's call for a critical consciousness, for reflexivity regarding society's development.[26] Writing prior to her country's dramatic collapse, Naumann-Beyer draws direct connections between Horkheimer and Adorno's theories and the situation of the GDR. She presents as urgent concerns the devastation of the environment, the domination of nature and the short-sightedness of scientific goals, and pushes for open and critical dialogue in the public sphere. Far from denying the convergence of socialism and capitalism, Naumann-Beyer questions the status quo in the GDR. By tracing Horkheimer and Adorno's development from devout Marxists in the twenties and thirties to their growing disenchantment in light of historical events in the 1940s, she justifies the broadened scope of their critique. Rather than read *Dialektik der Aufklärung* as ending only in pessimism, moreover, she translates its critique into a critical optimism. Unlike GDR publications of the early 1970s, Naumann-Beyer averts attention from factors such as Horkheimer and Adorno's skepticism regarding the revolutionary potential of the working class. Instead she focuses on the need for an open reading of their theories, in other words, for an open-ended Marxism. By contextualizing *Dialektik der Aufklärung* and drawing parallels to the present, she advocates a reading of the text in line with the "new thinking" ushered in by Gorbachev's reforms in the mid- to late 1980s:

> Fasse es nicht als wissenschaftliche Prognose auf, die Unheil voraussagt, sondern als negative Utopie, die durch Übertreiben warnen will! Versteh' es als ein Menetekel, das Fehler und Verhängnisse des alten Denkens vergrößert und so für ein *neues Denken* wirbt. Dann wirst du vielleicht vernehmen, was ich aus ihm herausgehört habe: Die Aufforderung, die alte Logik des Gleich um Gleich, von Drohung und Gegendrohung oder—wenn du willst—von Rüstung und Gegenrüstung endlich außer Kraft zu setzen! (1228)

The GDR's practical reassessment of Critical Marxism in the late 1980s, as exemplified by the publication of *Dialektik der Aufklärung*, underlines the growing recognition of the gross inadequacies of socialism. Predating this by approximately twenty years is the indirect and positive literary reception of the Frankfurt School's "modern" Marxism, a discourse that runs counter to the official rejection of their ideas until shortly before the country's collapse.

As mentioned in the previous chapter, within the context of the post-Wall *Literaturstreit* Richard Herzinger and Heinz-Peter Preußer refute the thesis that representations of progress in later GDR literature seriously undermined the regime's legitimacy.[27] While they acknowledge the *Zivilisationskritik* inherent in works of Wolf and GDR writers such as Heiner Müller, Volker Braun and Christoph Hein, they view this critique not as a counter-discourse, but as a sign of consensus between the socialist state and its literary intellectuals. Central to their thesis is the premise that this literary *Zivilisationskritik* did not address specific developments in the GDR, but rather served as a warning against the alienation and instrumentalization associated with the capitalist West. They explain:

> Dem auf Zerstörung durch Profitmaximierung programmierten Welt-markt dürfte der Sozialismus sich nicht ausliefern. Allein seine Resistenz gegenüber der trügerisch glizernden und doch todgeweihten westlichen Zivilisation legitimiert den real existierenden Sozialismus als Gegenposition, aus der das "Andere" denkbar bleibt. (196)

Since industrialization proceeded much more rapidly in the West, the East bloc in their view came to constitute a refuge of slowness and underdevelopment that forestalled the negative consequences of technological progress: "Nicht mehr aus seiner eigenen fortschritts- und technikbegeisterten Ideologie, sondern gerade aus seinem Versagen, aus dem Mangel gegenüber dem Überfluß der westlich-bürgerlichen Gesellschaft heraus wird nun der Sozialismus legitimiert" (196). As I accentuate in the interpretations that follow, for Wolf, Maron and Königsdorf concerns arising from unfettered scientific-technological progress are irreducible to capitalism or socialism. Instead, negative consequences such as environmental degradation (e.g., in *Der geteilte Himmel, Flugasche*), alienation (*Nachdenken über Christa T., Kein Ort. Nirgends, Die Überläuferin),* cybernetics ("Die neuen Lebensansichten eines Katers," "Selbstversuch"), and nuclear threat (*Kassandra, Störfall, Respektloser Umgang*) are endemic to the ideology of progress in Western, patriarchal societies to which the GDR certainly counts. Herzinger and Preußer postulate that the slow process of modernization in the GDR constituted an ideal ground, even a prerequisite, for the cultivation of "sisterliness" and those "feminine values" (206) that these writers uphold as working against Western civilization's destructive course. As they target precisely these "anti-modern" values, Herzinger and Preußer present an affront against Wolf's particular brand of feminism.

Notes

1   Quoted in Wolfgang Emmerich, "'Dialektik der Aufklärung' in der jüngeren DDR-Literatur," *Die Literatur der DDR. 1976–1986. Akten der internationalen Konferenz. Pisa. Mai 1987*, ed. Anna Chiarloni, Gemma

Sartori and Fabrizio Cambi (Pisa: Giardini, 1988) 407.

2 James Schmitt and James Miller, "Aspects of Technology in Marx and Rousseau," *The Technological Imagination*, ed. Teresa de Lauretis, Andreas Huyssen and Kathleen Woodward (Milwaukee/Madison: University of Wisconsin Press, 1980) 88–89.

3 M. Buhr and G. Kröber, *Mensch—Wissenschaft—Technik. Versuch einer marxistischen Analyse der wissenschaflich-technischen Revolution* (Köln: Pahl-Rugenstein, 1977). First published in Russian. See also Alexander Stephan, "Die wissenschaftlich-technische Revolution in der Literatur der DDR," *Der Deutschunterricht* 2 (1978): 17–34.

4 See Roger Shattuck, *Forbidden Knowledge. From Prometheus to Pornography* (New York: St. Martin's Press, 1996).

5 Alfons Auer, "Darf der Mensch, was er kann?" *Wissenschaft, Technik, Humanität: Beiträge zu einer konkreten Ethik*, ed. Alois Buch and Jörg Splett (Frankfurt a. M.: Verlag Josef Knecht, 1982) 15.

6 Immanuel Kant, "Beantwortung der Frage: Was ist Aufklärung,?" *Was ist Aufklärung? Thesen und Definitionen*, ed. Ehrhard Bahr (Stuttgart: Reclam, 1986) 9.

7 Albrecht Wellmer, *Kritische Gesellschaftstheorie und Positivismus* (Frankfurt a. M.: Suhrkamp, 1969) 77.

8 *Akteneinsicht Christa Wolf. Zerrspiegel im Dialog*, ed. Hermann Vinke (Hamburg: Luchterhand, 1993) documents Wolf's collaboration and her observation by the *Stasi*. An assessment of Wolf by the *Stasi* in 1960 reads: "Sie ist sehr parteiverbunden, tritt überall als Genossin auf, hat ein sicheres ideologisches Urteil…" (97).

9 Gisela Schultz, "Ein überraschender Erstling," *Neue Deutsche Literatur* 9.7 (1961): 129.

10 Christa Wolf, "... mit der Jugend zu rechnen als mit einem Aktivposten. Gespräch mit Christa Wolf," *Christa Wolf. Ein Arbeitsbuch. Studien— Dokumente—Bibliographie*, ed. Angela Drescher (Berlin/Weimar: Aufbau, 1989) 7–8.

11 Dietrich Allert and Hubert Wetzelt, "Die große Liebe," in Martin Reso, *"Der geteilte Himmel" und seine Kritiker; Dokumentation mit einem Nachwort des Herausgebers* (Halle: Mitteldeutscher Verlag, 1965) 78.

12 Günther Wirth, "Den Blick zum klaren Horizont gewonnen," *"Der geteilte Himmel" und seine Kritiker* 19.

13 This debate is documented in *"Der geteilte Himmel" und seine Kritiker*, a collection of reviews written predominately by GDR critics.

14 Alfred Kurella, "Begründung der Zuteilung des Heinrich-Mann-Preises. Deutsche Akademie der Künste, Sektion Dichtkunst und Sprachpflege," *"Der geteilte Himmel" und seine Kritiker* 29.

15 Felix J. Weil, quoted in Martin Jay, *The Dialectical Imagination* (Oxford:

Little, Brown and Co., 1973) 5. Although Weil spoke of "true" and "pure" Marxism, Jay stresses that this should not be understood as a retreat to dogmatism or a declaration of the eternal laws of history.

16   Theodor Adorno and Max W. Horkheimer, *Dialektik der Aufklärung* (Frankfurt a. M.: Fischer, 1988; 1969) 9. Hereafter noted parenthetically with the abbreviation DA.

17   Jürgen Habermas, "Die Verschlingung von Mythos und Aufklärung. Bemerkungen zur Dialektik der Aufklärung—nach einer erneuten Lektüre," *Mythos und Moderne: Begriff und Bild einer Rekonstruktion*, ed. Karl Heinz Bohrer (Frankfurt a. M.: Suhrkamp, 1983) 420.

18   Max Horkheimer, *Kritische Theorie*, Vol. II (Frankfurt a. M.: Fischer, 1968) viii.

19   Max Horkheimer, *Kritische Theorie*, Vol. I (Frankfurt a. M.: Fischer, 1968) x.

20   Waltraud Naumann-Beyer, "Empfang einer Flaschenpost," *Sinn und Form* 6 (1989): 1221–1222.

21   Heinrich Heiseler et al. ed., *Die "Frankfurter Schule" im Lichte des Marxismus*. (Frankfurt a. M.: Verlag Marxistische Blätter, 1974) 178–179.

22   Wilhelm Raimund Beyer, *Die Sünden der Frankfurter Schule* (Frankfurt a. M.: Verlag Marxistische Blätter, 1971) 4.

23   Walter Jopke, "Grundlagen der Erkenntnis- und Gesellschaftstheorie Adornos und Horkheimers," *Die "Frankfurter Schule" im Lichte des Marxismus*, 48–69.

24   Horkheimer, *Kritische Theorie*, Vol. I, x.

25   Andras Gedö, "Dialektik der Negation oder Negation der Dialekik," *Die "Frankfurter Schule" im Lichte des Marxismus* 22.

26   Naumann-Beyer, "Empfang einer Flaschenpost," 1209. Naumann-Beyer consructs her essay on *Dialektik der Aufklärung* as a dialogue between Euphrandor and Theokles. I read the statements of these figures as expressions of the author's viewpoint.

27   Richard Herzinger and Heinz-Peter Preußer, "Vom Äußersten zum Ersten. DDR Literatur in der Tradition deutscher Zivilisationskritik," *Text und Kritik. Literatur der DDR. Rückblicke* (München: text + kritik, 1991) 195.

CHAPTER THREE

Gender and the "Dialectic of Enlightenment"

> *Erst jetzt wird uns bewußt, daß die gesellschaftlichen und ökonomischen Grundlagen der Emanzipation—obwohl außerordentlich wichtig—doch nicht alles sind: daß wir nicht den Spuren der Männer folgen sollen, weil dies zur Vernichtung "weiblicher" Eigenschaften geführt hat.*
>
> Christa Wolf, 1976

Representations of progress in the works of Wolf, Maron and Königsdorf draw on and refigure central tropes of the Frankfurt School to reveal how concepts of progress are inflected by gender. Before turning more specifically to a discussion of gender and the "dialectic of enlightenment," it is useful to highlight some fundamental differences between women's literary production in the two Germanies that can be attributed to the divergent political, social and economic developments in East and West. In the Federal Republic, for one, women's activities in the student movement, their involvement in the League of German Socialist Students (SDS) and in the campaign for abortion rights spurred a "second wave" of feminism. In the GDR, by contrast, no organized student movement or women's movement took place. As implied by the popular feminist slogan "the personal is political," women became increasingly aware of the inextricable relationship between the private and the public, between the everyday oppression they experienced and the overriding structures of patriarchal society. In the Federal Republic, the nature of women's literary production in the late 1960s and 1970s reflects theoretical shifts within the New Women's Movement. Sigrid Weigel distinguishes three phases of women's writing: an initial "documentation-agitation" phase (1968–1974) of reportage and protocol literature that sought to enlighten, inform and create an awareness of feminist concerns such as equality, abortion rights and single motherhood; a second phase in the mid-1970s of subjective, predominantly autobiographical texts; and, finally, a phase characterized by diverse literary production by women.[1]

The literature of the first two phases has been referred to as *Frauenliteratur* ("women's literature"), a term that links this literature to explicit feminist goals, describing a literature *by* women, *for* women and *about* women.[2] Weigel emphasizes that the goal of the second phase was "das *'spezifisch Weibliche'* von Erfahrungen, Wahrnehmungen, Kenntnisse und Sehweisen etc. zu entdecken und dafür Ausdrucksformen (in der Sprache) zu finden."[3] Verena Stefan's much-debated text *Häutungen* (1975) has come to exemplify this phase. *Häutungen* relates Stefan's own growth in feminist consciousness that arose from her work in the women's group "Brot & Rosen" and her engagement for abortion rights. Centering on highly subjective themes of relationships and female sexuality, *Häutungen* progresses from initially showing the female narrator under man's shadow, as "Schattenhaut," to a description of how she comes into her own close to nature and reveling in a woman-identified sexuality. Figuring women as essentially sensuous, emotional and "natural" beings, Stefan reveals how "shedding" the layers of patriarchal deformation will expose women's true identity. Accentuating those "feminine" qualities historically associated with women, *Häutungen* thus presents an important corrective to the historically asymmetric inscription of the feminine as an aberration from a male norm whose validity long went unquestioned. Yet Stefan fails to stop there: she also turns the tables to degrade masculinity by explicitly denigrating those qualities and experiences associated with men. "The endorsement of what is good about women," social psychologist Carol Tarvis reminds us in her discussion of such compensatory feminist impulses, "does not require a rejection of what is good about men."[4] Although *Häutungen* reflects the aesthetic expression of the new freedom afforded to women by the feminist movement, the separatist politics it endorses ultimately perpetuates and cements the age-old opposition of masculinity and femininity.

The separatist feminism advocated by Stefan and typical of the second phase of the West German women's movement can be termed "cultural feminism." Linda Alcoff describes cultural feminism as "the ideology of a female nature or female essence reappropriated by feminists themselves in an effort to revalidate undervalued female attributes."[5] Beyond the celebration of female virtues, cultural feminists assert that "the enemy of women is not merely a social system or economic institution or set of backward beliefs but masculinity itself and in some cases male biology" (Alcoff 408). Alcoff also underscores that cultural feminist politics seeks to establish an environment free of "masculinist values" in which female nature can flourish. The distinction between these elements will be drawn on in following chapters to distinguish Christa Wolf's specific brand of feminism from cultural feminism. Wolf's later works variously undertake a positive revaluation of "feminine" attributes, a project that can be construed as romanticizing woman's historical association with nature and apart from the interminable vices of culture. As feminist philosopher Genevieve Lloyd argues with regard to women's exclusion from "male" modes of thought: "To have been largely excluded from the dominant, and supposedly more 'advanced', forms of abstract thought or moral consciousness can be seen as a source of strength when their defects and impoverishments become apparent."[6] Yet Lloyd also reminds us, as does Wolf, that feminine virtues are related to women's social position and roles, "they are strengths that derive from exclusion; and the merits of such 'minority consciousness' depend on avoiding asserting it as a rival norm" (106). Re-inscribing the feminine as Other, this time on the part of women who had little or no part in defining "woman," runs the risk of constructing anew the myth of woman/the feminine and makes it difficult to envision an alternate future.

By the late 1970s, many West German writers and critics acknowledged that advocating a distinct "women's literature" could imply that women's experiences and problems were solely women's concern, and consequently result in "eine Ghettosierung ihrer literarischen Produkte [...] und damit auch die Probleme, die in ihrer Literatur zur Darstellung kommen" (Heuser 123) In other words, while the term "women's literature" proved initially useful for designat-ing the consonance of texts by women with the New Women's Movement's politics and goals, it also created apprehensions that the issues addressed in "women's texts" would be viewed as marginal. The phrase *literature by women*, by contrast, draws attention to the diversity of women's literary production that eventually emerged in the West.

Within the GDR's specific cultural context the terms "feminist" and "feminism" figure as Western labels that GDR authors commonly avoided when describing themselves or their works. GDR literary critic Eva Kaufmann, writing in 1989–1990, explains that GDR women writers rejected calling their works "feminist" for a variety of reasons. These include "Schwierigkeiten mit dem Begriff; der Anspruch, nach allgemeinen, nicht nach besonderen Frauen-Kunstnormen bewertet werden zu wollen; Abneigung, für feministische 'Parteilichkeit' in Anspruch genommen zu werden; allgemeine Ideologie-verdrossenheit und anderes mehr."[7] Many rejected Western feminism itself because they associated it with separatist politics. In an interview with Karin Huffzky in 1974, for example, Irmtraud Morgner defines herself explicitly as a communist rather than a feminist since in her view feminism implies "daß die Menschwerdung der Frau nur eine Frauensache sein könnte."[8] Morgner goes on to assert: "Da wird aber ein Menschheitsproblem aufgeworfen. Emanzipation der Frauen ist ohne Emanzipation der Männer unerreichbar und umgekehrt" (328). Despite her trenchant critique of patriarchal structures, Wolf likewise stresses the "human" potential of both sexes and distances herself outright from those branches of feminist theory, as reflected in *Häutungen*, that draw on essentialist, pre-social notions of masculinity and femininity without reference to the sociohistoric contexts that produce gender differences. She focuses her critique not on individual men, but rather on social structures and norms, "die Sitten, die die Männer oft daran hindern, sich Frauen gegenüber menschlich zu verhalten" (Huffzky 329).

In Marxist theory, moreover, the "woman question" was answered by women's integration into the realm of production. Paragraph 123 of the GDR *Gesetzbuch der Arbeit* makes the programmatic claim: "Die Gleichberechtigung der Frau in der sozialistischen Gesellschaft wird durch die Teilnahme am Arbeitsprozeß und die Mitwirkung an der Leitung von Staat und Wirtschaft voll verwirklicht."[9] With the guarantee of legal and economic parity, women's oppression came to be regarded as a "Nebenwiderspruch," a secondary contradiction that would be resolved with the progress of socialist society. No doubt, the state took many concrete measures to improve women's lot, such as guaranteeing reproductive rights, childcare and shortened workdays for mothers. In fact, the severe reduction of such rights in the aftermath of unification has highlighted the degree to which GDR women had come to view them as fundamental. By continuing to equate woman's role with mothering, however, the GDR's official policy failed essentially to challenge traditional gender roles. Like most fully employed women in the capitalist West, the vast majority of GDR women returned home from work only to begin a so-called "second shift" of domestic chores and childcare. Privileging the realm of production, the official definition failed to account for significant dimensions of women's experience. Women writers in turn came to critique not only the one-sided emphasis on production, but also the privileging of those values attributed to it—such as reason, objectivity, rationalism—over the values of emotion, subjectivity and sensitivity typically associated with the realm of reproduction.

Reflecting in 1989 on her long-held belief that the struggle for emancipation must take place within the worker's movement, Morgner divulged that her belief in socialism's ability to bring about significant changes in women's lives waned as her disillusionment with the GDR's Stalinist socialism grew. She explained:

> Emanzipation der Frau: Nebenwiderspruch, hat man ihnen lange gesagt. Und ich glaubte ja auch früher, wenn der Sozialismus aufgebaut wird, ist die Frauenfrage ein sekundäres Problem und erledigt sich irgendwie von selbst. Aber wir haben die Erfahrung machen müssen, daß jedenfalls ein stalinischer Sozialismus das Frauenproblem weder lösen kann noch will, weil er eine Männergesellschaft ist.[10]

Despite its ideology of gender equality, then, GDR socialism—like capitalism—was a patriarchal social system that valorized those institutions and practices oriented toward a male norm. GDR sociologist Irene Dölling terms her country's social politics "paternal-patriarchal."[11] Rather than marking an end to gender hierarchies related to the capitalist mode of production, Dölling explains, the alignment of official proclamations of gender equality with the actual autonomy afforded women veiled the continuation of gender hierarchies and also increased women's dependence on the state. Dölling exclaims: "Wie der pater familias [...] übernimmt 'die Partei' mit ihrer zentralistisch-hierarchischen Struktur und ihrem Generalsekretär als dem 'Vater des Staatsvolks' an der Spitze die Funktion, im Interesse aller zu sprechen, zu wissen, was für alle gut ist" (129). In other words, the governing elite took responsibility not only *for* but also *from* its citizens, like a paternal father obviating the possibility of self-determination and self-representation.

The growth in the number of literary texts written by women in the GDR and focusing on women's issues can also be related to the heightened awareness of gender issues adumbrated by the women's movement in the West. In an interview with Alice Schwarzer, Morgner stresses the considerable influence of the Western feminist movement, commenting: "Ohne diese Frauenbewegung hätte es sicher in der DDR diese Literatur nicht gegeben. [...] Also für mich kann ich sagen, die Denkanstöße der Bewegung haben mir überhaupt erst möglich gemacht, das Thema in einem größeren Zusammenhang anzufassen" (35). Although Morgner draws our attention to the significant impact of the New Women's Movement on women writers, it must also be noted that "feminist" literature by GDR women also had a marked effect on feminist theory and practice in the West. Angelika Bammer stresses the particular appeal of GDR texts for American feminists who, strongly influenced by traditional Marxism and Critical Theory, sought, as does the protagonist of Morgner's *Leben und Abenteuer der Troubadora Beatriz nach Zeugnissen ihrer Spielfrau Laura*, "eine dritte Ordnung, eine Alternative zu bürgerlichem Feminismus einerseits und patriarchalischem Sozialismus andererseits."[12]

In addition to impulses from the West, the liberalization of cultural policy after the VIII Parteitag (1971) further encouraged women's literary production. To recall Honecker's (in)famous words: "Wenn man von der festen Position des Sozialismus ausgeht, kann es meines Erachtens auf dem Gebiet von Kunst und Literatur keine Tabus geben. Das betrifft sowohl die Fragen der inhaltlichen Gestalt als auch des Stils."[13] Honecker's proclamation on the one hand gave official sanction to the expression of greater subjectivity and aesthetic experimentation. On the other hand, the notion of the "firm position of socialism," the equation of GDR socialism with socialism per se, accentuated the disparity between actual conditions and the socialist ideal.

In 1974 three major novels by and about women appeared in the GDR: Gerti Tetzer's *Karin W.*, Brigitte Reimann's *Fransiska Linkerhand* and Irmtraud Morgner's *Leben und Abenteuer der Trobadora Beatriz*. The publication in 1975 of the anthology *Blitz aus heiterm Himmel,* a collection of stories by seven authors (four men and three women) each consigned to write a story centering on a sex change, further underscores the growing preoccupation with and critical assessment of gender roles. This volume includes Christa Wolf's "Selbstversuch" (first published 1972) discussed in the next chapter. Two documentary texts, Sarah Kirsch's *Die Panterfrau* (1973) and Maxie Wander's *Guten Morgen, du Schöne* (1978) also attest to the strong interest in the conditions of women's lives. Consigned by the GDR's Aufbau publishing house in conjunction with the International Women's Year, *Die Panterfrau* contains Kirsch's transcription of five interviews she conducted with GDR women. Its primary focus is on women's issues related to the realm of production. Wander's interviews, by contrast, bring to light subjective experiences. The women discuss relationships, their families, sexuality, and offer insight into conflicting expectations, personal trials and individual triumphs. The nineteen interviewees illuminate how the new possibilities open to women in the public realm engendered feelings of strength and independence. These new opportunities and experiences also gave rise to greater expectations and heightened women's awareness of the inadequacies of a patriarchal society in which many personal desires and hopes remained unfulfilled. "Frauen, durch ihre Auseinandersetzungen mit realen und belangvollen Erfahrungen bereift," writes Christa Wolf in her introduction to *Guten Morgen, du Schöne*, "signalisieren einen radikalen Anspruch: als ganzer Mensch zu leben, von allen Sinnen und Fähligkeiten Gebrauch machen zu können."[14]

While it is possible to detect feminist impulses in GDR literature, it proves more difficult to locate feminism in GDR society itself. With feminism denounced in the political realm, women's groups developed primarily in conjunction with peace and environmental groups that formed within the protective realm of the church. Literature, as one of the few realms of the public sphere where tempered opposition could be voiced, hence served as the primary avenue to express feminist sentiments and theories. Kaufmann emphasizes: "Da in der DDR jede selbständige Regung und Bewegung von Frauen als 'Emanzentum' verpönt und politisch denunziert wurde [...] übte die Belletristik gerade auch in der Kritik des Patriarchats die vielberedete Ersatzfunktion aus" (113). Yet GDR women writers rarely represented gender issues in isolation. Rather, they set gender in relation to global issues such as war, ecological degradation and developments in the Third World.

Claims that reason, science, and/or nature are structured by gender are quick to be discredited as based on gross stereotypes. To be sure, the common feminist analytic paradigm of sex (as essence) and gender (as construction) fails to account for complex configurations of gender. In this context, the differentiation between "symbolic," "structural" and "individual gender" explicated by feminist philosopher Sandra Harding proves particularly useful.[15] Harding notes that as symbols "masculinity" and "femininity" are constructed through mutual exclusion: "central to the notion of masculinity is its rejection of everything that is defined in culture as feminine and its legitimated control of whatever counts as feminine" (54). At least symbolically, masculinity and femininity are necessarily asymmetrical. A focus on science's symbolic "maleness" shifts attention away from individual men or women to questions of social construction, which nonetheless have very real implications and effects. Symbolic gender, then, interacts with structural gender (the division of labor and social activity by gender) and individual gender, i.e., what constitutes masculine and feminine identity and behavior.

In *Dialektik der Aufklärung*, Horkheimer and Adorno argue that reason as an instrument of domination functions through man's suppression of and mastery over nature, myth, magic, the body, and woman—all elements of the symbolic feminine.[16] Drawing heavily on the Western philosophical tradition which, steeped in sexual metaphors,[17] defines reason symbolically through its "maleness" and consequently constitutes the "feminine" through exclusion, Horkheimer and Adorno cast woman as the Other of male reason. In the excursus "Odysseus oder Mythos und Aufklärung," she is represented as a "zaubernde Hetäre" and "Rätselbild von Unwiderstehlichkeit und Ohnmacht" (DA 79). Horkheimer and Adorno likewise accentuate structural gender when they ground woman's subjugation in the gendered division of human activity. Although they fail to escape defining woman as Other and at times slide into essentialism, they unambiguously plot woman's—and man's—identity as constructed primarily through social and historical forces. Indeed, as Leslie Adelson has pointed out, "the Frankfurt School of Critical Theory has been faulted for overemphasizing ideology while paying insufficient critical attention to the role of the body in twentieth-century history and, further, denying the human body any possible role in effective political resistance to structures of domination."[18] The overdetermination of the body by structural factors obviates notions of subjective agency and renders individual gender, that which constitutes gendered identities and behavior in particular, peripheral in *Dialektik der Aufklärung*.

As elucidated earlier, Horkheimer and Adorno describe the process of enlightenment as the domination of outer and inner (human) nature through reason, stating: "Was die Menschen von der Natur lernen wollen ist, sie anzuwenden, um sie und die Menschen vollends zu beherrschen" (DA 10). Employing the term "patriarchal" (DA 10) to define this process, they clearly view this domination as a product of male-dominated society and its institutions. Horkheimer and Adorno accentuate woman's position within patriarchal society in the philosophical fragment of *Dialektik der Aufklärung* entitled "Mensch und Tier, " explaining woman's subordination in terms of her biological function that, historically, has subordinated her, placed her closer to nature. The (patriarchal) process of enlightenment further marginalized woman and relegated her activities to the private realm:

Diese [die Frauen] habe keinen selbständigen Anteil an der Tüchtigkeit, aus welcher diese Zivilisation hervorging. Der Mann muß hinaus ins feindliche Leben, muß wirken und streben. Die Frau ist nicht Subjekt. Sie produziert nicht, sondern pflegt die Produzierenden, ein lebendiges Denkmal längst entschwundener Zeiten der geschlossenen Hauswirtschaft. Ihr war die vom Mann erzwungene Arbeitsteilung wenig günstig. Sie wurde zur Verkörperung der biologischen Funktion, zum Bild der Natur, in deren Unterdrückung der Ruhmestitel dieser Zivilisation bestand. Grenzenlos Natur zu beherrschen, den Kosmos in ein unendliches Jagdgebiet zu verwandeln, war der Wunschtraum der Jahrtausende. Darauf war die Idee des Menschen in der Männer-gesellschaft abgestimmt. (DA 264)

Confined to the private sphere, reduced to her biological function, woman became the "image of nature" and the object of domination. Although she distinguishes herself from the rest of "nature" by belonging to the world of culture, woman's role in culture nonetheless remains subordinate, her identity fractured: "Sie selbst erreichte für die ganze ausgebeutete Natur die Aufnahme in der Welt der Herrschaft, aber als gebrochene. Sie speigelt, unterjocht, dem Sieger seinen Sieg in ihrer spontanen Unterwerfung wider ..." (DA 265).

While both men and women are objectified in the process of enlightenment, woman's marginality renders her position more complex and ambiguous: she has functioned to mirror male victory, her subordination solidifying his domination of her and of nature. It is hence impossible to construe woman as separate from man, as outside the progress of Western civilization and purely as the victim of this progress. In supporting man's position, she perpetuates the status quo and must also assume responsibility for social conditions.

A basic question arising from women's equation with nature is whether the woman/nature connection provides a rationale for women's continuing sub-ordination or constitutes a potentially emancipatory position.[19] In her classic 1974 study, feminist anthropologist Sherry Ortner posed the question, "Is female to male as nature is to culture?"[20] In searching for an explanation for women's secondary social status, which she sees as "one of the true universals, a pan-cultural fact" (67),[21] Ortner looks to other cultural universals and reaches the conclusion that, despite varied manifestations of the domination of nature in diverse cultures, nature—like woman—is universally subordinated. Within the dichotomy of nature/culture, moreover, culture is equated "with the notion of human consciousness (i.e. systems of thought and technology), by means of which humanity attempts to assert control over nature" (72). Though she is part of culture, then, woman's close alignment with nature identifies her with some-thing universally devalued and dominated. One may surely question the validity of Ortner's thesis in describing *all* cultures, yet her work nonetheless sheds light on central aspects of the relationships between woman, nature and culture. Foremost, Ortner draws attention to woman's double position as at once part of culture and, like nature, subordinate within it.

Arguments supporting woman's proximity to nature generally boil down to women's physiology, i.e., their responsibility for human reproduction and the social roles consequently assigned to them.[22] The social roles and characteristics associated with women's assigned roles of mother and caretaker point to the legacy and continuation of biological determinism: women's social roles have become viewed as "natural" and accordingly reproduced and institutionalized in culture. "The result," Ortner asserts, "is a (sadly) efficient feedback system: various aspects of woman's situation (physical, social, psychological) contribute to her being seen as closer to nature, while the view of her as closer to nature is in turn embodied in institutional forms that reproduce her situation" (87).

One might argue that Horkheimer and Adorno reinforce age-old beliefs of women's biological "inferiority," remaining locked in an androcentric model that offers no alternative interpretations to stereotypical gender roles.[23] Indeed, they go no further in examining woman's complex position within the dialectic of enlightenment. Yet while they figure woman as the Other of patriarchal society, she is at the same time part of the dialectic which ultimately plots man as an object as well. Within their critique of enlightenment, i.e., within their critique of patriarchal society and the domination of nature, then, Horkheimer and Adorno express an immanent critique of those mechanisms that have led to the domination of both woman and nature. In his article "A Feminine Dialectic of Enlightnement? Horkeimer and Adorno Revisited," Andrew Hewitt points to the potentially emancipatory function of women's position, suggesting that in *Dialektik der Aufklärung*, "Man does not dominate woman and identify her with nature—he dominates woman by identifying her with nature. In this repressive identification, of course, will be bound up the utopian instrumentalization of woman as the means of a (copulative) reconciliation with nature."[24] Echoing the argument laid out by Friedrich Engels in *Ursprung der Familie*, namely that man's oppression of woman constitutes the first class oppression and would vanish with the withering away of the capitalist mode of production, Horkheimer and Adorno at once affirm and critique women's subordinate position in capitalist society.

Weigel further illuminates the function of woman in the history of enlightenment. Criticizing the feminist tendency to perpetuate the equation of woman with the Other of reason, with the twist of upholding the "feminine" and rejecting the "masculine," Weigel recognizes the emergence of a new myth of the feminine/woman, one that simply results in "verkehrte Spiegelbilder männlicher Entwürfe."[25] Weigel delineates the complex "Ort der Frau" within enlightenment discourse, and describes woman's position as follows:

Der Ort des Weiblichen Subjekts ist nicht nur weitaus komplizierter als der des männlichen, er führt auch eine *doppelt ver-kehrte Perspektive* in die Dialektik ein: den Blick und die Rede des anderen Geschlechts, das wünscht, zum Platz des einen hinüberzuwechseln, ohne seine Herkunft von der Kehrseite einfach abschütteln zu können—und das sich zudem nicht einmal so sicher ist, wie begehrenswert der ihm lange verwehrte Platz überhaupt sei. (22)

Woman's complex position in Weigel's view affords her a *"doppelt ver-kehrte Perspektive,"* a structural perspective that reveals the drawbacks and the benefits of man's position: while she seeks to attain the status of man long denied her, she simultaneously questions how desirable "the masculine" really is.

In theorizing gender relations, feminist standpoint theorists such as Nancy Hartsock and Sandra Harding likewise focus on the structural difference between men's and women's lives. Unlike their Frankfurt School predecessors, however, they argue that the sexual division of labor affords women a particular and privileged position that allows for the possibility of female agency. To legitimize a feminist standpoint, Hartsock draws on historical materialism's insight that being determines consciousness, that factors such as race, class, gender and sexual orientation structure our view of the world. Hartsock details how feminists can use the epistemological perspective theorized by Marx regarding the enlarged perspective of the proletariat to gain insight into the sexual division of labor from the perspective that this position affords women.[26] In contrast to men's "partial" and "perverse" perspective, women's lives are seen to provide a "particular and privileged vantage point on male supremacy" (Hartsock 284). Women have "vision," are better able to see what Christa Wolf terms society's "blind spot." Hartsock stresses the liberatory potential of standpoint theory, claiming that "because it provides the basis for revealing the perversion of both life and thought, the inhumanity of human relations, a standpoint can be the basis for moving beyond these relations" (303). In "Berührung," Wolf reflects this line of reasoning. She claims: "Ich behaupte nicht, Frauen seien von Natur aus mehr als Männer vor politischen Wahndenken, vor Wirklichkeitsflucht gefeit. Nur: Eine bestimmte geschichtliche Phase hat ihnen Voraussetzungen gegeben, einen Lebensanspruch für Männer mit auszudrücken" (LS 220).

Like East German women writers, Hartsock broadens Marx's class analysis to include "all human activity," reproduction as well as production. In her view, the female experience of reproduction provides an enhancement and modification of the proletarian vision theorized by Marx. To avoid misunderstandings that standpoint theory is grounded solely on the experience of motherhood, she stresses the degree to which the institution of motherhood structures social practice. Drawing on object relations theory as articulated by Nancy Chodorow and Jane Flax, she also illuminates how the process of differentiation and individuation from the primary caretaker (understood to be female) varies for boys and girls. Through the dynamic process of separation from the mother, females develop more flexible ego boundaries and, as a consequence, develop a greater capacity for empathy, experience others as part of the self and themselves as connected to others and the world. Males, by contrast, develop more rigid ego boundaries, which leads them to perceive themselves as separate and distinct from others. Institutional structures reproduce and perpetuate the divergent experiences engendered by the division of labor in child raising. "These different (psychic) experiences," Hartsock states, "both structure and are reinforced by the differing patterns of male and female activity required by the sexual division of labor, and are thereby replicated as epistemology and ontology" (296).

The wide range of women's cultural, economic, social and sexual identities has led postmodernists to question standpoint theory's seemingly unified positioning of women. Yet Harding and Hartsock refute that standpoint theory makes such universal claims. Harding underscores that standpoint theorists ground their arguments in "the objective perspective *from women's lives*" and neither give "transhistorical privilege" to women's perspective nor base their assumptions on women's biology, intuition, or experience.[27] Moreover, although they focus on gender difference, standpoint theorists fully recognize the significance of other factors in structuring views of the world; they acknowledge that identity is always fractured and that "the subject of feminist knowledge ... must be multiple and contradictory" (167).

Attempting to articulate a feminist theory from the position of women's lives without resorting to cultural feminism's essentialist trappings or to poststructuralism's dismantling of gender as an analytic category, Alcoff develops a positional definition of woman. This positional definition "makes her identity relative to a constantly shifting context, to a situation that includes a network of elements involving others, the objective economic conditions, cultural and political institutions and ideologies" (Alcoff 413–414). With its emphasis on historical specificity and the fluidity of social and discursive relationships, positionality draws attention to women's historical construction as second-degree objects in an asymmetrical gender hierarchy, while it opens up the possibility of theorizing female agency in a non-essential manner. "Positionality," Adelson underlines, "does not demarcate a place, nor does it consist of choice alone (although it does entail a standpoint). Rather, it characterizes a set of specific social and discursive relations in a given historical moment. These relations concern and also produce gender, race, class, sexuality, ethnicity, and other practices through which power is constructed, exercised, resisted and challenged" (64).[28]

Within the context of the GDR, the state's omnipotence and invasiveness makes it difficult to dissociate the external locus of power from its internalization and effects, and thus clearly to discern a subject's agency and possibilities for resistance. Yet subjects, Teresa de Lauretis reminds us, are not only constructed by their social reality, but also contribute to its construction, they are "both subject-ed to social constraint and yet subject in the active sense of maker as well as user of culture, intent on self-definition and self-determination."[29] Reading the texts of Wolf, Königsdorf and Maron through the lens of positionality illuminates the extent to which their representations of gender are socially constructed.

Notes

1 Sigrid Weigel, "'Woman Begins Relating to Herself': Contemporary German Women's Literature. Part One," *New German Critique* 31 (Winter 1984): 53–94.

2 See Magdalene Heuser, "Literatur von Frauen/Frauen in der Literatur," *Feminismus. Inspektion der Herrenkultur*, ed. Luise Pusch (Frankfurt a. M.: Suhrkamp, 1983) 122.

3 Sigrid Weigel, *Die Stimme der Medusa* (Reinbek bei Hamburg: Rowolt, 1989) 50.

4 Carol Tarvis, *The Mismeasure of Woman* (New York: Simon & Schuster, 1992) 62.

5 Linda Alcoff, "Cultural Feminism versus Post-Structuralism: The Identity Crisis in Feminist Theory," *Signs* (Spring 1988): 408.

6 Genevieve Lloyd, *The Man of Reason. "Male" & "Female" in Western Philosophy*. 2nd ed. (Minneapolis: University of Minnesota Press, 1993).

7 Eva Kaufmann, "Irmtraud Morgner, Christa Wolf und andere. Feminismus in der DDR," *Text und Kritik. Literatur in der DDR. Rückblicke* (München: text + kritik, 1991) 115.

8 Karin Huffzky, "'Irmtraud Morgner. Produktivkraft Sexualität souverän nutzen.' Ein Gespräch mit der DDR-Schriftstellerin," *Grundlagentexte zur Emanzipation der Frau*, 3rd. ed., ed. Jutta Menschnik (Köln: Pahl-Rugenstein, 1980) 328.

9 Quoted in Gisela Bahr, "Blitz aus heiterm Himmel. Ein Versuch zur Emanzipation in der DDR," *Die Frau als Heldin und Autorin*, ed. Wolfgang Paulsen (Bern: Franke, 1979) 223–236.

10 See Alice Schwarzer, "Jetzt oder nie! Die Frauen sind die Hälfte des Volkes! Interview with Irmtraud Morgner," *Emma* 2 (1990): 34.

11 See Irene Dölling, "Alte und neue Dilemmata: Frauen in der ehemaligen DDR," *Women in German Yearbook* 7 (1991): 121–136. Gerd Meyer offers a detailed discussion of paternalism in the GDR in *Die DDR-Machtelite in der Ära Honecker*. Tübinger Mittel- und Osteuropastudien–Politik, Gesellschaft, Kultur, Vol. 3 (Tübingen: Franke, 1991).

12 Angelika Bammer, "Trobadora in Amerika," *Irmtraud Morgner. Texten, Daten, Bilder*, ed. Marlis Gerhardt (Frankfurt a. M.: Luchterhand, 1990) 201.

13 Quoted in Wolfgang Emmerich, *Kleine Literaturgeschichte der DDR* (Frankfurt a. M.: Luchterhand, 1989) 243.

14 "Berührung," Wolf's introductory essay to *Guten Morgen, du Schöne*, is reprinted in *Lesen und Schreiben. Neue Sammlung* (Frankfurt a. M: Luchterhand, 1980) 209–221, here 219.

15 See Sandra Harding, *The Science Question in Feminism* (Ithaca: Cornell University Press, 1986), in particular pages 52–57.

16 See also Weigel, "Wilden und Fremden," *Topographien der Geschlechter. Kulturgeschichtliche Studien zur Literatur* (Reinbek bei Hamburg: Rowolt, 1990) 20–21.

17 In *The Man of Reason*, Lloyd offers an excellent overview of the use of sexual metaphor in Western philosophy.

18 Leslie A. Adelson, *Making Bodies, Making History: Feminism & German Identity* (Lincoln and London: University of Nebraska Press, 1993) 64.

19 See Ynestra King, "Healing the Wounds: Feminism, Ecology, and the Nature/Culture Dualism," *Reweaving the world: the emergence of ecofeminism*, ed. Irene Diamond and Gloria Feman Orenstein (San Francisco: Sierra Club Press, 1990) 110.

20 Sherry Ortner, "Is Female to Male as Nature is to Culture?" *Woman, Culture & Society*, ed. Michelle Rosaldo and Louise Lamphere (Stanford: Stanford University Press, 1974) 67–87.

21 See also Nancy Chodorow, *The Reproduction of Mothering. Psychoanalysis and the Sociology of Gender* (Berkeley: University of California Press, 1978).

22 See Ortner 81–82.

23 For this argument, see Christine Kulke, "Die Kritik der instrumentellen Rationalität—ein männlicher Mythos," *Die Aktualität der "Dialektik der Aufklärung,"* ed. Harry Kunneman and Hent de Vries (Frankfurt a. M.: Campus, 1989) 128–149.

24 Andrew Hewitt, "A Feminine Dialectic of Enlightenment? Horkheimer and Adorno Revisited," *New German Critique* 56 (Spring 1992): 153

25 Sigrid Weigel, *Topographien der Geschlechter* 20–21.

26 Nancy Hartsock, "The Feminist Standpoint: Developing the Ground for a Specifically Feminist Historical Materialism," *Discovering Reality*, ed. Sandra Harding and Merrill B. Hintikka (Dordrecht, Holland: D. Reidel Publishing Co., 1983) 283–310.

27 Sandra Harding, *Whose Science? Whose Knowledge? Thinking from Women's Lives* (Ithaca: Cornell University Press, 1991) 167.

28   Adelson accentuates the fluidity of positionality and argues that despite Alcoff's critique of essentialism, by defining woman *as* positionality and drawing on identity politics, Alcoff ultimately falls into the essentialist trap.

29   Teresa de Lauretis, "Feminist Studies/Critical Studies: Issues, Terms, Contexts," *Feminist Studies/Critical Studies*, ed. Teresa de Lauretis (Bloomington: Indiana University Press, 1986) 10.

CHAPTER FOUR

"Self-Experiments":
Nachdenken über Christa T. and *Unter den Linden*

> *Unser wissenschaftliches Zeitalter wird nicht sein, was es sein könnte und sein muß—bei Strafe einer unerhörten Katastrophe—, wenn nicht die Kunst sich dazu aufschwingt, dem Zeitgenossen, an den sie sich wendet, große Fragen zu stellen … Ihn zu ermutigen, er selbst zu werden…*
>
> Christa Wolf, "Selbstinterview"

The VI. Party Congress of the SED in 1963 initiated a new long-term economic system, the NÖS (Neue Ökonomische System der Planung und Leitung), to promote greater efficiency and productivity through increased rationalization of the economic system. According to Wolfgang Emmerich the NÖS penetrated all realms of society and, in conjunction with the scientific-technological revolution, ushered in a "kaum zu bremsende Bestreben, den 'realen' Sozialismus 'systematisch' zu verwissenschaftlichen, gleichsam zu technologisieren."[1] The process of rationalization reduced social production to its scientific aspect and obviated all notions of human agency and individuality. The human consequences of instrumental reason, however, failed to enter into official discourse. Emmerich stresses: "Die […] Möglichkeit einer 'Dialektik der Aufklärung', eines Umschlagens von menschenfreundlicher Rationalität in einen den Menschen instrumentalisierenden Absolutismus der Ratio, wurde nicht als Gefahr erkannt" (173). In her essay collection *Lesen und Schreiben* (1968), Wolf explores literature's role in the scientific age: "Der Prosaautor," she ponders, "was sagt er seinen Zeitgenossen, die dabei sind, den stromlinienförmigen Menschen zu konstruieren" (LS 17). Wolf provides a response to this question with *Nachdenken über Christa T.* (1968), a work in which she asserts the power of fiction to represent "eine Wahrheit jenseits der wichtigen Welt der Fakten" (LS 37). In *Nachdenken über Christa T.*, Wolf turns her attention to the internal conflicts of an individual who struggles to live life to its fullest. Drawing attention to broader historical implications, David Bathrick argues that this work signals a

> radical move inward—a break with a discursive paradigm based upon a dialectical materialist, i.e. an objectivist epistemology—but beyond that

a problematizing of all the categories which had heretofore been accepted notions of socialist discourse: of history, of science, of one's political role, of the private sphere, of the situation and nature of the individual subject.[2]

In a society that demands conformity and assimilation, Christa T. attempts to say "I."

Wolf seeks to legitimate this radical conceptual turn in the essay "Lesen und Schreiben," arguing that literature must reflect the new vision of the socialist age. She opens her essay with the proclamation: "Das Bedürfnis, auf eine neue Art zu schreiben, folgt, wenn auch mit Abstand, einer neuen Art, in der Welt zu sein" (LS 9). As in her controversial speech at the 11th Plenum in 1965, Wolf justifies her break with an aesthetic that "objectively" represents the real development of socialism as consonant with the proclaimed ideal. Referring to Newton, Einstein and Heisenberg, Wolf aligns her aesthetic shift with larger cultural paradigm shifts. She validates her move away from the atomistic worldview of Newtonian mechanics to a worldview that reflects Heisenberg's principle of indeterminacy. The Newtonian paradigm stresses the independence of the observer—"Feste Objekte bewegen sich fortgesetzt auf berechneten Bahnen und wirken nach berechenbaren Gesetzen aufeinander ein" (LS 28)—while Heisenberg accounts for the interaction of observer and system and introduces the concept of potentiality. In *Physics and Philosophy* (1958), Heisenberg contends that artistic style "arises out of the interplay between the world and ourselves, or more specifically between the spirit of the time and the artist. The spirit of the time is probably a fact as objective as any fact in natural science...."[3] Taking up this line of reasoning, Wolf argues that in the consciousness of the writer, past, present and future coalesce and engender a perception of "depth": "die Koordinate der Tiefe, der Zeitgenossenschaft, des unvermeidlichen Engagements" (LS 32). In an interview with Hans Kaufmann in 1973, Wolf describes this authorial "fourth dimension" in the text as "subjective authenticity" (DiA2 797). She relates the interaction between the author and her time directly to the difficulty of saying "I" central to *Nachdenken über Christa T.*: "Man sieht eine andere Realität als zuvor ... es wird viel schwerer, 'ich' zu sagen, und doch zugleich oft unerläßlich. Die Suche nach einer Methode, dieser Realität schreibend gerecht zu werden, möchte ich vorläufig 'subjektive Authentizität' nennen" (DiA2 780–781).

"Subjective authenticity" has become a hallmark of Wolf's prose. In *Nachdenken über Christa T.*, the dialogic, non-linear and reflective style in which narrator and subject at times merge to become one marks the dimension of the author.[4] Wolf acknowledges in "Selbstinterview" that the object of her narrative was not only Christa T., but also Christa Wolf: "Ich stand auf einmal mir selbst gegenüber" (LS 51), she states. The question that prefaces

Nachkdenken über Christa T., "Was ist das: Dieses Zu-sich-selber-kommen des Menschen,?" signals the narrative's interrogation of the possibilities for self-actualization. Excerpted from the diary of Johannes R. Becher, this statement announces a radical departure from the collective ideal Wolf still clung to in *Der geteilte Himmel*. Indeed, Christa T.'s individuality, her status as an outsider, and her defiance of social norms—her quest, "*man selbst zu sein*" (N 9)—is what compels the narrator to reconstruct the life of her former classmate and friend who died at the young age of thirty-five. Drawing on memory, diary sketches and other real-life sources, the first-person narrator relates the story of this unique individual so that Christa T.'s own quest may serve as an example. "Halten wir also fest," she urges her readers, "es ist unseretwegen, denn es scheint, wir brauchen sie" (N 10). The narrator hopes that the spontaneous non-conformity that characterized Christa T.'s own process of self-inquiry will spur those who hear her story to undertake a similar process of self-reflection.

Through "nach-denken," an explorative process of memory and commemoration, the narrator traces Christa T.'s life course against the backdrop of a society where facts reign and "truth" remains a superficial slogan. Unlike those around her, Christa T. unabashedly confronts the status quo and considers her personal development within the context of socialist progress. "Christa T., sehr früh, wenn man es heute bedenkt, fing an, sich zu fragen, was denn das heißt: Veränderung. Die neuen Worte? Das neue Haus? Machinen, größere Felder? Der neue Mensch, hörte sie sagen, und begann, in sich hineinzublicken" (N 71–72). While her support for socialism remains steadfast, Christa T. questions its inevitability. Her position comes to light in a dialog concerning socialism's ideal development: "Was halten sie für unerläßlich für den Fortbestand der Menschheit?" (N 171). To recall, Wolf's *Moskauer Novelle* similarly poses this question, to which the pragmatist Blasing responds that humanity's future depends on the exploitation of the world's energy sources, a "truth" that goes unquestioned in that narrative. By contrast, Christa T. defies the prevailing worldview: for her, humankind's survival demands morality, conscience and fantasy. The personal stake she sets in society's future distinguishes Christa T. from those around her: "sie meinte nicht, was viele dachten: dazu gehöre nichts als ein bißchen Mut, nichts als die Oberfläche der Geschehnisse, die man leicht Wahrheit nennt, nichts als ein bißchen Rede von Vorangekommensein" (N 142).

Wolf opposes the notion that in an age of reason non-fictional genres will be viewed as the sole purveyors of "'Wahrheit' [...], das heißt: wie es wirklich gewesen ist" (LS 17). In *Nachdenken über Christa T.*, she advocates a concept of "truth" that defies the historicist representation of a unified picture of the past "wie es wirklich gewesen ist." Promoted by nineteenth-century historian Theodor Ranke, historicism upholds the history of the victors through the representation of great events, deeds, and men. With *Nachdenken über Christa*

T., Wolf turns her attention instead to an individual silenced by the relentless flow of history. Her historiographic project reflects that advocated by Walter Benjamin in his "Theses on the Philosophy of History": Wolf sees it as her task to "brush history against the grain," to undertake a re-vision of history from the perspective of the marginalized and oppressed.[5] She seeks to etch into the reader's memory the unrecorded past of a woman excluded from representation.

The divergent connotations of sputnik in *Der geteilte Himmel* and *Nachdenken über Christa T.* likewise mark the fundamental shift in Wolf's assessment and representation of progress. As discussed earlier, in *Der geteilte Himmel* the successful Soviet satellite—"the news"—provided a concrete symbol of socialism's scientific-technological advances. In *Nachdenken über Christa T.*, by contrast, Wolf depicts the heralding of scientific-technological progress as mere propaganda. As Christa T. and the narrator step out onto the balcony one evening to perhaps catch a glimpse of the "new star," sputnik, on the horizon and to toast the advances of the scientific age, the "new star" fails to appear. The narrator recalls the sobering recognition she shared with Christa T.: "[d]ie glückliche, allen Anfängen günstige Zeit früher Unbefangenheit war vertan, wir wußten es. Wir schütteten den letzten Wein in den Apfelbaum. Der neue Stern hatte sich nicht gezeigt" (N 142). At a time when technology was proclaimed as a "new god" and embraced with religious fervor, if not blind faith, Wolf suggests through the religious symbolism of spilling wine onto the apple tree, as J. H. Reid points out, that "technology is *not* the new messiah."[6] The failure of the "new star" to materialize in the evening sky, or the failure of Christa T. and her friends to see it, implies that scientific-technological progress will not propel the GDR into a utopian future. The official buzzwords of Freedom, Reason, and The Scientific Age have lost their validity: "Frieden war plötzlich ein Wort, das gelten sollte, Vernunft dachten wir, Wissenschaft: das wissenschaftliche Zeitalter" (N 142).

With *Nachdenken über Christa T.*, Wolf established herself as one of the first GDR writers to illuminate the consequences for the individual of unfettered scientific-technological progress, bringing to light, "[d]aß im NÖS eine gefährliche Fetischisierung von Rationalismus und Technik angelegt sein könnte" (Emmerich 174). The new world of socialism Wolf represents is not one of the proclaimed "Neue Mensch," but rather the "neu[e] Welt der Phantasielosen. Der Tatsachenmenschen. Der Hopp-Hopp Menschen" (N 55). As Anna Kuhn points out, "Christa T. watches the rise not of the new human being, but of the one-dimensional human being."[7] Christa T. recognizes that unreflected progress, the instrumentalization of social processes and the reign of facts and mechanical laws lead to the erasure of the self: "man erfreute sich an der absoluten Perfektion und Zweckmäßigkeit des Apparats, den reibungslos in Gang zu halten kein Opfer zu groß schien—selbst nicht das: sich auslöschen. Schräubchen sein" (N 60). Christa T. aspires to be more than a simple cog in the wheel of history; her goal, plainly stated, is "Mensch sein" (N 40). In this vein, Helen Fehervary is right to argue that, to a society defined in terms of production and efficiency, Christa T. represents a burden: "Her labor and goal rest solely in asserting her own place in history, and thereby she disturbs the streamlining of the historical continuum."[8]

Although highly critical of the course of Western civilization, Wolf is quick to distinguish her position from Western anti-Enlightenment critiques. Echoing Kant's definition of Enlightenment, she underscores the central role of reason for progress: "So bleibt der schmale Weg der Vernunft, des Erwachsenwerdens, der Reife des menschlichen Bewußtseins, der bewußte Schritt aus der Vorgeschichte in die Geschichte. Bleibt der Entschluß, mündig zu werden" (LS 47). Prose, in Wolf's view, should accompany and guide individuals on the path to self-knowledge and self-actualization. Although GDR newspapers, films, and books represent the ideals of self-actualization, humane relationships and morality, their "schrecklich strahlende Helden" (N 60) fail to conform to the reality Christa T. experiences. Instead, she recognizes a world concealed by the world of facts, an existence beyond the objective and rational: the quotidian life of subjectivity and emotions. Telling in this regard is the note she scribbles in the margin of her journal: "Der Pilot [...] der die Bombe auf Hiroshima geworfen hat, ist ins Irrenhaus gegangen" (N 61–62). Rather than reflect a scientific reality "von der die Kenn-Nummer Mensch sein kaum noch als widerstehendes, aufbegehrendes, rebellierendes Individuum abhebt" (LS 31), Wolf insists on subjectivity.

The continuity of past behaviors on the part of GDR youth in the 1960s, who represent society's future, further underscores that the socialist ideal of the "new human being" had yet to be realized. The lack of humanitarianism, a passive acceptance of the status quo, the persistence of authoritarianism and the enduring failure of individuals to take responsibility for their actions—all characteristic of fascist Germany—become visible in the questionable ethics and actions of the new generation represented by Christa T.'s pupils. The school outing on which one of Christa T.'s students, Hammurabi, stakes a bet with his peers that he wins by brutally biting off the head of a live toad offers a prime example of the continuation of past behavioral patterns. For Christa T., seventeen years of age at the war's end, this detestable action ushers in a flood of memories of equally senseless acts she had witnessed in the Nazi period: "Da knallt der schwarze Kater noch einmal an die Stallwand. Da zerschellen noch einmal die Elstereier am Stein. Das wird noch einmal der Schnee von einem steifen kleinen Gesicht gewischt. Noch einmal schnappen die Zähne zu. Das hört nie auf" (N 109). These inhumane actions unite past and present. As the continuation of the Hammurabi story suggests, individuals remain unaccountable for their actions. The narrator draws out the scenario that likely followed the toad incident: rather than indict the perpetrator himself,

Hammurabi's parents and the school principal place the blame squarely on Christa T.'s shoulders. According to the logic of an authoritarian state, the episode would have been avoided had Christa T. properly educated her students. The program of the 6th Party Congress in 1963 accents the role of ethics and morality, "Für den sozialistischen Menschen, der im Kampf um die Vollendung des Sozialismus heranwachst, gehören Menschenwürde und Gerechtigkeit zu den Grundsätzen seines Lebens."[9] Christa T.'s experience proves otherwise. Unwilling to accept her reality, she fabricates an alternative ending to the Hammurabi story. In this conclusion, penned in Christa T.'s journal, an emotional Hammurabi shows regret after his boorish act and seeks cleansing: he rinses out his mouth, brushes his teeth, throws himself down and weeps like a child (N 110). Christa T.'s vision, then, implies that Hammurabi learns from the past and will in the future act morally and ethically.

Another of Christa T.'s students exposes the degree to which the new generation has internalized a conformist ideology. This former student, who went on to become a physician, announces with pride the wisdom he gained over the years, summed up in his statement: "Der Kern der Gesundheit ist Anpassung" (N 112). In other words, those who wish to be healthy conform, those who refuse grow ill. Thus while Christa T. reportedly succumbs to leukemia, her illness is also a metaphor for her unwillingness to conform and adapt to societal pressures—her inability to live in her time. The symptoms of this illness include "Sehnsucht" (N 90), "Unruhe" (N 148), "unverbraucht[e] Gefühle" (N 155), "Unglück" (N 156), "die Schwierigkeit, 'ich' zu sagen" (N 166). When the narrator imagines asking Gertrud Born, a former classmate of Christa T.'s who acquiesces to the status quo, if Born thinks Christa T. died of leukemia, Born responds with an unequivocal "no" (N 54). Born, under the married name Dölling, further remarks that Christa T. was always at risk because of her powers of imagination: "Sie hat es nicht fertiggebracht, die Grenzen anzuerkennen, die einem nun einmal gesetzt sind" (N 51). Before the signs of leukemia set in, a doctor provides the following diagnosis of Christa T.'s "illness": "Todeswunsch als Krankheit. Neurose als mangelnde Anpassungsfähigkeit an gegebene Umstände" (N 75). Yet Christa T. is incapable of following the doctor's advice for her recovery: a woman of her intelligence, he suggests, must and will learn to conform (N 76). In the GDR, the only means to treat her illness is "Dämme bauen gegen unmäßige Ansprüche, phantastische Wünsche, ausschweifende Träume" (N 122). Although this treatment perhaps impedes Christa T.'s death, it ultimately fails because it targets the symptoms of the illness but not the underlying cause. Christa T., then, represents a tragic casualty of rationalized society. In the end, however, the narrative sustains the belief that the GDR could develop into a truly socialist society. Shortly before Christa T.'s death, subtle social changes become evident: "Es beginnt, was sie so schmerzhaft vermißt hatte: daß wir uns selber sehen;

deutlich fühlt sie, wie die Zeit für sie arbeitet, und muß sich doch sagen: Ich bin zu früh geboren. Denn sie weiß: Nicht mehr lange wird an dieser Krankheit gestorben werden" (N 180).

In drawing attention toward the individual and the inner world, Wolf breaks with prevalent political and cultural norms. Unlike Rita in *Der geteilte Himmel*, who successfully integrates into the realm of production, into the collective "we," Christa T. charts an opposing course: she withdraws from the productive realm and attempts to say "I." For Sonja Hilzinger, Christa T.'s life presents a "Paradigma [...] für das Nicht-Ankommen im Sozialismus, so wie er in der DDR entwickelt ist."[10] Along similar lines, Helen Fehervary argues that *Nachdenken über Christa T.* can be read as "anti-*Bildungsliteratur*": Christa T. is "asocial, writes fragments that are never published, prefers a contemplative country life to a career, is uncomfortable with the constraints of the traditional family structure" (99). These characterizations brings to the fore the extent to which Christa T. differs from the positive heroes of Socialist Realism who, rooted in industrial production and in the collective, legitimized the state. Extending Fehervary's argument, one can claim that Christa T.'s labor can only be termed "unproductive" within a society that equates productivity solely with rationalization and efficiency in the public sphere, a definition that excludes the reproductive, caring labor which women have been socialized to perform. As Hilary Rose argues in another context, a unity of reason and emotion, of "hand, brain and heart" is a precondition for the expression of an alternative epistemology.[11] *Nachdenken über Christa T.* targets not only the privileged status of the realm of production, but the privileging of those values attributed to it (reason, objectivity, rationalism) over the values associated with the realm of reproduction (caring, subjectivity, sensitivity). A pivotal work, it represents an early model of the gendered critique explicit in Wolf's later texts.

Nachdenken über Chista T.'s representation of an alternate epistemology and ontology has led numerous feminist literary critics to highlight the significance of gender in the work. In her illuminating article "Christa Wolf and Feminism: Breaking the Patriarchal Connection," Myra Love points to three feminist characteristics of Wolf's novel: "the subversive potential of female subjectivity expressed in the figure of Christa T.; the relationship of the two female protagonists as a counter-patriarchal example of female friendship and solidarity; and the possibility of a new mode of appropriating experience, perception and expression."[12] With the "two female protagonists," Love refers to the narrator and Christa T., whose subjectivity is constructed through a dialogic process of identification. Anna Kuhn similarly states: "[w]hile it can be assumed that Christa Wolf at the time of writing *Christa T.* was not consciously criticizing patriarchy, it is also clear that the alternative model of human interrelationship that she creates stems from women's experience" (94). Focusing on Christa T.'s moral stance and its affinity to psychologist Carol

Gilligan's research on women's moral reasoning, which Gilligan sees as based to a greater extent on principles of compassion and care than men's, Kuhn accentuates an important facet of Christa T.'s way of knowing. Although discredited in a patriarchal, scientific society, Christa T.'s moral vision is essential for the humanizing of such a society. The point is not that women's intimate "moral voice" should supplant men's independent and abstract sense of morality, that women's "moral voice" is necessarily better, but rather that society should also value a sense of morality based on an ethic of care and attachment. In breaking down dichotomies and moving beyond a binary mode of thinking, Wolf offers an alternative, feminine model, what Katharina von Hammerstein terms "ein Modell der Ganzheit-bildenden Vielheit."[13]

Within the context of Western science's tendency to disenchant the world, Christa T.'s insistence on the "halb reale, halb phantastische Existenz des Menschen" (N 111) is an attempt at re-enchantment that seeks to free men and women from the dictates of instrumental reason. As feminist philosopher Sandra Harding argues, beyond the world of facts "there is another world—the world of emotions, feelings, political values, of the individual and collective unconscious [...] and the world within which we all live most of our waking and dreaming hours under constant threat of its increasing reorganization by scientific rationality."[14] Feminist theory, Harding continues, should seek to reveal the relationships between these "two worlds."

Elaborating on Wolf's insistence on a multi-dimensional view of the individual in an increasingly one-dimensional society, Love has pointed to supernatural and paranormal elements in Wolf's works that blur "categories of thought and feeling that we normally take to be separate."[15] Love convincingly reads Christa T.'s encounter with a clairvoyant, "der Generool," as symbolizing her rejection of the world of facts, of that which society deems to be logical and scientific. Not limited to the rational but suffused with emotion, Christa T.'s mode of thinking also resembles that of the clairvoyant. It hence comes as no surprise that the clairvoyant correctly diagnoses her illness: in contrast to the doctor who asserts that Christa T. will learn to conform and in this way be cured, the clairvoyant recognizes Christa T.'s fate, that she will die young.

Wolf's rejection of a scientific worldview has fostered much of the political and philosophical criticism of her work. "The radicalism of Wolf's prose," Love argues, "is a function of its deviation from the narrowly conceived naturalism and materialism of the 'scientific' world-view that constitutes the consensus reality of socialists and capitalist alike" (3). The reception of *Nachdenken über Christa T.* documents the degree to which Wolf's repudiation of a cybernetic society incensed cultural officials. Though it eventually appeared in the GDR, the work's publication was initially delayed, and it was then printed in a limited edition, a clear sign that it did not sit well with cultural officials.[16] While it does not fault socialism per se, *Nachdenken über Christa T.* certainly indicts the status quo by rejecting a rationalized worldview, focusing on an "unproductive" individual and exposing the negative effects of scientific-technological progress. These factors sufficed to spark considerable controversy in the GDR. In "Selbstinterview" (1968), an essay staged as an interview about *Nachdenken über Christa T.*, Wolf anticipates that her work would be critiqued for its associative structure, its failure to reflect the ideal development of socialism, and its subjective focus on an individual who withdraws into private life (LS 51–55). As with the essay "Lesen und Schreiben," Wolf defends her aesthetics and reveals its ultimate affinity with the socialist ideals.

Since *Der geteilte Himmel*, critics in both East and West have accused Wolf of being blind to the positive advances of science and technology. This accusation marks the assessment of *Nachdenken über Christa T.* by GDR critic Horst Haase.[17] For Haase, science and technology comprise the primary forces of socialist progress, indeed constitute the very foundation of any "useful" existence: "Bleibt dieser [der Wissenschaft.] seit Jahrhunderten wesentlicher Faktor menschlichen Fortschreitens. Bleibt, was Marx die Grundlage sinnvollen Tuns auch im Bereich menschlichen Zusammenlebens ist" (Haase 181). While he acknowledges science's destructive and annihilating potential, Haase argues that in creating "ganze Menschen," "Verantwortungsbewußtsein" and "Moral," the socialist system establishes the necessary preconditions for science's humane and beneficial use (182). Interestingly, responsibility and morality are the very qualities that Christa T. sees as threatened by instrumental reason. Because Wolf rejects the scientific definitions and laws that for Haase form the very basis for moral and conscientious thoughts and actions, Haase accuses her of relativism and a lack of clarity, of too little "wissenschaftlich[en] Ernst" and "sachlich[e] Nüchternheit" (182–183).

In effect, Haase faults Wolf for failing to engage in the ideological battle of the Cold War. Rather than explicitly and unequivocally triumphing socialist progress, she in his view erroneously projects onto the GDR traits of a bourgeois, capitalist society: "Die drohende Zerstörung der Persönlichkeit! Die Vernichtung des menschlichen Selbstgefühls! Solche Kennzeichen einer antihumanistischen Gesellschaftsordnung in unsere sozialistische Welt zu projizieren, muß den Realismus der Darstellung im starkem Maße beeinträchtigen" (184). For orthodox GDR critics, the aesthetic representation of science was to replicate the ideals of socialism, not address conflicts and contradictions. Haase goes so far as to deny the relevance for the GDR of the Becher motto that prefaces *Nachdenken über Christa T.,* "Was ist das: Dieses Zu-sich-selber-Kommen des Menschen," pointing out that Wolf omits the words that follow in Becher's text, namely "Aus dem Leben eines bürgerlichen Menschen unserer Zeit" (184). In its failure optimistically to portray GDR reality, *Nachdenken über Christa T.* presented an affront to the ideological role many GDR political and cultural officials held of literature. Drawing attention to the radicalism of

Wolf's text for its time, GDR poet Sarah Kirsch writes to Wolf upon reading *Nachdenken über Christa T*: "Die Frechheit am ganzen finde ich, daß Du über die Dinge so redest, als könnte man längst über sie reden...."[18]

Unter den Linden

An analysis of the personal consequences of unfettered progress constitutes a cornerstone of Wolf's texts. In an interview with Hans Kaufmann in 1973, Wolf decries the teleology of historical materialism:

> Ich kann und will mich nicht einlassen auf einen blanken historischen Determinismus, der in Individuen, Schichten, Klassen, Völkern nur die Objekte einer sich unumstößlich durchsetzenden historischen Gesetzmäßigkeit sähe und dem eine vollkommen fatalistische Geschichtsphilosophie entspräche; ebensowenig aber auf einen öden Pragmatismus, der in der Moral von Klassen und Individuen nichts sieht als ein Mittel zum Zweck, beliebig manipulierbar, beliebig ignorierbar, mal nützliches, mal unnützliches Vehikel. (LS 98)

In her collection of "three improbable stories" entitled *Unter den Linden* (1974), a volume that includes the title story "Unter den Linden" (1969), "Neue Lebensansichten eines Katers" (1970) and "Selbstversuch. Traktat zu einem Protokoll" (1972), Wolf focuses on the relations and mediations between the reified oppositions of object and subject, rational and irrational, fact and fiction, realism and the fantasy, man and woman. The first-person narrator of the title story recognizes, for example, that dreams free her from the "facts" and allow her to approach the "truth": "Nicht mehr bin ich an die Tatsachen gekettet," she states, "Ich kann frei die Wahrheit sagen" (UdL 65). In the "improbable stories," the opposition of facts and truth, two concepts often viewed as identical, forces readers to question the veracity of objective, factual/realistic accounts and thereby alerts them to the stories' realism: though "improbable," the narratives clearly relate to and emerge from societal conditions. Particularly in "Neue Lebensansichten" and "Selbstversuch," Wolf lays bare the deformation within and between individuals brought about by increased rationalization. In "Selbstversuch," moreover, Wolf specifically addresses the status of women in the GDR. Representing the exaggerated gender stereotype inherent in the binary opposition man/woman, she illuminates the persistence of entrenched roles and the need to work towards their dismantling.

In all three of her "improbable stories," Wolf employs narrative techniques such as dreams, fantasy, satire and irony to subvert the traditional realist narrative paradigm and rational discourse, creating an aesthetic realm in which she plays out possibilities for social change. In a society with literary censorship, the ability of the fantastic indirectly to articulate social criticism is an important consideration. The growing popularity of this genre among GDR writers in the 1970s can also be attributed to Honecker's proclamation of a liberalized cultural sphere, of "no more taboos" for artistic production, and to the GDR's renewed reception of Romanticism. Wolf's "Neue Lebensansichten eines Katers" (1970), a re-vision of E. T. A. Hoffmann's tale *Lebensansichten des Katers Murr* (1821), testifies to the latter trend. Wolf explains in her interview with Kaufmann how the "unrealistic" narrative techniques she employs in *Unter den Linden* serve to illuminate problems confronting the GDR: "ihre Verlegung in Traum, Utopie, Groteske kann einen Verfremdungseffekt in bezug auf Vorgänge, Zustände und Denkweisen erzeugen, an die wir uns schon zu sehr gewöhnt haben, als daß sie uns noch auffallen und stören würden" (LS 95). *Unter den Linden* highlights the reification of societal processes, the objectification of individuals and the lack of gender equality. Through exaggerated and distorted representations, Wolf draws attention to current problems to heighten awareness of social ills and potentially inspire their correction. Illuminating the gap between the "no longer" and the "not yet," she points to a utopian space in which possibilities for the future become visible.

Addressing the genre of the fantastic in GDR literature of the 1970s, Rainer Nägele identifies three spheres of displacement or "Verrückung": "Verrückung von Rationalem und Irrationalem (Dialektik der Aufklärung), des Verhältnisses von Besonderem und Allgemeinen (Dialektik der Totalität) und des Verhältnisses von Subjekt und Objekt (Dialektik der Identität)."[19] This dialectic displacement, as Nägele states, serves a critical function: "In dieser dreifachen Verrückung und Dialektik arbeitet die Kritik sich am Wirklichen ab: an der Tendenz der sozialistischen Gesellschaft zur Rationalisierung, zur Totalisierung und zum Terror der Identität" (207). Although Nägele elaborates on these spheres of displacement in reference to *Anti-Geisterbahn*, a collection of fantastic short stories penned by GDR writers, they also pertain to *Unter den Linden*. Wolf's narratives similarly reveal the dialectic between the rational and irrational, the particular and the general, the individual and society, and between subject and object.

In his review of *Unter den Linden*, GDR critic Rulo Melchert downplays the critical potential of fantastic narrative techniques, pointing instead to how the fantastic allows Wolf to explore new aesthetic forms and to expose aspects of the relationship between the individual and society. Although Melchert, like Wolf, stresses the fragility of the individual and the need for self-reflection, he empties these concerns of their specific historical context by abstracting them into sweeping generalities about the human condition. For example, rather than present a woman's struggle for love and recognition, "Unter den Linden" in his view symbolizes harmony between the individual and society "überstrahlt vom

Glück der Befreiung im Wiederfindung unseres Selbst" (442). Addressing "Neue Lebensansichten eines Katers" he affirms that it caricatures "ein System-Denken und eine System-Praxis, die menschliches Zusammenleben nicht befördert, sondern gefährdet," but makes no concrete reference to the enthusiastic reception and implementation of systems theory in the GDR (443). In the case of "Selbstversuch," Melchert similarly directs attention away from Wolf's critique of women's incomplete emancipation in the GDR to assert: Diese Gegenüberstellung von Mann und Frau, Frau und Mann, will nicht die soziale Emanzipation der Frau diskutieren, sondern das Verhältnis zwischen Individuum und Gesellschaft, Probleme der Selbstverwirklichung des Menschen als Einzelwesen und als Gattung (445). To be sure, Wolf's texts express human concerns that obtain well beyond the GDR's borders. Yet they also have a critical core her readers surely recognize.

While his interpretation presents a more differentiated reading than Melchert's, GDR critic Hans Georg Werner employs a similar critical strategy in his review of *Unter den Linden*.[20] Werner acknowledges that Wolf's critique of rationalization and of the suppression of individuality pertains to the GDR, yet ultimately undercuts the contemporary relevance of Wolf's critique by grounding the problems of rationalization and self-alienation squarely in bourgeois society. Werner relates these issues to the significant influence of the Romantics and of the Austrian writer Ingeborg Bachmann on Wolf's "improbable stories," faulting Wolf's uncritical acceptance of "die romantische Aversionen gegen Rationalismus, Leistungswillen, materielle Produktivität" (59). Attributing to capitalism the negative relationship of the individual to society, Werner emphatically denies that this relationship characterizes socialist society as well: "sie [die kapitalistische Gesellschaft] verwickelte den Menschen in einen gesellschaftlichen Kreislauf, der die kapitalistische Entfremdung des Menschen nicht nur reproduzierte, sondern immer weiter verschärfte" (61). Upholding the official emphasis on self-actualization through production, Werner also denounces Wolf's focus on self-actualization in and through inter-personal relationships. Moreover, he sees as unfounded Wolf's fear that science, technology and economics will become ends in themselves and censures Wolf's representation of "ein romantisiertes Weltbild [...], in dem die Gesetze der materiellen Produktion den aus der Subjektivität kommenden Anforderungen der Humanität entgegenstehen" (59). By representing productivity only in subjective and individualistic terms, Wolf in his view discounts the interaction of subjective and objective production processes: "bliebe ein wesentliches Moment nahezu unfaßbar: die praktischen Möglichkeiten der Subjektivität auf ihre Umwelt produktiv einzuwirken" (60). Werner fails to acknowledge that Wolf addresses the intimate and crucial relationship between the individual subject and societal processes, that in her works the personal is political.

To varying degrees, all three "improbable" stories view the rationalization and functionalization of the individual through the lens of gender. Sonja Hilzinger illuminates the following pattern of gender relationships as paradigmatic: "Die Frau, fähig zu lieben, Erkennen des Mannes und Hingabe, wünscht sich eine ebensolche erkennende Liebe; der Mann, den sie liebt, ist nicht nur unfähig dazu [...] sondern er begreift nicht einmal den Wunsch der Frau."[21] The tropes of recognition, in its dual meanings of *kennen* and *erkennen*, self-actualization and the "ability to love" figure significantly in Wolf's critique of science. The latter trope, when cast negatively as "men's inability to love," easily strikes a critical nerve, particularly when it conflates with the "masculine" realm of science. Unlike the cultural feminist perspective on "women's way of loving" that posits the cultivation and maintenance of relationships and intimacy as endemic to women's nature, Wolf sees this quality as neither inherent to women nor completely foreign to men. While she suggests that women generally have a greater need and capacity for love and connection because of their social roles, she explores the consequences for men *and* women of a dualistic culture that perpetuates the equation and devaluation of the private realm of woman, emotion, and nature. These binaries hinder both men's and women's "ability to love."

Both at the beginning and end of the title story "Unter den Linden," the narrator reminds us, "[d]enn höher als alles, schätzen wir die Lust, erkannt zu sein" (UdL 65, 116). In all three stories, women seek recognition through the private realm of relationships, men through the public realm of work: "Herr Jedermann gibt sein Geld aus, damit die Volkswirtschaft floriert, aber er spart sich seine Gefühle. Kollege Jedermann wird konkurrenzfähig. Genosse Jedermann hat Erfolg" (UdL 98–99). In "Unter den Linden," Peter's unhappiness stems from professional setbacks (UdL 71), reasons the narrator herself finds quite banal. Her grief results from personal setbacks: unrequited love, a failed relationship, too much passion in a society that demands the suppression of emotion for success in the public realm. Within the dominant masculine paradigm, Wolf exposes the costs of progress in the personal realm of feelings and love which is increasingly at risk: "[s]owas kommt heute weniger vor [...], man ist nicht mehr so für das Abstrakte" (UdL 90).

"Die neuen Lebensansichten eines Katers"

In the following, I focus more closely on "Neue Lebensansichten eines Katers" and "Selbstversuch," the two narratives set in the realm of science. "Neue Lebensansichten eines Katers" presents an absurd satire of societal rationalization and its effects. Through humor, the story issues a scathing indictment of an increasingly one-dimensional and makes explicit the criticism of a cybernetically-rationalized society in *Nachdenken über Christa T.*. The tale is narrated from the perspective of a highly rational tomcat who reflects, "wenn ich ein Mensch wäre, ich widmete mich wie mein Professor der totalen Ausbreitung der alles erkennenden, alles erklärenden, alles regelnden Ratio" (NL 123). The narrative centers around three professors, Professor Barzel, an applied psychologist, Dr. Fettback, a food scientist and physio-therapist, and Dr. Hinz, a cybernetic sociologist, who attempt to develop a cybernetic system of TOMEGL ("TOTALES MENSCHENGLÜCK") to predict, control and regulate human happiness. As Hinz emphasizes, "nur die Kybernetik sei imstande, ihm jenes absolut vollständige Verzeichnis sämtlicher menschlicher Unglücksfälle in sämtlichen denkbaren Kombinationen zu liefern" (NL 123). The goal of TOMEGL, simply stated, is "Abschaffung der Tragödie" (NL 123), in other words the programming and regulation of life along cybernetic lines, "nichts Geringeres als die erschöpfende Programmierung derjenigen Zeitfolge, welch die Menschen mit dem antiquierten Wort LEBEN belegt haben" (NL 134). According to the professors, human beings' "mystic" relationship to life has resulted only in "Unordnung, Zeitverschwendung, unökonomischer Kräfte-verschleiß" (NL 135).

Although the tomcat and professors are certainly caricatures, as Ludo Abicht points out they also "fit a new breed of real planners, people who are trying to make their system work by eliminating all human problems, need and feeling from their plan."[22] GDR critic Therese Hörnigk likewise argues that despite its grotesque exaggeration of scientific thought, "Neue Lebensansichten" must be read as a "Warnbild" in light of the attempted rationalization of GDR society along cybernetic lines since the mid-1960s.[23]

The science of cybernetics had begun to make great inroads in the Soviet Union in the post-Stalin period. Based on the possibilities attributed to artificial intelligence, cybernetic principles of control and self-regulation became viewed as applicable to a wide array of disciplines. Helmar Frank explains:

Die Kybernetik bezeichnet die Bestrebungen, verschiedene wissen-schaftliche Disziplinen vermittels einheitlicher Gesichtspunkte (insbe-sondere vermittels der regelungs- und der informationstheoretischen Terminologie) durch eine gemeinsame Methodik zu verbinden. Damit hängt auf das engste der Vergleich von Prozessen aus dem Gegen-standsbereich *einer* Wissenschaft mit formal entsprechenden, von einer *anderen* Wissenschaft untersuchten Prozessen zusammen, also insbesondere die Simulierung biologischer, psychologischer oder logischer Prozesse durch die informationsverarbeitende (kybernetische) Maschine.[24]

Although cybernetic principles are most commonly applied to biology and technology, some theorists, in particular those in the former Soviet Union, went so far as to claim the universal validity. Within the fields of psychology and sociology, for example, cybernetics describes individual and social development in terms of predictable processes and behavior.

The attempt of social cybernetics to explain complex human behaviors has stirred much debate, centering foremost on the controversial assertion that the human mind and artificial intelligence function along similar lines. One extreme is expressed by the Soviet cyberneticist A. N. Kolmogorov, who maintained that "it is theoretically possible for a cybernetic automaton to experience every human activity, including emotion."[25] This belief in the capacity of automated machines to express human feelings signals great faith in the possibilities of artificial intelligence. More problematically, it implies that all human capacities are explicable and hence controllable: if a machine could be capable of human emotions, then human emotion must be predictable, controllable and perhaps even programmable.

Despite considerable enthusiasm for cybernetics in the Soviet Union, this science proved to be quite controversial.[26] Not only did some Soviet theorists reject the notion that electronic machines can "think," but staunch ideologues questioned whether cybernetics presents an all-encompassing ideological system whose principles oppose those of Marxism, that is, whether the mechanistic laws of cybernetics contradict the dialectic of historical materialism. This fundamental issue was skirted by (re)defining cybernetics so as to imply that "Marxism is so much more general an intellectual system than cybernetics that the two do not conflict."[27] As Marxist-Leninism became a reified theory, a cybernetic approach that focuses on objective principles of control, predictability and regulation appeared entirely compatible with the mechanistic laws of Marxist-Leninism, particularly when one considers the role of conformity and accommodation both systems ascribe to the individual. Manfred Behn explains:

> Die Versuche, die Ergebnisse der Kybernetik als allgemeine Systemtheorie des "Entwickelten gesellschaftlichen Systems des Sozialismus" auszuwerten [...] begünstigten [...] die euphorischen Erwartungen auf einen saturierten gesellschaftlichen Zustand sich ständig vollkommenender wissenschaftlich-technischer Progression, in den sich die Individuen nur noch 'einzuregeln' hätten.[28]

In "Neue Lebensansichten," Wolf polarizes the realms of science and emotion, underscoring the reification and one-dimensionality of the scientific realm. As Abicht states with regard to the type of society Wolf depicts: "[t]his scientifically regulated, completely controlled world with its extreme division of labor is a total deviation from the Marxist model of the potential socialist society" (168). Abicht makes explicit how far the GDR has departed from this

original model by citing the utopian vision of a communist society spelled out
by Marx in *The German Ideology*:

> [I]n a communist society, where nobody has one exclusive sphere of
> activity but each can become accomplished in any branch he wishes,
> society regulates the general production and thus makes it possible for
> me to do one thing today and another tomorrow, to hunt in the
> morning, fish in the afternoon, rear cattle in the evening, criticize after
> dinner....[29]

Marx's vision of a society characterized by immense personal freedoms and
productive diversity represents a striking contrast to the one-dimensional norm
depicted by Wolf.

In "Unter den Linden," Wolf paints an ominous picture of a fully
rationalized world where all are alienated from themselves, where emotions are
no longer expressed—where all are blind to the soul. "Bald verbindet uns nichts
als unsere Seelenblindheit. [...] Da wir alle die Sünde der Lieblosigkeit kennen,
wird niemand sich mehr ihrer erinnern" (UdL 114), the narrator states. In "Neue
Lebensansichten" the professors developing the cybernetic system agree, "daß
die Seele eine reaktionäre Einbildung sei, die viel unnützes Leid über die
Menschheit gebracht und, unter anderem, solchen unproduktiven Wirtschafts-
zweigen wie der Belletristik ein lukratives Dasein ermöglicht habe" (NL 121).
While literature may reserve a special place for the soul, for sensuality and
emotion, these features are seen to have no reasonable purpose in science or in
the regulated cybernetic society the professors envision. The cyberneticist, Dr.
Hinz, contends that all human problems, such as the soul, which slow or deter
scientific-technological progress can be easily schematized, and must ultimately
be eliminated in order to succeed with the "abolition of tragedy." Drawing
attention to the dismissal of the soul, an utterly unscientific concept, Max
Horkheimer states in his *Critique of Instrumental Reason*: "as progress imposes
stricter limitations on life and regulates behavior more fully, imagination is
replaced by purposive systematic procedures, active emotions by reliable
emotions, and feeling by reason. [...] Reason divorced from feeling is now
becoming the opposite of *Anima* or soul."[30] The separation of reason from
emotion informs the professors' attempt to systematize and eliminate from their
system those human characteristics that affect physical and mental health. These
include "the pleasures of life," "dangers to civilization," "sexuality," "family,"
"leisure time," nutrition" and "hygiene" (NL 134). When Max, the utterly
rational tomcat, inadvertently files the index card "ability to conform" from the
box "social norms" into the box "pleasures of life," the professors laud his
cleverness. Consequently, in a move that reveals the underlying chaos of even
the most rational of systems, the pleasure of conformity becomes the supporting

pillar of their SYMAGE (System der maximalen körperlichen und seelischen Gesundheit). The struggle against conformity of Christa T. and the female narrator of "Unter den Linden" attest to the bitter irony of this central principle.

The professors' quest to create a regulated social system "mit einem Freiheitsspielraum von plus minus null in genau voraussagbarer Weise auf Reize antwortet: ein vollkommenes Reflexwesen" (NL 141) evinces the extreme degree of conformity they seek. Ironically, this ideally systematized being can only function in an environment devoid of all external influences (NL 141). Reading "Neue Lebensansichten" as a satire of GDR society, SYMAGE becomes an analogy for the GDR's reified, non-dialectic Marxism that was to provide the necessary foundation for complete human happiness and fulfillment. The need for a closed, completely stable system is a direct reference to the securing of the GDR's borders in 1961. GDR officials justified the construction of the Wall by arguing that it was an "antifaschistischer Schutzwall," a necessary means of keeping the detrimental, fascist influences of the capitalist West at bay. It also provided a way to ensure socialism's unfettered development in the GDR.

Because humans fail readily to conform, the pragmatic professors suggest that they must be forced into their happiness. Since their system's troubling and unstable variable is "die Größe Mensch" (NL 144), they proceed to abolish from their catalog all the superfluous characteristics that make up "Normalmensch" such as "schöpferisches Denken" (NL 145). Dr. Fettback, however, argues that "creative thought" and the definition "human" should not be conceived of as contradictory to their cybernetic system for human happiness. Personality in his view is integral to creativity and "höchstes Glück der Erdenkinder" (NL 145). Yet although creative thought conforms to the human image, the professors contend that, like the soul, it can be fostered in literature and art and disregarded for scientific purposes. They hence eliminate from their system "secondary" personality traits such as courage, selflessness, and the ability to perceive beauty, those unique qualities that distinguish humans from machines. It is ironic, then, that the computer, not the scientists, stages the ultimate revolt against these omissions.

The computer's failure leaves Dr. Barzel utterly distraught and drives him to behave in ways that from Max's perspective are completely "irrational." These include Barzel's infatuation with the seventeen-year-old neighbor, Regina. For Max, who has never before witnessed any show of emotion from the professors, this can only be explained as an illness. Likewise he adduces from the emotions expressed by Barzel's rebellious daughter Isa, "daß Lächeln und Weinen infantile Überbleibsel aus der Entwicklungsgeschichte der Menschheit sind und von voll gereiften Exemplaren dieser Gattung etwa um das fünfundzwanzigste Lebensjahr herum abgestoßen werden" (NL 138). In Max's utterly rational view, further progress would ideally lead to the elimination of all such sentiments.

A closer look at gender relations makes apparent the contradictions inherent within a system that defines human happiness in terms of a lack of emotion. The world of the male professors contrasts sharply with that of the female characters. For example, Professor Barzel confesses that women are more apt to evade the progressive scientific testing methods he is attempting to develop. However, neither he nor the tomcat openly express this recognition, "um nicht in den Verdacht verstreckter Gegnerschaft zur Frauenemanzipation zu kommen, und um den Frauen, die ja samt und sonders unter ihrem Defekt leiden, keine Männer zu sein, ihre mißliche Lage nicht noch zu erschweren" (NL 120). Without question, the masculine, along with the "Idealbild," the computer Heinrich, represents the norm for human progress; women, from the male perspective, are viewed as aberrations. Anita, Barzel's wife, is a lonely, affection-starved woman who takes to drink, spends her evenings reading detective novels and eating pralines, and holds monologues about "die Enttäuschungen des Lebens, besonders aber die des Frauenlebens, und besonders die Enttäuschungen, die die allernächsten Personen, zum Beispiel der eigene Ehemann einem zufügen ..." (NL 125). Frustrated as her husband begins to spend nights in the office with Heinrich, she consummates an affair with Dr. Hinz. Like Dr. Barzel, the tomcat neglects his fatherly duties on the pretext that he is pursuing scientific inquiry (NL 131). The professor's teenage daughter Isa also exhibits behavior anathema to the professor's rational facade, as exemplified by her "uncivilized" romp with her scantily clothed friends in the family swimming pool. Holding to a very different conception of human progress and happiness, she views her narrow-minded father as a stuffy "Fortschrittsspießer" (NL 141). Even the Beckmann's female cat possesses stereotypically feminine attributes: she is "zierlich," "anmutig," and "verführerisch," although "in ihrem Inneren leider frech und anmaßend und gierig [...], kurzum: ein Weib" (NL 120).

Despite their attempts to create the perfect cybernetic system and "annihilate the tragedy," the professors are ultimately incapable of living without emotion. Fettback extols the significance of personality and individuality, Hinz has an affair with Anita, and Barzel, who already suffers from a stomach ulcer, sleeplessness and impotence, takes to drink when Regina rejects him. In a final crazed monologue, he addresses Regina and iterates how through SYMAGE he will force her into a life of happiness with him:

> Eines Tages nämlich werden Sie mich mögen müssen, mein Fräulein. Bloß dann werden Sie ... ein Reflexwesen sein wie jedermann, und den Stolz werde ich dir als nebensächlich weggeformt haben, und anstatt mit deinem faden blonden Motorradjüngling werde ich dich mit SYMAGE verheiraten. (NL 149)

At the end of the next "improbable" story, "Selbstversuch," the narrator envisions creating or discovering a man whom she can love, one who has the ability to love and express emotion. Barzel's vision, in turn, can be read as a sarcastic analog to the vision in "Selbstversuch." Barzel too is motivated by jealousy and love, but of a different sort: he will use SYMAGE to create the person who, with all emotions erased, will be forced to love him.

"Selbstversuch"

"Selbstversuch" was conceived as part of the anthology *Blitz aus heiterm Himmel* (1975), for which Edith Anderson commissioned GDR authors to write stories centered on the topic of sex change. Two years prior to its publication in Anderson's anthology, Wolf's narrative appeared in the journal *Sinn und Form*. "Selbstversuch" reflects Wolf's growing interest in the possibilities for women's self-actualization within patriarchal, socialist society already evident in *Nachdenken über Christa T.*. As in this earlier text, "Selbstversuch" represents individual fulfillment as a necessary aspect of socialism and renders problematic the official emphasis on self-actualization through acquiescence to a masculine norm. As Helen Fehervary and Sara Lennox note, "Selbstversuch" reflects Wolf's earlier texts in that it "combines a utopian vision with a critique of conformism, careerism, bureaucratization and technocracy."[31] Its distinguishing feature is its explicit focus on gender: in "Selbstversuch," they assert, "the 'self' is not just a human but a distinctly female personality" (110).

In its projection of a utopian future based on scientific-technological progress, "Selbstversuch" can be classified as a work of science fiction. It is set twenty years into the future, in the year 1992. This future brings with it the development of *Petersein masculinum 199*, a drug which, at least in terms of primary sexual traits, has the power to transform women into men. Far from a positive advance, this possibility reflects how the GDR's narrow definition of "women's emancipation" as equal integration into the realm of production excluded other wishes and needs.[32] Subjective needs comprise the treatise "Selbstversuch," written in the first person by the experimental test person, a thirty-three-year-old professor of physio-psychology, after she breaks off the sex-change experiment. The female scientist's own story, "Selbstversuch," serves as a corrective to the neutral, objective account written up by the male professor. In an interview in 1973, Wolf expresses her fear that "der radikale Ansatz, von dem wir ausgegangen sind ("Befreiung der Frau"), steckenzubleiben droht in der Selbstzufriedenheit über eine Vorstufe, die wir erklommen haben und von der aus neue radikale Fragestellungen uns weiterbringen müßten" (LS 93). Wolf's narrator accordingly speaks of the time she "threatened" to become a man, "Mann zu werden drohte" (SV 192).

For Sonja Hilzinger, Wolf's future orientation illuminates "einer sich zunehmend verselbständigen Wissenschaft, die menschliche Phantasie und Erkenntnisfähigkeiten gänzlich wegzurationalisieren droht" (169). As in "Neue Lebensansichten," Wolf draws the characters in "Selbstversuch" from the scientific realm. Both "Neue Lebensansichten" and "Selbstversuch" depict scientific attempts to alter and "perfect" the human being, in the former text through the development of a cybernetic system that manipulates external factors, in the latter through altering the genetic code. As previously noted, the cybernetic rationalization of GDR society constitutes a concrete referent for the technocratic nightmare Wolf depicts in "Neue Lebensansichten." "Selbstversuch" is likewise grounded in the contemporary issues of gender, science, and the individual. Wolf's 1969 essay "Ein Besuch," an account of her conversations with the biologist Hans Stubbe, testifies to her growing preoccupation with the dark side of the scientific age, not only the horrific possibilities of nuclear physics but also of genetic engineering. Both "Ein Besuch" and "Selbstversuch" warn that we must prepare ourselves for an age in which "bios," life itself, could become an object of scientific manipulation (DiA2 707).

Pursuing the possible intervention into genetic processes, Wolf notes in "Ein Besuch" that as early as 1865, Francis Galton suggested that principles of directed evolution in plant breeding could be applied to the control and guidance of human evolution. Galton hypothesized: "Es scheint, als ob die physische Beschaffenheit zukünftiger Generationen unter der Hand des Züchters fast so formbar wäre wie Lehm. Es ist meine Absicht zu zeigen [...] daß die geistigen Qualitäten ebenfalls kontrollierbar sind" (DiA2 714). The genetic control and manipulation of the human spirit theorized by Galton prefigures the correspondence of man and machine implied by cybernetics, as we saw in "Neue Lebensansichten," conjuring a vision of a society populated by clones or androids, by human forms but not by unique individuals. For Wolf, the possibility to manipulate the human genome suggests an "Eingriffsmöglichkeit in das so und nicht anders gewordene Individuum, das uns durch Tradition und Erziehung als Innerstes, Eigenstes, Unantastbares und Unberührbares vorkommt, als das Tabu aller Tabus" (DiA2 699–700).

Fearful that the individual will become the object of scientific manipulation, that genetics, like the GDR's scientific Marxism, will place increasing weight on the "usefulness" and "utility" of human beings, Wolf ponders what motivates the geneticists' quest for knowledge: "Ein bißchen lieber Gott sein wollen? Ein bißchen mehr Tempo, Vollkommenheit, Nützlichkeit und Verwendbarkeit in die große, aufreizende Gleichmut der Natur sich einzuschmuggeln?" (DiA2 706–707). In "Selbstversuch," as we shall see, the transformation of a woman into a man is motivated by scientific inquiry and the "Reduzierung einer fragwürdige Gattung" (SV 152): woman. In response to Wolf's concerns, Stubbe describes the scientists' sense of adventure and the creativity inherent in the pursuit of new discoveries (DiA2 707). Stubbe implies, moreover, that moral or ethical implications will not prevent the targeted interference in the human gene pool. His words echo the convictions many physicists expressed when faced with the potential use of nuclear energy for atomic warfare. Regarding the extent to which scientists should be held accountable for the potential misuse and abuse of their discoveries, Stubbe replies:

> Die Frage: Sollen wir weiterforschen? ist müßig. Wie werden weiter-
> forschen. Was erfindbar ist, wird erfunden werden. Aber wir werden
> unsere eigenen Erfindungen nur als Menschen überleben, als
> vernunftbegabte Wesen in vernünftig organisierten Gesellschaften—
> oder gar nicht.—Stellen Sie sich die Fähigkeit, Manipulationen an der
> menschlichen Erbmasse vorzunehmen, in der Hand faschistischer
> Regierungen vor.... (DiA2 724)

Wolf's and Stubbe's concerns are well-founded. One need only recall the Third Reich's recourse to Social Darwinism and Eugenics to preserve, purify and perpetuate the "Aryan" gene pool, to justify the "survival of the fittest" and put to death or sterilize those deemed weaker, including the mentally and physically handicapped, the diseased, Roma and Jews.

For both nuclear power and genetic engineering, the social benefits e.g., sufficient energy and treatment and cure of genetically-determined diseases, coexist with the immense threat of human annihilation. With the possibilities we now have to destroy life on earth, the rejection of a one-sided rationality that divorces the means from the ends becomes all the more crucial for survival. For Wolf, the notion of "Homo technicus, dieses Wesen von menschlicher Gestalt, das auf die Welt gesetzt wird, um in möglichst reibungsloser und technisch perfekter Weise materielle Güter zu schaffen" (DiA2 720) undermines not only her firm conviction that the imperfect human being can better herself or himself, but also her unwavering belief in literature's social role. "Der Prosaautor [...] was sagt er seinen Zeitgenossen, die dabei sind, den stromlinienförmigen Menschen zu konstruieren, fähig, sich allen Anforderungen der Zivilisation anzupassen?" (LS 17) she asked in *Lesen und Schreiben*. Molding the perfectible or "perfect" human, she fears, could render literature obsolete:

> jene finsteren biologischen Visionen von dem beliebig manipulierbaren
> menschenähnlichen Monstrum zerstören auch die Kunst. Keine
> Entscheidungsmöglichkeit—keine Konflikte; keine Auseinander-
> setzung mit den Grenzen der Natur—kein Schicksal. Ende des
> historischen Menschen. Keine Geschichte mehr und keine Geschichten.
> (DiA2 720)

Genetic engineering in her view would signal the end of "Identität, Verantwortung, Schicksal—die Dimension der Tiefe im menschlichen Leben" (DiA2
720).

In Stubbe's writings, however, Wolf discovers a statement suggesting that
scientists and writers share a common vision because they share a common
future: "Unsere Erde, dieser einmalig kostbare Planet, Geburtsstätte und Heimat
des Menschen" (DiA2 726). Stubbe's insistence on the individual, on
personality, sparks in Wolf the idea of a possible "fourth dimension" in science,
one that assures her of literature's continued relevance:

> Die Kunst, die sich selber ernst nimmt, arbeitet also auf ihre Weise
> daran mit, daß die Menschen den ungeheuerlichsten Entdeckung der
> Wissenschaft gewachsen sein können? Indem sie die Persönlichkeit
> stärkt? Indem sie, als Organ ihrer Gesellschaft, Bilder vom Menschen
> entwirft und die Möglichkeit erweitert, sich selbst zu sehen und zu
> erkennen. (DiA2 726)

In her works, Wolf reveals this fourth dimension of depth, the passionate
engagement with the issues of our time, reflection and subjectivity, as vital for
literature, for scientists, and for our very existence. The radical questions Wolf
poses express her persistent hope in a radical change in the position of women
and of humankind. Their impulse can be termed both feminist and utopian for,
as Marlene Barr and Nicholas Smith suggest, "Feminism today is the most
utopian project around. That is, it demands the most radical and truly
revolutionary transformation of present society."[33]

Fredric Jameson points out that science fiction reveals the limits of our
imagination in that it accentuates the impossibility of imagining a reality
different than our own. Jameson argues that

> the most characteristic science fiction does not seriously attempt to
> imagine the 'real' future of our social system. Rather, its multiple mock
> futures serve quite the different function of transforming our own
> present into the determinate past of something yet to come. Science
> fiction can thus be viewed as "future history," a term that highlights
> how this genre functions as a vehicle for representing the present as
> history and thereby defamiliarizing and estranging it.[34]

The transposition into another time is a technique of alienation that leads readers
to encounter their own present as estranged. Science fiction functions "not to
give us 'images' of the future [...] but rather to defamiliarize and restructure our
experience of our own *present*, and to do so in specific ways distinct from all
other forms of defamiliarization" (244). The alienating narrative perspective

Wolf employs in "Neue Lebensansichten" illuminates questions of cybernetics, while "Selbstversuch" focuses more closely on women's emancipation in the GDR. According to Jameson, such utopian representations lead to "the transformation of the cultural text into an auto-referential discourse, whose content is perpetual interrogation of its own conditions of possibility" (250).

Wolf's insistence on an alternate future has a clear utopian impulse. As Ernst Bloch stressed, utopias are not purely phantasms, but are based on concrete societal tendencies. Relating the concept of concrete utopia to texts by women, Sigrid Weigel theorizes the "Schreiben des Mangels als Produktion von Utopie."[35] Weigel argues that women's literature, in pointing out and working through the negative conditions and consequences of women's lives in patriarchal culture, makes visible the possibility of another way of living. In literature by women Weigel identifies "unterschiedliche Schreibweisen der *Doppelexistenz*: des Lebens im Muster der herrschenden Frauenbilder und in der Antizipation der befreiten Frau" (31). By negating the status quo, alternative possibilities come to light. Drawing on Bloch, Weigel situates women's "double existence" between the "no longer" and the "not yet" and identifies "Strategien der schreibenden Gestaltung des Mangels, des Hindurchgehens durch die vorhandenen Frauenbilder bis zu ihrer Zerstörung" (31). The demystification and destruction of the existing images of women create the possibility of "einer neuen, emanzipierten bzw. befreiten Frau" (33).

The focus on women's lives and the utopian possibilities of female perception, Fehervary and Lennox argue, comprises "the very radicalism of Wolf's work, not as an alternative to Marxism but as a qualitatively new and autonomous dimension that is a prerequisite for its renewal" (112). By rooting "Selbstversuch" within a specifically female way of knowing, Wolf suggests a possible mediation between socialism and feminism, though at that time "still tentative, obscure and to a large extent unarticulated, but therefore perhaps all the more credible and promising" (112). Centered on the construction of gender, "Selbstversuch" reveals a woman-centered ontology and epistemology: Wolf represents the male world as "positivisitic, or scientific in its worst sense," the female realm as holistic, "as the much richer interaction of objective fact and subjective response, a reality constituted by the act of mediation" (110–111). Moreover, in centering on patriarchy, "Selbstversuch" also targets the GDR's reified Marxist-Leninism.

The female protagonist of "Selbstversuch" is objectively equal to her male colleagues. She is a scientist, doctor of physio-psychology and head of the collective for sex transformation. However, her colleagues resent her attempts to advance her career. In the private realm, moreover, her partner Bertram feels neglected because of her professional commitments and therefore ends the relationship: "Frauen als Wissenschaftler, ja, hohe weibliche Intelligenzquotienten selbstverständlich; aber was einer Frau einfach nicht liegt ist der

Hang zum Absoluten" (SV 200). "Masculine" qualities appear to be tolerated only when women still fulfill their "feminine" function. For example, Bertram finds it intolerable that his partner occasionally spends evenings in the institute and evades the "problem" of a child because of career demands. Although women enjoy greater opportunities, men continue to prefer the traditional female role of jealousy, attachment and self-sacrifice (SV 201). Unlike the narrator, the woman whom Bertram eventually marries makes no attempt to be his equal. She willfully subordinates herself and, treasuring Bertram like a prized art object, finds it incomprehensible that someone would give up anything as "precious" as this man (SV 201). Wolf illustrates that for women, "Hochmut," "Ehelosigkeit," and "Ehe-Unlust" (SV 204) represent negative characteristics that offend the (masculine) law. Yet society recognizes, accepts and even valorizes such traits in men. Dr. Rüdiger, for example, garners respect as a bachelor while the notion of women as bachelors (or bachelorettes) goes against nature: such women, quite plainly, are "Unnatur" (SV 201). The narrator acknowledges: "Eine Frau, die den für ihr Geschlecht erfundenen Kompromiß ablehnt: der es nicht gelingen will, 'den Blick von sich abzuwenden und ihre Augen in ein Stück Wasser oder Himmel zu verwandeln'; die nicht gelebt werden will, sondern leben: Sie wird erfahren, was schuldig heißt" (SV 201). Women's ensuing bad conscience and guilt stem from their internalization of male norms, norms that both sexes continue to perpetuate.

The narrator's friend Beate, an accomplished chemist, gives the impression that she can successfully juggle her roles as a professional, a wife and a mother. Beate appears "die Glückliche. Die alles ins rechte Verhältnis zueinander brachte: den schwierigen Beruf, einen anspruchsvollen Mann, zwei Kinder" (SV 218). Why then does Beate volunteer to be the next test person, in other words, to become a man? And why does Anders's failure to complete the experiment leave her devastated? Her repose can only be read as a sign of her suppressed desires, of wishes that in her view can only be fulfilled as a man. The options available for intelligent women in patriarchal society leave them caught between multiple roles, and lead them to run, "zwischen Mann und Arbeitsdrang, Liebes-glück und Schöpfungswillen, Kinderwunsch und Ehrgeiz ein Leben lang zickzack [...] wie eine falsch programmierte kybernetische Maus" (SV 205). "Cybernetics" stems from the Greek "kybernetes" meaning pilot or governor. In "Selbstversuch," Wolf's shows man as the one who fills this role, the one who controls and programs.

Wolf's stereotypic representation of gender roles has been a recurrent point of critical contention. Gisela Bahr, for one, argues that "Selbstversuch" remains caught in clichés: "die in dieser Erzählung geschilderten Unterschiede gehören zu den stereotypen Vorstellungen von Mann und Frau, die wir endlich abbauen müssen, anstaat sie immerfort zu wiederholen" (226). To be sure, "Selbst-versuch" abounds with clichés, with "abgegriffene, durch allzu häufigen

Gebrauch verschlissene Bilder."[36] For example, in a psychological response test, the woman relates the word "red" to "love," the man to "anger"; to "child" she responds "soft," he "dirty" (SV 204). Likewise, women are figured as bad drivers and men prove their manliness by eating *Eisbein*. As objects of the male gaze, women receive "unverschämte Männerblicke" or "abschätzende Männerblicke," looks that degrade yet nonetheless confirm their presence, that they "are there" (SV 207). Women's gaze, by contrast, supports and strengthens men's self-confidence: as Anders the scientist receives a look from a woman, "der einen Regenwurm zum Manne gemacht hätte" (SV 203). The story goes so far as to suggest, "Mann und Frau leben auf verschiedenen Planeten" (SV 207). This assertion may appear timely in light of John Gray's pop-psychology bestseller *Men are from Mars, Women from Venus* (1995). Yet while Gray attributes traditional gender differences to nature and argues for their acceptance, Wolf seeks to disrupt stereotypic gender roles through sparking in both men and women a critical questioning of the status quo. The destruction of the dominant images of women, Weigel emphasizes, is a prerequiste for women's liberation: "Der Entwurf einer neuen, emanzipierten bzw. befreiten Frau wird möglich erst durch die Entzauberung bzw. Zerstörung der herrschenden Frauenbilder" (33).

The lack of analyses or models in *Selbstversuch* for how rigidly defined gender roles could be overcome is fundamental to Bahr's critique (235). Reflecting the tendency of American feminists to idealize the situation of women in the GDR, Bahr argues that Wolf fails to document the concrete advances toward equality in the East. She hence reads Wolf's narrative as "ahistorical" within the context of the GDR, "ja regressiv, denn sie fällt hinter das bereits Erreichte zurück" (227). To be sure, Wolf's extremely cliched representation points to traditional roles that no longer accurately reflect the status of women and men in GDR society. Yet they are at the same time not completely unrepresentative: through bringing to light socialized patterns of behavior and beliefs, they reveal more than a kernel of truth.

Like Bahr, GDR critics Sigrid Damm and Jürgen Engler claim that "Selbstversuch" perpetuates gender stereotypes and expresses too little credence in socialism's potential for bringing about equality in every sense of the term.[37] Criticizing in particular Wolf's negative representation of masculinity, Damm and Engler claim that while Wolf's assessment may reflect the radical, separatist feminism present in capitalist society, in a socialist society that "organically" links women's emancipation to class struggle it is largely unfounded (66). Wolf insists, by contrast, that despite socialism the GDR remained a patriarchal society, that the deformations caused by patriarchy were not overcome simply through a change in the economic system. Under both ideological systems, hierarchy, objectification and male domination remain the norm.

Damm and Engler, although applauding Wolf's critique of one-dimensional rationality and affirming that emotion is critical for the development of a truly socialist society, argue that Wolf goes too far in representing the split between reason and emotion in gendered terms. In positing this division as gendered, Wolf in their view uncritically follows in the footsteps of bourgeois authors who reflect the division between thinking and feeling in capitalist societies. They contend that with her focus on gender polarities and on the exigency of personal and moral engagement for human emancipation, Wolf fails to recognize the lack of complete gender equality

> als Problem der konkreten gesellschaftlichen Praxis, also vom Stand der gesellschaftlichen Entwicklung bestimmte Frage der Verbindung von Menschlichkeit und technisch-wissenschaftlichem bzw. ökonomischem Fortschritt, von Humanität und rationaler Organisation des gesellschaftlichen Lebens, von subjektiver Anstrengung aller Gemütskräfte und objektiven Verhältnissen. (46)

In contrast to Wolf, these critics see human progress ("emancipation") as inextricably linked to scientific-technological progress. Viewing as unequivocal the development resulting from objective societal processes, i.e., from the male realm, their field of vision excludes the possibility of a viable gendered critique. In their respective reviews, both Bahr and Damm/Engler suggest that Wolf reduces gender to essentialist traits, to "angeblich angeborenen, geschlechtsspezifischen Unterschiede" (Bahr 225).

German-American scholar Sabine Wilke likewise argues that in "Selbstversuch" Wolf takes recourse to an "authentic" female identity.[38] For Wilke, "Selbstversuch" marks Wolf's turn from a dialogic to an essentialist representation of gender. Wilke argues that unlike *Nachdenken über Christa T.*, "Selbstversuch" and Wolf's later works present gender not as an epistemological category but as a "quasi-ontologische Struktur der Authentizität, die vor allen Prozessen der kulturellen Einschreibung existiert" (87). Wilke bases her assertion about "Selbstversuch" on the persistence of the narrator's "original" female identity even after she is transformed into Anders, into a man (86). To be sure, since "Petersein Maskulinum 199" first acts upon her primary sexual traits, the narrator retains knowledge of her previous self. Only through interaction with her environment "as a man," from a position of power and privilege, does her "inner self" begin to change. To further support her thesis that "Selbstversuch" signals Wolf's essentialist turn, Wilke cites Wolf's narrator's query, "wie die Wörter 'menschlich' und männlich,' einer Wurzel entsprungen, unrettbar weit voneinander wegtrieben," and postulates that Wolf bases this view on "einer unverdorben Sprachebene […] die in der patriarchalischen Kultur und Zivilisation verdinglicht und in ein selbst-zerstörerisches Instrument gekehrt wird" (86). In contrast to Wilke, I would argue that the shared etymology of "menschlich" and "männlich" attests to Wolf's focus on symbolic and structural gender differences that interact with, but are irreducible to, individual gender. Defined through the exclusion of femininity, masculinity became raised to a cultural, "human" ideal and divorced from those other qualities captured in the "feminine." Affirming those values and activities associated with the "feminine," then, does not necessarily signify a recourse to essentialism. Furthermore, Wolf's affirmation of values other than "masculine" counters the assimilationist model of emancipation dominant in the GDR. Wolf asserts, "daß nicht der Mann das Modell von der Gesellschaft ist, sondern Mann und Frau" (DiA2 800).

In "Selbstversuch," Wolf draws attention to the central role of language in the maintenance of power hierarchies. Beyond the shared root of "menschlich" and "männlich," she shows how in the "masculine" realm of science words go unquestioned as signifiers of factual truth. By naming and giving meaning, man acts out and maintains his dominance. Calling the test person "Anders" ("Other"), for example, the professor identifies her in terms of her difference from the masculine norm—a difference that the sex change experiment seeks to eliminate. As the Other, the test person begins to lose her "inner" language, the "feminine" play with multiple and ambiguous meanings. As Anders, then, her difference is slowly erased. A close reading further reveals women's marginalization as attributable to structural gender differences based on power and privilege. Wolf casts women as unequal players in a power game controlled by men. He is "Spielmeister" (SV 214), the "Herr der Lage" (214) who determines the "heilig gehaltenen Spielregeln" (SV 213). The three W's, "Wirtschaft, Wissenschaft, Weltpolitik" (SV 221) characterize the male realm of objectivity and unequivocality whose "highest virtues" are "Nichteinmischung und Ungerührtheit" (SV 208).

"Selbstversuch" presents women's need for recognition as unfulfilled, yet the expression of the potential fulfillment of this wish substantiates the work's utopian impulse. Prior to her sex change, the female protagonist was incapable of expressing her own desires and conformed to social norms by defining herself only in terms of male society and its wishes. As Weigel emphasizes, "der Mangel eines *eigenen* Begehrens [...] herrscht, solange die Frau in den Regeln der männlichen Ordnung denkt und schreibt" (36). Women's lack of their own desires and wishes impedes the development of an alternate vision. Through her sex change, the protagonist comes to see the dark side of the masculine realm she had previously idealized: she discovers the professor's secret. In the treatise, which she directs at the professor, she writes: "Ihre heillose Arbeitswut, all Ihre Manöver, sich zu entziehen, waren nichts als der Versuch, sich vor der Entdeckung abzusichern: Daß Sie nicht lieben können und es wissen" (SV 225). The goal of a more humane society, she recognizes, can only be reached through a fundamental change in social conditions, one that fosters men's "ability to love." The process undergone by the narrator reflects the progression from liberal (equality) feminism to difference feminism as articulated in "Berührung," an essay Wolf conceived as the preface to Maxie Wander's *Guten Morgen, du Schöne* (1978): "Die Möglichkeit, die unsere Gesellschaft ihnen [den Frauen] gab: zu tun, was die Männer tun, haben sie, das war vorauszusehen, zu der Frage gebracht: Was tun die Männer überhaupt? Und will ich das eigentlich?" (LS 218). When she breaks off the experiment, the narrator begins to plan her own "unscientific" self-experiment: "Jetzt steht uns mein Experiment bevor: der Versuch zu lieben. Der übrigens auch zu phantastischen Erfindungen führt: zur Erfindung dessen, den man lieben kann" (SV 226).

In "Neue Lebensansichten" as in "Selbstversuch," scientists experiment with regulating human life through the elimination of the symbolic feminine, the elimination of attachment, emotion and subjectivity. The "new human being" they envision is a masculine being. Although clothed in fantasy, these experiments reflect the social regulation that Christa T. attempted to defy. Like the female narrator of "Selbstversuch," Christa T. recognizes the fundamental changes that must take place before her "Versuch, man selbst zu sein" (N 9) can be realized.

Notes

1 *Wolfgang Emmerich, Kleine Literaturgeschichte der DDR (Frankfurt a. M.: Luchterhand, 1989) 173.*

2 David Batrick, "Productive Mis-reading: GDR Literature in the USA," *GDR Bulletin* 16.2 (Fall 1990): 5.

3 Werner Heisenberg, *Physics and Philosophy. The Revolution of Modern Science* (New York: Harper & Brothers, 1958) 109.

4 In "Juninachmittag," published 1965, Wolf first experimented with this open and engaged style. The story's opening lines confront the formulaic prescription of socialist realism: "Eine Geschichte? Etwas Festes, Greifbares, wie ein Topf mit zwei Henkeln, zum Anfassen und Daraus-Trinken?" *Gesammelte Erzählungen* (Darmstadt/Neuwied: Luchterhand, 1980) 41.

5 Walter Benjamin, "Über den Begriff der Geschichte," *Gesammelte Schriften*, Vol. I.2, ed. R. Tiedemann and H. Schweppenhauser (Frankfurt a. M.: Suhrkamp, 1974) 697.

6 J. H. Reid, *Writing without taboos: the new east German literature* (Oxford: Berg, 1990) 200.

7 *Anna K. Kuhn, Christa Wolf's Utopian Vision: From Marxism to Feminism (Cambridge: Cambridge University Press, 1988) 75.*

8 Helen Fehervary, "Prometheus Rebound: Technology and the Dialectic of

Myth," *The Technological Imagination*, ed. Teresa de Lauretis, Andreas Huyssen and Kathleen Woodward (Milwaukee/Madison: University of Wisconsin Press, 1980) 99.

9   "Protokoll des VI. Parteitags der SED," quoted in Irma Hanke, "Vom neuen Menschen zur sozialistischen Persönlichkeit. Zum Menschenbild der SED," *Deutschland Archiv* 9.5 (1976): 503.

10   Sonja Hilzinger, "Als ganzer Mensch zu leben…," *Emanzipatorische Tendenzen in der neueren Frauen-Literatur der DDR* (Frankfurt a. M.: Peter Lang, 1985) 53.

11   Hilary Rose, "Hand, Brain and Heart: A Feminist Epistemology for the Natural Sciences," *Sex and Scientific Inquiry*, ed. Sandra Harding and Jean F. O'Barr (Chicago: University of Chicago Press, 1987) 265–282.

12   Myra Love, "Christa Wolf and Feminism: Breaking the Patriarchal Connection," *New German Critique* 16 (Winter 1979): 37.

13   Katharina von Hammerstein, "Warum nicht Christian T.? Christa Wolf zur Frauenfrage, untersucht an einem frühen Beispiel: *Nachdenken über Christa T.*," *New German Review* 1 (1985): 27.

14   Sandra Harding, "The Instability of the Analytical Categories of Feminist Theory," *Sex and Scientific Inquiry*, 288.

15   Myra Love, "'A Little Susceptible to the Supernatural?': On Christa Wolf," *Women in German Yearbook* 7 (1991) 13.

16   See Manfred Behn, ed., *Wirkungsgeschichte von Christa Wolf's "Nachdenken über Christa T."* Königstein/Ts.: Athenäum, 1978, and Angela Drescher, ed., *Dokumentation zu Christa Wolf "Nachdenken über Christa T."* (Hamburg: Luchterhand, 1991).

17   Horst Haase, "Nachdenken über ein Buch," *neue deutsche literatur* 4 (1969): 174–185.

18   "Sarah Kirsch an Christa Wolf." Letter written on 23. March, 1969. In: *Dokumentation zu Christa Wolf "Nachdenken über Christa T."* 74.

19   Rainer Nägele, "Trauer, Tropen und Phantasmen: Ver-rückte Geschichten aus der DDR," *Literatur der DDR in den siebziger Jahren* (Frankfurt a. M.: Suhrkamp, 1983) 207.

20   Hans-Georg Werner, "Zum Traditionsbezug der Erzählungen in Christa Wolfs "Unter den Linden," *Weimarer Beiträge* 4 (1976): 36–64.

21   Sonja Hilzinger, "Als ganzer Mensch zu leben …" 72.

22   Ludo Abicht, "Review of *Unter den Linden*," *New German Critique* 6 (1975): 168.

23   Therese Hörnigk, *Christa Wolf* (Göttingen: Steidel, 1989) 157.

24   Helmar Frank, *Kybernetik und Philosophie* (Berlin: Dunker & Humblot, 1969) 11.

25   *Marxism, Communism and Western Society. A Comparative Encyclopedia,*

ed. C. D. Dernig (New York: Herder & Herder, 1972) 299.

26 See *Marxism, Communism and Western Society* for more on the debate over cybernetics in the Soviet Union and the assessment of cybernetics in light of Marxist-Leninist theory.

27 *Marxism, Communism and Western Society* 299.

28 Manfred Behn, "Einleitung," *Wirkungsgeschichte von Christa Wolfs "Nachdenken über Christa T."* 3.

29 Quoted in Abicht 168.

30 Max Horkheimer, *The Critique of Instrumental Reason*, trans. Mathhew J. O'Connell et al. (New York: Seabury, 1974) 60.

31 Helen Fehervary and Sara Lennox, "Introduction to translation of 'Selbstversuch,'" *New German Critique* 13 (1978): 110.

32 It should also be noted that like in the United States, there was a "glass ceiling" in the GDR. Women held very few top-level positions and on the average earned less than men.

33 Marleen Barr and Nicolas Smith, *Women and Utopia* (Lanham: University Press of America, 1983) 151.

34 Fredric Jameson, "Progress vs. Utopia; or, Can We Imagine the Future?" *Art after Modernism. Rethinking Representation*, ed. Brian Wallis (New York: The New Museum of Contemporary Art, 1984) 245.

35 Sigrid Weigel, "Das Schreiben des Mangels als Produktion von Utopie," *Women in German Yearbook* 1 (1985) 29–38.

36 Gero von Wilpert, *Sachwörterbuch der Literatur* (Stuttgart: Kröner, 1969) 394.

37 Sigrid Damm and Jürgen Engler, "Notate des Zwiespalts und Allegorien der Vollendung," *Weimarer Beiträge* 7 (1975): 63.

38 Sabine Wilke, *Ausgraben und Erinnern. Zur Funktion von Geschichte, Subjekt und geschlechtlicher Identität in den Texten von Christa Wolf* (Würzburg: Königshausen und Neumann, 1993) 86–87.

CHAPTER FIVE

Flights of the Imagination:
Monika Maron's *Flugasche* and *Die Überläuferin*

> *Immer wieder überfiel sie die Vorstel-*
> *lung, sie lebte in einem Versuchslabor*
> *für Menschen, in dem Aufbegehren nur*
> *geduldet wurde, solange es der Verhal-*
> *tensforschung diente.*
>
> Monika Maron, *Die Überlauferin*

The texts of Monika Maron (1941–) offer a compelling contrast to those of Christa Wolf. Like Wolf, Maron interweaves in her works the themes of science, realism and gender. Upon its publication in the Federal Republic, for example, Maron's first literary work *Flugasche* (1981) was heralded both as the GDR's first "Umwelt-Roman"[1] and as a women's novel, a "Frauenroman." Like Wolf, Maron subverts the dominant rational pattern through narrative techniques such as fantasy and dreams. Yet Maron's more pointed indictment of "really existing socialism" prevented her from being published in the GDR: all her works, from *Flugasche* to her novel *Die Überläuferin* (1986) were granted publication only in the West. Although not part of the official literary canon of the GDR, Maron's texts still circulated in that country and, consumed as "forbidden fruit," afforded her a privileged status in the eyes of her secret readership.[2] With an official readership limited to the West, however, Maron finally left the GDR for Hamburg in 1988 on a three-year visa. During and after the *Wende*, Maron's numerous and often controversial essays on unification, many collected in the volume *Nach Maßgabe meiner Begreifungskraft* (1993), and her novel *Stille Zeile Sechs* (1992) garnered her significant acclaim. More recently, disclosure in 1995 of Maron's *Stasi* collaboration in late 1976 and 1977 as the IM ("Inoffizieller Mitarbeiter") "Mitsu" has fueled the polemic on the oppositional status of GDR writers as diverse as Maron and Christa Wolf.[3]

Written shortly after Wolf Biermann's expatriation, *Flugasche* reveals the effects of intricate mechanisms of social control, in particular the suppression of oppositional voice. Biermann's satirical commentaries on the GDR provoked censure (he was banned from performing in the GDR in 1965), irritation and ultimately spurred his expatriation: after a concert tour in the West in November 1976, government officials barred Biermann from reentering the GDR. David Bathrick remarks on how Biermann's expulsion brought about a fundamental shift in the nature of dissent among critical GDR writers, and brings to the fore how dissidence meshes with a critique of instrumental reason. "What these writers had begun to understand," Bathrick argues, "is the extent to which the *language* of a supposedly progressive, scientifically rationalized, dialectical materialism was irrevocably linked to repressive power structures in the GDR, and that any genuine struggle for social change would also mean a recasting of the entire value system around which it would cohere."[4] The crackdown on dissidence in all its guises is the cultural backdrop of Wolf's controversial narrative *Was bleibt*. Written in 1979, revised in 1989 and finally published 1990 after the regime's collapse, *Was bleibt* documents the effects on literary production of the regime's increasing dogmatism and suppression of oppositional sentiment, which Wolf expresses indirectly through the early Romantics in *Kein Ort. Nirgends*. Comparing *Flugasche* and *Was bleibt*, Silvia Klötzer accentuates that both works are highly autobiographical, sparked by the personal crisis of a fragmented self, thematize a crisis of language, and "portray a state of disillusionment, stagnation, and crisis of the protagonist [...] when her support of the GDR can no longer be sustained."[5] These themes likewise characterize *Kein Ort. Nirgends*.

A look at the case "Mitsu" offers further insight into official and unofficial discourses of progress and lends *Flugsasche* a sense of biographical immediacy.[6] The case "Mitsu" and Maron's own work as a journalist evince that Maron initially attempted to reform the system from within the official framework of language and power. While Maron's collaboration seems particularly paradoxical given the radical disassociation from the state that characterizes both her later life and the trajectory of her female protagonists, her early biography presents a model of integration and acquiescence. The child of communists and anti-fascists, Maron moved from West to East Berlin in 1951 and became an active participant in the communist youth organization, the FDJ. Her stepfather Karl Maron was one of the GDR's founding fathers, a member of the "Gruppe Ulbricht," head of the *Volkspolizei* and, from 1955–1963, the GDR's Minister of the Interior. After the *Abitur*, Maron herself took employment in a factory, studied theater and art history, worked for GDR television and the Berlin *Schauspielschule*, and subsequently as a journalist for the women's magazine *Für Dich* and for the weekly *Wochenpost*. She left the latter position in 1976 to become a freelance writer. From 1965 to 1978 Maron was also a member of the SED, joining, she claims, with the hope of reforming the party from within, and leaving after Rudolf Bahro, a key figure of inner-party opposition, was imprisoned for publishing *Die Alternative*, his extensive critique of "real existing socialism," in the West.[7]

In addition to curiosity and a sense of adventure, Maron cites among the motivations for her *Stasi* activities the desire to travel to the West (her previous visa applications had all been denied) and to gather information for the novel she was writing at that time, namely *Flugasche*. Maron's collaboration animates a retroactive reading of the case "Mitsu" within the context of this novel, which was completed 1978 and published, after initial acceptance and subsequent rejection by the GDR Greifenverlag, three years later in the Federal Republic. The fifty page *Stasi*-file on "Mitsu" documents that the GDR secret police contacted Maron in 1976, after which she undertook eleven informational "missions" to West Berlin between January and June of 1977.[8] Thereafter Maron submitted a candid report that chronicled her impressions, proclaiming that the state's resounding yet empty promises and the lack of a public sphere in which individual critique could be voiced left her no choice but to express her sentiments directly.[9] In a report that anticipates the critical tenor of her literary texts, Maron lays bare the gross deviation of "really existing socialism" from the original socialist project. She criticizes the West Berlin Socialist Unity Party for its unrealistic and "euphoric repression" of socialism's readily apparent deficits. She counters West Berlin's diversity, vitality, and openness with East Berlin's rigidity and monotony, and praises the profit-based capitalist economy for the creativity it demands. Illuminating the degree of openness and the non-threatening nature of political discussions she experienced in the West, she censures the squelching of oppositional sentiment in the GDR. Furthermore, she describes the atmosphere of unity and solidarity at a West Berlin concert by the Greek freedom fighter Mikis Theodorakis. Though heralded as intrinsic to socialism, Maron had yet to experience such a feeling in the East. In this regard she remarks on the state's disingenuous proclamations: "Ich empfand, um wieviel Möglichkeiten und Gefühle, die wir in uns haben, wir betrogen werden. Der Verzicht auf einen gewissen Wohlstand, auf Konsum und spanische Austern ist nichts und gar nichts im Vergleich zum Verzicht auf eine freiwillige Gemeinschaft, die lebendig ist in ihren Zielen und ihrer Arbeit."[10] This sense of personal restriction and betrayal, a trait Wolf's female protagonists share, figures centrally in *Flugasche*.

The essay's acerbic tenor evinces that while Maron chose to work within the system, she employed her status as an informant to voice a direct and caustic critique that significantly undermined the regime's legitimacy. The August 4, 1977 entry on Maron's activities underlines her dissent: "Die Haltung der KP [Kontaktperson] zur Politik von Partei und Regierung unserer Republik ist unsachlich, nicht objektiv und artet in vielen Fragen in eine linksradikale Opposition aus."[11] Maron's knotty entanglement with the state appears in the statement that follows: "Sie will eine grundsätzlich andere DDR, in der die Presse- und Meinungsfreiheit besteht und die Freiheit der Persönlichkeit geachtet wird. Sie ist Verfechterin des 'menschlichen Sozialismus'" (149). At the time of her *Stasi* cooperation, then, Maron advocated "socialism with a human face," which the *Stasi* equates with the desire for a "fundamentally different" GDR. Its protocols further describe Maron as a sparse provider of information and a continuing source of irritation, noting in particular her harping on Biermann's recent expatriation. In May 1978, she terminated her role as "contact person" with the blatant explanation, "daß sie die DDR öde und den inhaftierten SED-Dissidenten Rudolf Bahro gut finde" (149). In allying herself with both Biermann and Bahro, Maron conveys her firm endorsement of opposition vis-à-vis the regime. It hence comes as no surprise that upon her break with the *Stasi* "Mitsu" herself became the object of surveillance under the unflattering, yet seemingly appropriate code name of "Wildsau"—a wild and unruly sow.

The documentary nature of *Flugasche* sheds light on the process of censorship and raises critical questions about literature's role in the public sphere. Maron's work in journalism figures prominently in her casting of *Flugasche*'s protagonist Josefa Nadler, a reporter for the *Illustrierte Woche* who is assigned to report on B.(itterfeld), the heavily polluted industrial city whose enormous coal-powered chemical plant emitted 180 tons of flight ash daily and came to epitomize the nature of industrial progress in the GDR. In his review of *Flugasche*, Tilman Jens notes that in 1974 Maron herself traveled to Bitterfeld as a journalist for the *Wochenpost*.[12] While her initial report focused on official promises to build a cleaner plant powered by natural gas, her subsequent reports grew virulent as prospects for modernization dwindled and the harsh realities of this worker's town came to light. As Jens observes, "Doch nicht um technischen Fortschritt zu bejubeln, war die eigenwillige Journalistin nach Bitterfeld gefahren—sie wollte die düstere Kehrseite des Fortschritts beleuchten, vom oft unwürdigen Leben der Menschen dort erzählen, die in Qualm und Gestank leben müssen." With Maron no longer toeing the official line, the party intervened and pressured the *Wochenpost* and its reporter; Jens remarks, "die lästige Nestbe-schmutzerin wird allmählich kaltgestellt." Silenced, Maron left journalism and proceeded to cast her experiences into literary form. The resulting novel *Flugasche*, however, was ultimately censored as well.

At the 1981 Leipzig Book Fair, Minister of Culture Klaus Höpke justified the censoring of *Flugasche* on the grounds that it expressed contempt for the GDR's concept of work. To be sure, in a country heralded as a "worker's and peasant's state" Maron subverts ideological and aesthetic conventions and documents the continuation of power structures and inequality, the physical and mental consequences of brutal work conditions, and the cynicism of the working class towards higher authorities.

The degree to which Maron's depiction of industrial labor undermines socialist realist doctrine is apparent when juxtaposed with the propagandistic glorification of industrial areas such as Bitterfeld. The opening statement of the 1959 Bitterfeld Conference claims:

> In solchen Zentren des sozialistischen Aufbaus werden die großen Heldentaten im Kampf um die Erfüllung unserer wirtschaftlichen Aufgaben vollbracht; hier wächst ein neuer sozialistischer Mensch, der

mit hervorragender Arbeit und schöpferischen Erfindungskraft [...] mitwirkt, [...] hier findet der Künstler die Gestalten für seine Werke, die uns neue Kraft zu neuen Taten geben.[13]

While Maron herself entered into the factory world and drew her characters from that milieu, the "center of socialist construction" she depicts in *Flugasche* fails to evoke great deeds. Instead, the filth and stench emanating from local chemical plants infect the city's inhabitants:

> Diese Schornsteine, die wie Kanonenrohre in den Himmel zielen und ihre Dreckladung Tag für Tag und Nacht für Nacht auf die Stadt schießen [...] Und diese Dünste, die als Wegweiser dienen könnten. Bitte gehen Sie geradeaus bis zum Ammoniak, dann links bis zur Salpetersäure. Wenn Sie einen stechenden Schmerz in Hals und Bronchien verspüren, kehren Sie um und rufen den Arzt, das ist der Schwefeldioxyd. (F 16)

In *Der geteilte Himmel* (1963), Christa Wolf offers a similar description of the industrial city Halle when she writes:

> Jedes Kind konnnte hier die Richtung des Windes nach dem vorherrschenden Geruch bestimmen: Chemie oder Malzkaffee oder Braunkohle. Über allem diese Dunstglocke, Industrieabgase, die sich schwer atmen. Die Himmelsrichtungen bestimmete man hier nach den Schornsteinsilhouetten der großen Chemiebetriebe, die wie Festungen im Vorfeld der Stadt lagen. (GH 27)

As remarked in the previous discussion, the resounding optimism of of *Der geteilte Himmel* ameliorates this dreary picture. In showing how Rita integrates into the collective and draws strength from her co-workers, Wolf's work serves as a point of contrast for *Flugasche*. Unlike Rita, Josefa grows isolated and is eventually deserted by her colleagues and her partner Christian when she attempts to assert her own desires.

Josefa's distance from the workers' plight draws attention to the cleft between intellectuals and workers which the Bitterfeld conference addressed and sought to diminish. Maron portrays a power hierarchy in which workers ultimately remain on the bottom, as implied by Alfred Thal's gesturing "nach oben" (F 19) to higher authorities when Josefa asks who determines whether the old power plant will remain open even after a new one is built. Illustrating how norms of productivity remain the foremost concern, Maron exposes the toils of labor. The workers' bodies, rather than reflect the ideal of the "new socialist being," are marked by physical hardship: "Geschundene Wirbelsäulen, zerstandene Beine, taube Ohren, Auswüchse an den Knochen. Ganz zu schweigen von den unsichtbaren Deformationen durch ewiges und einziges Signal an das Gehirn" (F 81). The accidental death of the stoker Hodriwitzka under the wheels of a bus further parodies and diverts the idealized trajectory of the socialist realist hero.

Flugasche documents the growing concern in the GDR and FRG about environmental degradation. In exposing the human consequences of the scientific-technological revolution, Maron suggests a convergence or "symmetry" between socialism and capitalism. The incompatibility of the notions "convergence" and "symmetry" with orthodox socialism comes to the fore in a 1979 letter exchange between writer Günter Kunert and the editor of *Sinn und Form*, Wilhelm Girnus. The exchange was sparked by Kunert's use of the word "symmetrisch," a word that to Girnus implied, "daß Industrialisierung überall in der Welt 'spiegelsymmetrisch,' also 'gleichermaßen' Umweltzerstörung bedeute."[14] In a lengthy response to Kunert, Girnus categorically rejects any notion of symmetry. Taking recourse to the immanent progressiveness of Marxist-Leninism, he argues: "Das Hauptkriterium dafür, daß es Deine 'Symmetrie' in der Welt nicht gibt, ist gerade, daß es für diese Angst vor der Zivilisation in der sozialistischen Welt keinen Boden gibt."[15] That GDR censors rejected Maron's *Flugasche* wholesale should therefore come as no surprise.

The degree to which Maron's critique of progress was sure to have provoked cultural authorities comes into view when we look at the controversy sparked by Hanns Cibulka's *Swantow*. While thematically related to *Flugasche*, *Swantow* was granted publication in the GDR. It first appeared in *Sinn und Form* in 1981, and was then published separately in revised form in 1982. Like *Flugasche*, *Swantow* represents the ecological devastation in the GDR and expresses a deep-seated skepticism toward progress in the East.[16] In his review of Cibulka's text, Höpke sheds light on additional ideological grounds for the ultimate rejection of *Flugasche*. While he shares the ecological concerns expressed in *Swantow*, Höpke denies their implications: the convergence of problems and solutions in East and West; their relation to the socialist economic system or science; the existence of power hierarchies in the GDR. Moreover, Höpke takes issue with the lack of attention Cibulka pays to nuclear proliferation and the West's "imperialist aggression" given what Höpke sees as the inherent and superior ability of socialist ideology to address these concerns and to harmonize the relationship between humans and nature.[17] To recall, Höpke justified censoring *Flugasche* because it failed to uphold the socialist concept of work. Yet Maron goes even farther: she not only lays bare the environmental degradation of B., but holds the party and state accountable; she not only suggests a symmetry between East and West, but focuses on "die dreckigste europäische Stadt ausgerechnet in einem sozialistischen Land" (F 32).

In contrast to writers such as Wolf who were able to locate and negotiate a space within a hegemonic system of state censorship by expressing, however tenuously, their continued belief in socialism, in her texts Maron rejects the state at its very foundation. By representing the conformity that Josefa's work as a journalist demands, Maron highlights contradictions between "reality" and its official representation. Josefa recognizes how her own journalistic work offers a skewed perspective on society: "Jede Woche steht etwas in der Zeitung über B., über ein neues Produkt, über eine Veranstaltung im Kulturpalast, über vorfristig erfüllte Pläne, über den Orden des Kollegen soundso. Nichts über das Kraftwerk, kein Wort von den Aschekammern, die das Schlimmste sind" (F 20–21). When she interviews Hodriwitzka, the question-answer exchange initially follows the prescribed formula, emulating a "verkrampfte sinnlose Zirkusvorstellung, in der man sich gegenseitig begafft wie durch Gitter und jeder vom anderen denkt, er stünde im Käfig" (F 50). Struck by the disingenuousness of her position, Josefa is suddenly beset by a "spontanen, inneren Protest gegen die Journalistenrolle" (F 50). She breaks with journalistic protocol by bluntly asking Hodriwitzka why he does nothing to improve the abysmal conditions: "Warum wehren Sie sich nicht,?" she asks, "Sie sind doch schließlich die herrschende Klasse" (F 50).

Josefa succeeds in motivating Hodriwitzka to document the debilitating conditions in B., yet upon his sudden death she takes the cause of depicting the "Versäumnisse beim Aufbau des Sozialismus" (F 176–177) into her own hands. Josefa's protest, then, restages Maron's own decision no longer to uphold the status quo through her work in journalism as well as "Mitsu's" submission to the highest authorities of a statement documenting socialism's deficits. However, Josefa's motivation to write the "whole" truth lies beyond the confines of B.: she not only endeavors to write this story, but to find a biography she can call her own: "Das Eigentliche, nach dem sie suchte, war die ihr gemäße Biografie" (F 99).[18] In Maron's novels, "biographies" belong only to those whose life course merges with the state's master narrative, that is to the generation of the country's founding fathers who legitimate their past and present actions through recourse to the GDR's foundational narrative of antifascism. In *Flugasche*, Josefa's senior colleague and mentor Luise exemplifies this status: Luise counters Josefa's sense of betrayal by the socialist state with her more horrific past under fascism (F 80). Like Christa Wolf, Luise belongs to a generation which came of age in fascist Germany. For Luise and Wolf, the atrocities of the German past motivated an incipiently positive identification with the anti-fascist and socialist Germany they were helping to build. By contrast, Josefa, like Maron, came of age under socialism and judges the present not by the past, but by the utopian promises of the future. She thus sees only irreconcilable contradictions. Josefa's role as a journalist demands that she alter this generational perspective and shore up the past in view of the present. "Aber ich soll die Revolutionen von hundertachtzig Tonnen Flugasche reinwaschen, soll sie putzen und polieren mit Glanzmitteln aus der Sprühdose und soll sie als PS-gewaltiges Gefährt in die Zukunft auf Zeitungspapier anpreisen" (F 120), she exclaims. The complacent acceptance of the status quo on the part of Josefa's partner Christian, who expresses a strong aversion to feminist sentiments, underscores that Josefa's dissent is attributable not only to her generation, but also to her gender.

Through depicting the regime of censorship, Maron brings to light mechanisms of control that reflect broader restrictions on thinking and being. As Josefa contemplates, "Es ist nur ein kurzer Weg von undrückbar zu undenkbar, sobald man sich darauf eingelassen hat, die Wirklichkeit nach diesem Maß zu messen; dazwischen liegt nur unaussprechbar" (F 32). Progress and reason, as Horkheimer and Adorno argue, have led to the manipulation and ultimate negation of the individual. In *Flugasche*, Josefa attempts to depict the pestilence of B., and also views her own life as a slow death. She fears "Das Bett, in dem ich sterben werde. Die Leben, die ich nicht lebe. Die Monotonie bis zum Zerfall und danach" (F 13). Like Maron, Josefa ultimately rejects the self-censorship required of public speech; she refuses to speak with a forked tongue. Living in a society whose highest commandments are "Ordnung, Disziplin, Treue, Verleugnung der Gefühle," Josefa recognizes the gradual disappearance of her own *un*conventional characteristics and thoughts (F 78). Echoing Wittgenstein's maxim that the limits of one's language are the limits of one's world, she dreads that truth and falsehood will become indistinguishable, that the "*Un*mechanismus endgültig einrastet und mir das *Un*druckbare, das *Un*aussprechliche, das *Un*denkbare zur *Un*wahrheit werden wird, weil ich so wenig wie die anderen ausgehalten habe, das Bewegendste und das Aufregendste nicht zu schreiben, nicht zu sagen, nicht zu bedenken" (F 33). Maron represents the process of identity formation as a process of self-control that ultimately leads to a dis-integration of the self, of what Horkheimer and Adorno term "das Lebendige" (DA 62). In *Flugasche*, Josefa struggles against the process of rationalization which in her mind has the same effect. She imagines a highly regulated future world: "Armselige kretinöse Geschöpfe werden heranwachsen, und die Schöpferischen unter ihnen werden eine unbestimmte Trauer empfinden und eine Sehnsucht nach Lebendigem" (F 79). In her next novel, *Die Überläuferin* (1986), Maron takes this process to the extreme when she writes of the state's co-optation of the individual: "Deine Rentabilität ist veranschlagt und wird erwartet [...] Deinen Kopf bauen sie einer Maschine ein, deine Arme machen sie zu Kränen, deinen Brustkorb zum Karteikasten, deinen Bauch zur Müllhalde" (ÜB 51).

Although she initially seeks self-realization through work and personal relationships, at the novel's close Josefa is physically and mentally isolated, her room the final refuge from uninhabitable professional and personal relationships. As Elizabeth Boa emphasizes in reference to women writers such as

Maron, Virginia Woolf, and Ingeborg Bachmann, the domestic space of the narrator's room often figures as a central chronotope as well as a metaphor for the "Kern des Selbsts, in das sich das Subjekt unter Druck zurückzieht."[19] Boa articulates the multivalence of this chronotope as a locus of control and a realm of freedom, and poses a crucial question: "Solches Sichzurückziehen, das aber zur völligen Isolation führen kann, bleibt mehrdeutig: ist es eine Überlebensart, eine Todesart oder gar die letzte Möglichkeit des Widerstands im Extremis?" (133) Through her struggle for emancipation Josefa transforms in Christian's eyes from a passive, stereotypically feminine embodiment of the "good" and "beautiful" into the opposite, a witch (F 95)—a woman whose wisdom and status on society's margins has historically been regarded as a demonic threat to the established patriarchal order. From the perspective of his own complacent acceptance of the status quo, Christian attributes Josefa's defection to a psychiatric defect on her part that demands treatment (F 100). For Josefa, the illness lies in society itself. She hence rightly questions whether counseling and medication can kill off the "Bazillus Zweifel" (F 107) that Christian and her colleagues diagnose as having infected her system. As we have seen, the metaphor of illness also figures prominently in Wolf's texts. In *Der geteilte Himmel*, self-doubt drives Rita to her suicide attempt, a "disease" from which she recovers by integrating into the collective. Christa T. eventually succumbs to her illness, to her "Neurose als mangelde Anpassungsfähigkeit an gegebene Umstände" (N 75). Like Christa T., Josefa asserts her individuality and attempts to say "I."

Maron's "ex-centric" protagonist calls into question official dictates of identity and seeks a radical transformation of the social order.[20] Spurred by Hodriwitzka's death, Josefa begins to reassess the meaning of her life and comes to recognize the ultimate futility of her attempts to effect change through official channels. Recalling Marx's vision of human productivity, she ponders: "Warum setzen wir uns nicht unter die Sterne, bauen Gemüse an, melken die Kuh, scheren das Schaf und weben an dunklen Abenden den Stoff für unsere Jeans" (F 106). Drawing a line between the "absurd" and the "natural," she redefines "life" in terms of its most basic elements. Beset by the longing, "den Schatten ihrer Kreatur zu fliehen, das zwanzigste Jahrhundert vor und hinter sich zu lassen und nur zu sein" (F 155), she looks to Christian to reach this timeless space. "Eine verzweifelte Lust zu lieben befiel sie, die Sucht, Schmerz zu empfinden und Schmerz zuzufügen, und sie liebte Christian, weil er ihr folgte an die animalischen Abgründe, auf die sie zuraste, als fände sie in ihnen die Rettung" (F 156). Only at night is she able to escape the dictates of her mind that control her physical desires and experience a unity with Christian that transcends temporal, spatial and corporeal boundaries (F 154), as the lovers transform into winged cuttlefish that inhabit both aquatic and ethereal realms. Yet by day Josefa cannot reconcile her nocturnal desire to lose herself in

Christian with his derision of her struggle for autonomy (F 154).

The irreconcilability of this division is mirrored in the abrupt shift in *Flugasche* from first- to third-person narration, a shift that reflects Josefa's process of identity formation or deformation. Boa points out that this change in narrative voice occurs shortly after Josefa exclaims "Alles was ich bin, darf ich nicht sein" (F 78), in Boa's view an aesthetic reenactment of the disappearance of the autobiographical first person who has been deceived of her self (137–138). Upon this switch to third-person narration, Josefa observes her own story from a distance through the eyes of other figures such as Christian. Silvia Klötzer notes that the shift in narrative voice also coincides with the rejection of Josefa's report, which constitutes an end to her "Illusion, Subjekt sein zu können" (254). Both in Josefa's attempt to write a truthful report and her search for her "true" biography, gender figures centrally.

Prior to the disappearance of the first-person voice, Josefa contemplates how gender relations between sons and mothers are marked by the increasing alienation and subordination of the female (F 92). Her desire to break this socialized pattern in raising her own son then blends with her memories of the chief editor, Strutzer, as he conveys his decision to report her unorthodox account to higher authorities. Finally, it merges with her longing for harmony with Christian. This chain of thoughts reveals how patriarchal hierarchies determine Josefa's relationships—with her son, with her partner, with her superior, with the state.[21] Pointing to the enmeshment of the personal and the political, Josefa's ponders, "Hat es das überhaupt schon mal gegeben, eine herrschende Klasse, die nicht in den Betten herrschte?" (F 141). That the narrative shift occurs precisely between Josefa's expression of longing for Christian and his statement "'Du bist ein Idiot'" uttered in response to her declaration that she submitted the uncensored report reveals the chasm between her desire for support and Christian's derision of her struggle. The reader learns that Josefa broke off her five year relationship with Christian three years previously with the explanation, "Ich will allein leben [...]. Ich wollte kein siamesischer Zwilling sein" (F 22). Yet society expects "emancipated" women to adapt to the male norm: "Aber emanzipierte Frauen frieren nicht, heulen schon gar nicht, und das Wort Sehnsucht haben sie aus ihrem Vokabular gestrichen. Ich friere, ich heule, ich habe Sehnsucht" (F 22). Josefa seeks comfort and happiness with Christian, yet also wants independence, a conflict that leads her to vacillate between her desire to lose her self in the relationship, "[d]ie exzessive Sehnsucht, sich aufzulösen" (F 154) and to exert her autonomy.

Maron employs the metaphor of "Schneewittchen im Sarg" (F 16) to express Josefa's existence as a "living corpse." This metaphor indicts the GDR's environmental and social policies as harbingers of death and also codes Josefa's salvation as male. Yet while Josefa toys with the notion that she is "waiting for Prince Charming" (F 15), she rejects the traditional trajectory of the fairy tale and acts to change her predicament. Her failed subversion of social norms in turn reflects the limited possibilities for (female) resistance. Although she moves from an initial imitation of male norms to an eventual protest against them, her struggle ultimately ends in disillusionment and regression. As Sigrid Weigel asserts: "Entsagung und Aufbegehren, Selbständigkeit und Unterwerfung, Mut und Verzweifelung liegen häufig so nah beieinander, daß es notwendig ist, die darin verborgene Struktur weiblicher Ausdrucksmöglichkeiten in einer patriarchalischen Kultur zu entschlüsseln."[22] In *Flugasche*, these contradictions suggest the lack of a cultural or social space for Josefa to play out her desires. Josefa, one can argue drawing on Bloch, remains caught between the "no longer" and the "not yet." With little ability to effect change and thus to anticipate a different future, she must struggle to make this liminal space productive.

The novel's u-topian flight scenes allude to a possible escape. Josefa first takes flight when she submits the "true" report. Freed from her previous complacency, she soars above Berlin where she encounters her grandfather Pawel,[23] for her the embodiment of resistance against rational norms. "Die Verrücktheit des Großvaters war verlockend, verrückte Menschen erscheinen mir freier als normale" she states earlier in the novel (F 9). Yet even in this other realm of fantasy, Maron mediates Josefa's sense of freedom by evoking the myth of Daedalus, i.e., the synchronicity of her flight "zur Sonne, Dädalus, [...] zur Sonne, zur Freiheit" and her catastrophic demise (F 71). Accordingly, Josefa's defeat at the hands of Strutzer leads her to lose her ability to fly: "Jetzt werde ich nicht einmal mehr zum Alex fliegen können, ich werde laufen müssen" (F 173), she recongnizes. Similarly, her utopian longing for a love relationship unrestricted by social norms is figured as a longing for flight that is antithetical to her growing isolation and restriction, to her perception "sie stünde in einem Käfig" (F 233).

Maron reweaves the themes of restriction and gender in Josefa's dreams. In the dream world, those characteristics emerge of which the "uniform human being" has been robbed: "Anfangs zuckt sein mißhandelter Charakter noch unter den Zwängen, aber langsam stirbt er ab, wagt sich nur noch in den Träumen hervor" (F 79). Early in the narrative, Josefa's dreams enact her rebellion against conformity. For example, she finds herself on a broad street as barriers and large vehicles, "monsters," close in on her. Though initially fearful and threatened, she confronts the encroaching obstacles with courage and remains intent on continuing along her path: "Ich habe keine Angst mehr. Ich muß weitergehn, muß ..." (F 67).

A later dream vividly stages the conflicting elements of affection and control that characterize Josefa's relationship with Luise. In the dream the daughter expresses her desire to learn to read, write, and finally to escape the confines and uniformity of her purple room. "Ich will nicht immer in dem

Zimmer sein, Mama, es ist so lila" (F 148), she pleads, only to be reprimanded and kept illiterate by the mother. As in reality, statements of truth (the daughter's claim that the room is purple) are punished, and the actions of both women are ultimately controlled by a male figure. In contrast to the purple women, he wears black and stands at the center of room, in the center of the daughter's world. Both women, then, must ultimately bow to higher authorities figured in the dream world as male.

A more humorous dream reenacts the celebration of International Women's Day. The dream is stimulated by a large front-page newspaper headline, printed in red, that reads "Gruß unseren Frauen und Mädchen" (F 157). Under the headline is a photograph of nine proud men lined up next to the one woman being honored, her knees dipped in a thankful curtsey (F 157). After seeing this article, Josefa's dreams of the speech "über das Glück, eine Frau zu sein" (F 157) that she would hold upon were she to receive a similar honor. In a highly ironic speech, she heralds the traditional gender division and image of women in socialist society, accents the absurdity of the "weaker" sex's demand for equal pay, thanks men for helping women to discover their female sexuality and allowing them entrance into the "clitoral epoch," and delineates the advantages of being judged by beauty rather than by actions or physical strength. "Gerechter könnte es nicht zugehen" (F 160), she concludes with regard to women's present situation in socialist society. Through exaggeration, the speech draws attention to prevalent arguments against women's equality. When her final provocative statement to the women in the audience, "Wenn ihr so weiterschreitet nach Gleichberechtigung, dann nehmen sie uns eines Tages noch in die Regierung, dann wären wir gefangen und müßten mitspielen nach der Männer Regeln" (F 161), is greeted with loud applause, Josefa recognizes that the audience has failed to recognize the irony of her speech. In effect, then, the women applaud their lack of equality and their powerlessness.

Increasingly dark, Josefa's dreams play out her prescribed roles and pressures, depicting her as controlled, dis-integrated and, finally, as corpse. Staging a violent encounter between a man and a woman, the final dream departs from the novel's otherwise more subtle casting of gender relations. In the dream the female expresses her belief in "das unmenschlich Große, an das Ungesehene [...] an den Ozean" (F 210) and her longing to reach this utopian space, an endless expanse engulfing Josefa in her memories. The male counters that it is too late. Rendered speechless by the woman's verbal attack on his indolence and timidity, he turns to physical violence to regain control. His blows disfigure the woman's face, he blinds her, rapes her, and in a violent subversion of her dream, kills her: "Da hast du deinen Ozean, schrie der Mann und stieß sich tief in die Frau .... Ohne sie anzusehen, fragte er: War es gut?   Die Frau war tot" (F 212). Boa likens the woman's blindness and death in the dream to the transformation Josefa undergoes when Christian removes his glasses before berating Josefa, a gesture "unter dem [Josefa] ihre Verwandlung erlebte in die unscharfe, sich auflösende Josefa, nicht nur gesichtslos, auch körperlos. So, unerreichbar für sie, verschanzt hinter einem Nebel, gegen den nur ihre Stimme ankam, aber kein Lächeln, kein Schreck in den Augen, so konnte er sprechen" (F 214). Positioning Josefa at a safe distance, Christian protects himself from "seeing" her and being vulnerable to her desires.[24] Aware of his frequent repetition of this gesture, Josefa takes part in her own transformation: internalizing Christian's disaffection, she experiences how she becomes bodiless and faceless. At the novel's close, confined to her room, she stages her own disappearance.

In a type of novelistic epitaph to Josefa's story, Flugasche's final paragraph discloses the ironic coincidence of Josefa's censure by her colleagues on the grounds of her unwillingness to revise her report on B. with the party's decision to shut down the old power plant (F 244). While the state's action on behalf of B.'s citizens may signal hope for the future, the reaction of Josefa's colleagues highlights the obliteration of the individual who acts independently of the collective will. Far from shedding a positive light on dissent, Maron illuminates Josefa's disillusionment and regression. Retreating to her bed, Josefa numbs the pain of personal and professional isolation with sedatives and alcohol. The nature of this withdrawal leads Genia Schulz aptly to interpret the novel as "der Zusammenprall einer Frau mit den gesellschaftlichen Normen der Strategie und Taktik, bis sie sich zunehmend resignierend auf weiblich konnotierte Verhaltensmuster zurückzieht. Sie kann nicht mehr sprechen, nimmt am herrschenden Diskurs ('Diskussionen') nicht mehr teil, läßt den Körper sprechen, wird krank."[25] Ultimately, Josefa's failure to conform transforms her into the docile body that Christian and patriarchal society figured her to be in the first place.

Die Überläuferin

The dream sequences that increase towards the end of Flugasche and signal its break from realist narration form the core of Maron's next major literary work. Die Überläuferin (1986) in effect begins where the former novel leaves off, with the numbed protagonist confined to her room, completely cut off from society. At the outset of this surreal novel, Rosalind Polkowski awakes one morning to find her legs paralyzed, a metaphor for her physical confinement in the GDR and the mental paralysis resulting from the stultifying routine and banality of her life. A historian by profession, Rosalind had trained her mind to focus exclusively on a prescribed topic and to steer it towards a concrete outcome: in other words, she had become a master at "zielstrebiges wissenschaftliches Denken" (ÜB 98). Although stripped of the realist elements and distanced from the realm of production that inform Flugasche, Die Überläuferin continues to play out the state's attempts to norm and control (female) identity.

Rosalind's paralysis magnifies not only her rejection of the world, but its rejection of her: that her phone has failed to ring in the three days since her Kafkaesque metamorphosis attests to her extreme isolation. Despite her physical absence, she has not been missed. Although now unable physically to cross the threshold to the outside world, Rosalind delights in the recognition that her mind has been freed to traverse topographical and chronological barriers, transforming her room into a temporal space in which she can conjure up and commingle past memories and desired futures in a never-ending present (ÜB 13). Her retreat from the outside world and from the urges of her body allows her to nurture her fantasies of freedom.

Despite this perceived freedom, Rosalind initially remains entrapped by painful memories and surreal fantasies that play out the mechanisms of social control she has internalized. Addressing the topics of order and security, family, identity and fantasy, the novel's satirical intermezzos stage the state's scientific prescription of behavioral norms. In the first "Zwischenspiel," The Man in the Red Uniform, a caricature of orthodox party functionaries and the figure who governs the intermezzos, sounds the official chord that echoes throughout *Die Überläuferin*: "Punkt eins: Ordnung und Sicherheit. Punkt zwei: Sicherheit und Ordnung" (ÜB 35). The second intermezzo centers on the family. With frequent reference to Marx, The Man in the Red Uniform delineates familial happiness and gender relations through recourse to scientific theory. Discounting as destructive all emotional or personal responses to the topic, he demands "scientifically-constructive" thought (ÜB 89). He goes on to dictate his "scientific" views, for example that "unfreiwillig familienlose Frauen mit oder ohne Kind" like Rosalind pose the greatest threat to society because of their permanent dissatisfaction and high potential for "feminist machinations": "Sie greifen die Männer an, propagieren die Frauenliebe und zersprengen so, siehe Marxengels, das kleinste Fruchtbläschen" (ÜB 93). Though absurd, his statement nonetheless recalls institutionalized stereotypes that continue to confine and define women, such as the contingency of female satisfaction on men, marriage and children.

The third intermezzo discusses the problem of identity and underlines how the GDR's collectivist ideology represses individuality. Representing the "Staatliche Behörde für Psychokontrolle" (ÜB 122), the Man in the Red Uniform exclaims that the dissatisfaction symptomatic of identity crises results from mistakenly attributing one's discontentment to a partner, job, or even to the government, rather than to oneself (ÜB 125). The "right" conviction, he proclaims, will lead down the "right" path to happiness (ÜB 126). Following this path, however, requires that the outer world intersect with the inner world, that the self accepts its prescribed identity. When accused by a state representative of a "Rückzug ins Private," Rosalind counters that for her the word "private" has no meaning since the state has in effect robbed her of her self: "Ich weiß gar nicht was das ist," Rosalind claims, "Ich gehöre mir nicht" (ÜB 65). Like Wolf's female protagonists, Maron's female figures refuse to conform to the state's master narrative: they withdraw from the collective and attempt to say "I." In the final "Zwischenspiel" Rosalind is put on trial for her socially destructive fantasies: "Die Anklage lautet: Phantasie in Tateinheit mit Benutzung derselben im Wiederholungsfall" (ÜB 170). For her country's leaders, fantasy means "der feste Glaube an das Gute," defined as belief in the good of the people, the functioning of the economy and the ability of the press to influence public opinion (ÜB 173). Official "fantasy" reinscribes the status quo: it works to maintain the reality from which Rosalind attempts to flee. The dictate of "order and security" becomes the "die Sicherheit und Ordnung des Kopfes" (ÜB 174).

An extreme manifestation of identity prescription is the male clone Rosalind encounters. Named only "k 239," the clone's sole function is to further scientific knowledge. The experimental subject of a scientific work in progress entitled, "Die Entwicklung der Persönlichkeit unter realen und klinischen Bedingungen," the clone sets the scientific norm against which his Original is then judged. Comparing clone and Original, scientists determine the effects on human productivity and efficiency of such "abnormal" influences as interaction with the opposite sex and alcohol. The clone proudly states: "Dank meiner Arbeit wissen wir, daß jederart extreme Empfindung auf ihn leistungsmindernd wirkt" (ÜB 206). The association of the "ab-normal" Original with illness echoes the metaphor of illness in Wolf's works, in which "illness" often figures as an effect of opposition to the one-dimensional, rational norm. As in the satire "Neue Lebensansichten eines Katers," the goal here is to create a cybernetic society devoid of human emotion. In *Die Überläuferin*, the knowledge gained through the "self-experiment" is used further to control and norm the Original. With this feedback system, the clone actually comes to embody the "eigentliche, unverfälschte Original [...], das vermeintliche Original hingegen nur eine beliebige, oftmals sogar krankhafte Abweichung" (ÜB 208.

Given the opposition of "illness" and "abstract rationality," it follows that illness becomes a state for which Rosalind longs. Relating "illness," the unusual presence of the "other being in herself," to her alter ego Martha, she acknowledges: "Die Krankheit wurde der Zustand, nach der ich mich sehnte" (ÜB 103). Guided by Martha, Rosalind ventures down side roads and into unsanctioned territories of the mind to confront those dimensions of thought numbed by repressive social relations. Not the chronotope of the room but the train station, a nexus of constant change and exchange, of departure, arrival and adventure, best describes Martha's mental topography. Living by her own moral standards, she rebels against social norms: she lies, steals, and cheats. Martha opposes the artificial, mechanized future human being, incarnated as the clone, with the

Other of reason, "das Besondere, das Unberechenbare, Seele, Poesie, Musik [...] eben das, was niemand wissen konnte, ehe der Mensch geboren war" (ÜB 51). Encouraging Rosalind to locate and cherish this repressed part of her self, she emphasizes: "Dieses scheinbar nutzloseste Stück von dir, die mußt du finden und bewahren, das ist der Anfang deiner Biographie" (ÜB 51). Following Martha, Rosalind eventually takes off "mit dem Kopf durch die Wand" (ÜB 130) fantastically to explore and incorporate unrealized dimensions of her self.

Far from glorifying Rosalind's defection with Martha, Maron figures Rosalind's border crossings as encounters with the abject: with the stench and blood of violent street wars, with an old Nazi who urinates on her face, with a vampire who sucks the blood from Martha's/Rosalind's neck. Rosalind's final sadomasochistic sex act with a filthy derelict on the sweltering streets of the Bowery, an act that follows and diametrically opposes her disillusioning encounter with the clone, represents the extreme debasement necessary for Rosalind to invigorate her corporeal numbness and become one with Martha.

Upon her return, Rosalind's perspective on her room has changed. It appears smaller, narrower: "Als würde sie vom falschen Ende durch ein Fernglas sehen, schrumpfte alles, was sie umgab, auf ein fernes, unwirkliches Maß" (ÜB 221). This "reverse telescoping" suggests that Rosalind's physical paralysis and the subsequent temporal and spatial transgressions have repositioned her room/life within a broader social and historical whole.[26] The air in her room has become uncomfortably dry, and she gazes longingly at the rain falling outside her window, an allusion to her continued search for unity of mind and body and harmony with the outer world. Earlier Martha related how, when caught in a sudden, inescapable downpour, she did not attempt in vain to protect herself, but rather succumbed to the inevitable: "...anfangs gleichmütig, später lustvoll. Ich öffnete den Mund, ließ das Wasser in mir hineinlaufen [...] Ein unbekanntes Gefühl von Einverständnis klang in mir nach wie ein wunderbarer Akkord" (ÜB 215–216). For Rosalind, this state of oneness with (human) nature can only be expressed in the subjunctive: "Den Mund weit öffnen und das Wasser in mich hineinlaufen lassen, naß werden, dachte sie, vom Regen naß werden, ja, das wäre schön" (ÜB 221). While she rebels in her mind, her physical defection cannot be realized.

Rosalind's second alter ego, Clara Winkelmann, embodies Rosalind's repressed corporeality. Excessive in girth and sexuality, Clairchen symbolizes insatiability. In contrast to Rosalind, she, like Martha, defies disciplining: she prostitutes herself, rapes, steals, lies, dances, and seduces, taking whatever measures necessary to find love. Yet, as in *Flugasche*, Maron represents the love Clairchen seeks as incompatible with social dictates. Martha, recognizing the bond between love and subordination in Western society, concludes: "die Gefühle liebender Europäer [sind, B.R.] ein nicht entwirrbares Chaos an Zuneigung, sadistischer Herrschaftssucht, masochistischer Unterwürfigkeit"

(ÜB 71). Susan C. Anderson underlines in this regard that Martha censures "not love itself, but the conditions under which love exists."[27] In other words, love independent of domination and subjugation exists only beyond the epistemologies and ontologies that confine Rosalind's (Western) world. Rosalind's escape from this confinement therefore necessitates that she banish the body/Clairchen from her self. Rosalind's material alter ego consequently takes her own life by hanging herself in a chestnut tree, an act that further symbolizes love as a recourse to a natural, atavistic state. In the drama "Ada und Evald" from which Maron develops this figure, Clairchen's unity with the chestnut tree takes on an added dimension of love's paradox: she first weds the tree before ultimately hanging herself in it.[28] As a state in which female desire and submission are inseparable, Maron represents heterosexual relationships as a microcosm of power in the public realm.

The state's attempt to suppress the Other—emotion, desire, imagination, fantasy, the "feminine"—is further exemplified in the censoring of Martha's work by "ein führendes Mitglied der Assoziation dichtender Männer" (ÜB 155), who accuses Rosalind's rebellious alter ego of crimes against the dominant masculine literary norms and against good taste. Characterizing Martha's oeuvre, he asserts: "Wir haben Romantizismen, Lyrismen, Pathos, Selbstmitleid, Infantilismus und modisches Feministengeplapper nachweisen können. Wörter wie Hoffnung, Sehnsucht, Schmerz, Leid [...] sind durchaus überrepresentiert" (ÜB 156). Such "feminine" sentiments as hope, longing, pain, and anguish inform Maron's work as they do Wolf's, pointing the inadequacy of the "masculine" status quo. As Martin Kane argues, the accusations against Martha represent "entirely justified grievances about the male-dominated, excessively rational and scientific world which seeks to shackle the imagination, and particularly the female one, in an ideological straitjacket."[29]

Calling into question the official dictate of identity, Rosalind seeks a radical transformation of the social order "Ich hätte gern ein Erdbeben" (ÜB 140), she exclaims. Recognizing the radical potential of Rosalind's retreat, Kane suggests that if in Maron's work the only solution is retreat, "then the brand of anarchic fantasy it proposes, the advocation by the heroine of the irrational and the mystical and her rejection of the notion that salvation may be found in 'progress' and scientific functionalism, constitute a profound threat—and not just to the GDR and other socialist societies" (233–234). Yet while Rosalind, like Josefa before her, transgresses social and personal boundaries, she does so only to find her structures of resistance limited by the very borders she attempts to traverse. The imaginary "other" realms of flight, dreams, fantasy and love she seeks or inhabits ultimately reveal the impossibility of locating a cultural or social space in which her desires can be played out. The threat of Maron's work, then, is its radical statement about women's position in contemporary society.

Notes

1 Jörg Bernhard Bilke, "Der erste Umwelt-Roman aus Ost-Berlin: Monika Marons *Flugasche*. Wo die Bronchien schmerzen," *Die Welt* 24 March 1981, 17.

2 Monika Maron, "Das neue Elend der Intellektuellen," *Nach Maßgabe meiner Begreifungskraft* (Frankfurt a. M.: Fischer) 85.

3 On the debate see: "Stasi-Deckname 'Mitsu,'" *Der Spiegel* (7 August 1995): 146–149; Karl Corino, "Die verfolgende Unschuld. Der Fall Maon alias Mitsu," *Neue Zürcher Zeitung* 19 October 1995; Wolf Biermann, "Verlogene Treue, "*Der Spiegel* 43 (23 October 1995): 39–44. Maron defends her collaboration in "Heuchelei und Niedertracht," *Frankfurter Allgemeine Zeitung* 14 October 1955.

4 David Bathrick, *The Powers of Speech. The Politics of Culture in the GDR* (Lincoln and London: University of Nebraska Press, 1995) 226.

5 Silvia Klötzer, "Patterns of Self-Destruction: Christa Wolf's What Remains and Monika Maron's Flight of Ashes," *Other Germanies: Questions of Identity in Women's Literature and Art*, ed. Karen Jankowsky and Carla Love (Albany: SUNY Press, 1997) 250.

6 I similarly interpret the case "Mitsu" in relation to *Flugasche* in "The Status of State and Subject: Reading Monika Maron from *Flugasche* to *Animal Triste*," *Wendezeiten/Zeitenwenden. Posistionsbestimmungen zur deutschsprachigen Literatur 1945*–1995, Weninger, Robert and Brigitte Rossbacher, ed. (Tübingen: Stauffenburg, 1997) 193–214.

7 For more on Bahro and Biermann within the context of intellectual opposition in the GDR, see Bathrick, *The Politics of Culture*, in particular 57–83.

8 "Stasi-Deckname 'Mitsu,'" 146–149.

9 Reprinted in Monika Maron, "'Zum Heulen—alles ist besser als bei uns,'" *Der Tagespiegel* 8 August 1995.

10 Maron, "'Zum Heulen.'"

11 "Stasi-Deckname'Mitsu,'" 147.

12 Tilman Jens, "Sand im Getriebe zweier Kulturen. M. Marons *Flugasche*— eine deutsch-deutsche Geschichte," *Deutsches Allgemeines Sonntagsblatt*, 22 March 1981.

13 Fritz Bressau, "Eröffnung der Konferenz," *Greif zur Feder Kumpel. Protokoll der Autorenkonfenz des Mitteldeutschen Verlags Halle (Saale) am 24. April 1959 im Kulturpalast des elektrochemischen Kombinats Bitterfeld* (Halle: Mitteldeutscher Verlag, 1959) 6.

14 "Um ein Wort. Ein Briefwechsel." Letter exchange between Günter Kunert and Armin Zellerl (in conjunction with Wilhelm Girnus, representing *Sinn und Form*). Armin writes in regard to a draft of a Kunert essay in which

Kunert mentions "die moderne Industriegessellschaft, die sich damals [1958/1959] symmetrisch abzuzeichnen begann." Regarding the implication of the term "symmetrical," Zeller responds: "Wäre es möglich, das Wörtchen 'symmetrisch' wegzulassen? Für mich würde der Satz nicht an Sinn verlieren, wenn es fehlte" (409).

15 Wilhelm Girnus, "Anläßlich Ritso. Ein Briefwechsel zwischen Günter Kunert und Wilhelm Girnus," *Sinn und Form* 31.4 (1979) 857.

16 For a discussion of *Swantow* and a comparison with *Flugasche*, see Michael Schenkel, *Fortschritts- und Modernitätskritik in der DDR-Literatur. Prosatexte der achtziger Jahre* (Tübingen: Stauffenburg, 1995).

17 Klaus Höpke, "Sicht auf Swantow—Überzeugendes und Bezweifelbares," *Sinn und Form* 36.1 (1984) 165–177.

18 Silvia Klötzer remarks that "B." refers not only to Bitterfeld but to Josefa's "Biographie Versuch." In "Perspektivenwechsel: Ich-Verlust bei Monika Maron," *Zwischen gestern und morgen: Schriftstellerinnen der DDR aus amerikanischer Sicht*, 252 (fn).

19 Elizabeth Boa, "Schwierigkeiten mit der ersten Person: Ingeborg Bachmanns *Malina* und Monika Marons *Flugasche, Die Überläuferin* und *Stille Zeile Sechs*," *Kritische Wege der Landnahme. Ingeborg Bachmann im Blickfeld der neunziger Jahre*. Londoner Symposium 1993 zum 20. Todestag der Dichterin (17.10.1973). Sonderpublikation der Grillparzergesellschaft, Vol. 2, ed. Robert Pichl and Alexander Stillmark (Wien: Hora Verlag, 1994) 133.

20 Linda Hutcheon elaborates on the notion of the "ex-centric" in *A Poetics of Postmodernism. History, Theory, Fiction* (London: Routledge, 1988).

21 The text suggests that this pattern of socialization will continue with her son: "Und eines Tages schläft er mit Frauen und sagt ihnen am Telefon, daß sie umsonst gekocht haben" (F 219).

22 Sigrid Weigel, "Der schielende Blick. Thesen zur Geschichte weiblicher Schreibpraxis," *Die verborgene Frau. Sechs Beiträge zu einer feministischen Literaturwissenschaft. Literatur im historische Prozeß*, Argument Sonderband, ed. Inge Stephan and Sigrid Weigel (Berlin: Argument, 1983): 96.

23 Maron explores the story of her grandfather, Pawel Iglarz, a Polish Jew, in *Pawels Briefe* (Frankfurt a. M.: Fischer, 1999).

24 See Boa 139.

25 Genia Schulz, "Kein Chorgesang. Neue Schreibweisen bei Autorinnen (aus) der DDR," *Bestandsaufnahme Gegenwartsliteratur. Text + Kritik Sonderband*, ed. Heinz Ludwig Arnold (München: edition text + kritik, 1988) 216.

26 Thomas Luckmann employs the term "reverse telescoping" to describe how biographies temporally integrate the short- and long-term: "Biographical

schemes endow the meaning of short-term action with long-term significance. One might say that this is a matter of 'reverse telescoping': what looms large when seen with the naked eye recedes into the background if one looks at it through the wrong end of the binoculars. The meaning of daily routines does not disappear in such telescoping but is set in relation to the vaster background of an entire lifetime." In "Constitution of Human Life in Time," *Chronotopes: The Construction of Time*, ed. John Bender and David E. Wellbery (Stanford: Stanford University Press, 1991) 161–162.

27   Susan C. Anderson, "Creativity and Non-Conformity in Monika Maron's *Die Überläuferin*," *Women in German Yearbook* 10 (1995): 152.

28   Monika Maron, *Das Mißverständnis. Vier Erzählungen und ein Stück* (Frankfurt a. M.: Fischer, 1982) 93–124.

29   Martin Kane, "Culpabilities of the Imagination: The Novels of Monika Maron," *Literature on the Threshold. The German Novel in the 1980s*, ed. Arthur Williams, Stuart Parkes and Roland Smith (Oxford: Berg, 1990) 233.

CHAPTER SIX

Beyond the "Dialectic of Enlightenment": *Kein Ort. Nirgends, Kassandra* and *Störfall*

> *Gab es Kreuz- und Wendepunkte, an denen die Menschheit, will sagen: die europäische und nordamerikanische Menschheit, Erfinder und Träger der technischen Zivilisation, andere Entscheidungen hätten treffen können, deren Verlauf nicht selbstzerstörerisch gewesen wäre?*
>
> Christa Wolf, 1983

In her narratives *Kein Ort. Nirgends* (1979), *Kassandra* (1983) and *Störfall* (1987), Christa Wolf turns to the past in attempt to locate the historical turning points that set Western society on its self-destructive course. In *Kein Ort. Nirgends*, she explores the negative dialectic of enlightenment at the time of the Enlightenment. Drawing analogies between the GDR in the late 1970s and Germany in the early 1800s, she accents the central role attributed to science and technology in the transformation from feudalism to a bourgeois society and in the transition from socialism to communism. While the industrial revolution sought to realize the promises of the Enlightenment, liberté, egalité, fraternité, the scientific-technological revolution was to usher in the "truly human" communist society. In *Kassandra*, Wolf looks further back in time to the transition from matriarchal to patriarchal culture. Focusing on the antagonism between the Greeks and the Trojans, she prefigures East–West relations in her own time and relates masculinist patterns of thought, the mentality of war and women's objectification in the past and the present. In *Störfall. Nachrichten eines Tages*, an autobiographical first-person narrative that Wolf penned shortly after the nuclear catastrophe of Chernobyl in April 1986 and completed a mere three months later, Wolf looks to human evolution for answers to humankind's self-destructiveness. "An welchem Kreuzweg ist womöglich die Evolution bei uns Menschen fehlgelaufen, daß wir Lustbefriedigung an Zerstörungsdrang gekoppelt haben?" (S 73), she ponders. Since the nuclear meltdown at Chernobyl confirmed her fears of science's destructiveness, it is understandable that *Störfall* represents Wolf's harshest critique of instrumental reason and abstract rationality. Wolfgang Emmerich goes so far as to read this work as depicting "eine in toto fehlgeschlagene Evolution der Species Mensch."[1]

Kein Ort. Nirgends

With a focus on the early Romantics and the onset of the industrial revolution, *Kein Ort. Nirgends* illuminates the aesthetic, personal and social consequences resulting from literary censorship, the division of labor and the marginalization of women. In addition to *Kein Ort. Nirgends*, Wolf composed three essays that further reflect her strong interest in writers of the early Romantic period: "Der Schatten eines Traumes. Karoline von Günderrode—Ein Entwurf" (1978), the forward to a collection of Günderrode's poems, prose, and letters; "Nun ja! Das nächste Leben geht aber heute an. Ein Brief über die Bettine" (1981), the afterword to Bettine von Arnim's epistolary novel, *Die Günderrode*; and "Kleists 'Penthesilea,'" the afterword to a GDR edition of Kleist's drama. Broadening the historical context of *Kein Ort. Nirgends*, these essays illuminate parallels to the present. In the narrative itself, Wolf blurs the boundaries between literary history and historical fiction with an intricate montage of authentic and imagined statements delivered as interior monologue and as dialog. Through frequent shifts between the first-, second- and third-person narrative voice, which at times merges with the authorial "we," she breaks down divisions between the figures themselves and between the narrated past and narrative present. Like Maron's *Flugasche*, *Kein Ort. Nirgends* also represents a reaction to the repressive cultural climate of the 1970s. While it would be a stretch to call *Kein Ort. Nirgends* autobiographical, Wolf certainly felt a strong kinship with the early Romantics, identifying with the obstacles they faced as (women) writers, their synthetic philosophy and their aesthetic innovations.

Kein Ort. Nirgends revolves around an "erwünschte Legende" (KON 6), the meeting in 1804 of two early Romantic writers, the dramatist Heinrich von Kleist and the poet Karoline von Günderrode. The setting is an afternoon tea party in Winkel am Rhein hosted by Joseph Merten, a wealthy wine merchant. Other guests include the lawyer Savingy (a previous love interest of Günderrode), the writers Clemens Brentano and Bettina von Arnim (Brentano's sister), the scientist Ness von Esenbeck and Kleist's physician, Wedekind. Similarly alienated by the mundane conversation at the pseudo-salon, Kleist and Günderrode depart for a stroll through the countryside on which they confide their inmost values and hopes, and share their apprehensions about the rising industrial age, rigid gender roles, and the changing relationship of the artist to society.

These themes resonate as well with the contemporary GDR context. Wolf began to pen this work directly after Wolf Biermann's expatriation in 1976. Numerous progressive GDR writers and intellectuals, among them Wolf, expressed their outrage towards the regime's disciplinary actions against Biermann with a public petition. This in turn provoked further punitive measures, including expulsion from the Berlin branch of Writer's Union in Wolf's case and expulsion from the SED in the case of her husband, Gerhard Wolf. The state's crackdown sent a clear message regarding the limits of dissent and the consequences for breaching those limits. In *Kein Ort. Nirgends*, Wolf clothes her reaction to the dogmatic cultural politics by turning to history, seeing in the early Romantics' critical relationship to their society a situation analogous to her own; they were likewise "Avantgarde ohne Hinterland" (LS 228).

In an interview with Frauke Meyer-Gossau, Wolf describes Biermann's expulsion in 1976 as a caesura in GDR cultural politics that for many of that country's intellectuals sparked an existential crisis:

> Eine Gruppe von Autoren wurde sich darüber klar, daß ihre direkte Mitarbeit in dem Sinne, wie sie sie selbst verantworten konnte und für richtig hielt, nicht mehr gebraucht wurde. Wir waren ja Sozialisten, wir lebten als Sozialisten in der DDR, weil wir dort uns einmischen, dort mitarbeiten wollten. Das reine Zurückgeworfensein auf die Literatur brachte den einzelnen in eine Krise; eine Krise, die existentiell war. (DiA2 878)

For Wolf, who adamantly believed in the writer's engagement in social processes and the ability of literature to guide and transform society and individuals, it was particularly devastating to see writers, even those deeply committed to socialism, relegated to the apolitical margins of society. In *Kein Ort. Nirgends* and in her controversial narrative *Was bleibt*, a work drafted in 1979, Wolf radically questions what remains for writers in a repressive regime. In *Was bleibt,* she makes explicit the effects on literary production of the regime's suppression of oppositional voice, effects she projects onto the predicaments of the early Romantic writers she figures in *Kein Ort. Nirgends*.[2] Looking at thematic similarites between *Was bleibt* and *Kein Ort. Nirgends*, Anna Kuhn notes their shared focus on the conditions of the writer and literature in a time of cultural repression, the common themes of aliention, self-alienation and community, and their similarly dystopic tenor.[3]

In "Ein Brief über die Bettine," Wolf sheds light on censorship in von Arnim's time and in her own. In a close reading of Wolf's Bettine essay, Georgina Paul shows how Wolf interweaves details about restrictive policies enacted to suppress revolutionary and democratic forces that were seen as posing a threat to restoration Germany. For example, Wolf calls attention to the "Karlsbader Beschlüsse" of 1819 and the "Sechzig-Artikel" of 1834 (30). These legal measures limited the autonomy of universities, legitimized observation of professors and students, and restricted the freedom of the press. Paul points out Wolf's strategic use of GDR parlance such as "Bespitzelung" and "Widersprüche" in discussing 1830 to highlight analogies with the present (31).

For example, Wolf characterizes the political context in which Bettine wrote as follows:

> Das Land Utopia, in dem es frei, gleich, und brüderlich zugehn sollte, weicht in den deutschen Kleinstaaten, besonders in Preußen, der Realität der Heiligen Allianz und der Karlsbader Beschlüsse; zerbricht in öffentliche Reaktion und privates Biedermeier; geht unter in Demagogenverfolgung, Zensur und Bespitzelung, in der zähen Fortdauer eines Gesellschaftswesens, welches [...] seine eigenen Widersprüche nicht zur Kenntnis nehmen will. (DiA2 577)

As Wolf revealed in *Nachdenken über Christa T.*, the GDR had yet to fulfill the utopian promises of freedom, equality and brotherhood: the realities of everyday life undermined the propaganda of socialist and Enlightenment progress.

In their contemporary context, *Kein Ort Nirgends* and Wolf's complementary essays exemplify the broad-based reassessment of Romanticism in the GDR. Up to the early 1970s, the GDR's selective literary canon drew primarily on the progressive tendencies of the Reformation, the Enlightenment, Classicism, the *Vormärz* and Realism. Diametrically opposing Classicism and Romanticism, the GDR upheld Goethe's dictum of the Classical as "healthy" and the Romantic as "sick." Georg Lukács also condemned Romantic writers, specifically Kleist, for evincing "Dekadenz," "Schwäche" and "Lebensuntüchtigkeit" (DiA2 512). Underscoring the Romantics "irrationality," moreover, Lukács pointed to the abuse of their texts in the Third Reich. In a state that defined itself explicitly as "anti-fascist," this misuse further justified exclusion from the literary canon.[4]

An additional reason for the omission of the Romantics from the GDR's literary heritage was their representation of the individual as "anti-social." Reflecting this dominant viewpoint, GDR critic Hans-Dietrich Dahnke argues: "Trotz humanistischer Ausgangspunkte und Ziele waren Antigesellschaftlichkeit und Antirealismus das Ergebnis."[5] Because the early Romantics drew attention to sociopolitical contradictions without offering productive solutions, their critique was perceived as a reactionary movement inward that severed literature from social circumstances. This "anti-realist" retreat into the world of the imagination stood at odds with the GDR's narrow concept of realism.

More important for this analysis, Herminghouse cites the understanding of Romanticism as a counter-movement and critique of the Enlightenment as a primary reason for its dismissal in the GDR (223). Given Marxism's Enlightenment heritage, to critique one of its fundamental tenets, the revolutionary role attributed to scientific-technological progress, was to critique Marxism itself. Dahnke points to the Romantic's negative conception of industrial production and labor:

Nicht in der praktisch wirklichkeitsaneignenden und -verändernden Tätigkeiten suchten die Romantiker eine Lösung; mit Schärfe lehnten sie alle Aktivitäten dieser Art ab und diskreditierten die Arbeit als das, was die Menschen aus dem Paradiese trieb. Vielmehr erstrebten sie einen Existenzzustand der innerlich-schöpferischen Aktivität, des kontemplativen Genießens. (69)

Dahnke's view of reflective thought as "unproductive" and irrelevant to social change implies that material labor constitutes the only type of "productive" labor. As discussed earlier, a similar line of argumentation characterized the negative GDR reviews of *Nachdenken über Christa T.*. Contemplative and unable to define herself through society, Christa T. is a truly "romantic" character.

Remarking on the disproportionate weight placed in the Enlightenment on economic and material processes in relation to subjective mental and cultural factors, Dahnke illuminates the early Romantics' protest against "Vorstellungen von Modellierung und Lenkung des konkreten Menschen, gegen das Übergewicht einer wissenschaftlich-theoretischen Erklärung und Bestimmung von Mensch und Welt."[6] Wolf's *Neue Lebensansichten eines Katers*, an early example of the re-vision of Romanticism, exemplifies this protest. As we have seen, since *Nachdenken über Christa T.* the "romantic" critique of the rationalized and normative conception of social progress and of the individual has come to characterize Wolf's oeuvre. The reevaluation of the Romantics, as Dahlke illuminates, fostered a critical examination of the contradictions within GDR society and resulted in a "verstärkte Auseinandersetzung mit dem Problem des Widerspruchs zwischen Ideal und Wirklichkeit, Theorie und Praxis, individuellen Bedürfnissen und gesellschaftlichen Realisierungsmöglichkeiten" (5).

In a 1983 interview at Ohio State, Wolf countered the critical assessment of her own work as "anti-Enlightenment." Wolf asserted that the idea that the GDR's renewed reception of the Romantics represents a rejection of the Enlightenment was decidely "undialectical" (DiA2 905). She explains: "Erstens sind weder Sturm und Drang noch Romantik, jedenfalls nicht die Frühromantik, antiaufklärerisch: man kann sie auch als Zweige der Aufklärung verstehen" (DiA2 905-906). Wolf relates her interest in this specific historical period to her attempt to locate the roots of the humankind's self-destructive course at a time when historical progress runs counter to the goals of the Enlightenment. In this regard she pursues the question that prefaces *Dialektik der Aufklärung*, namely "warum die Menschheit, anstatt in einen wahrhaft menschlichen Zustand einzutreten, in eine neue Art von Barbarei versinkt" (DA 1). Echoing Horkheimer and Adorno, Wolf's Kleist expresses the self-destruction of the Enlightenment: "Der Mensch hat ein unwiderstehliches Bedürfnis, sich aufzuklären, da er ohne

Aufklärung nicht viel mehr ist als ein Tier. Doch sobald wir in das Reich des Wissens treten, scheint ein böser Zauber die Anwendung, die wir von unsern Kenntnissen machen, gegen uns zu kehren" (KON 81). Like the authors of *Dialektik der Aufklärung*, Wolf traces the roots of current social problems to a scientific worldview that attempts to explain and control societal processes and the individual through normative, reductionist, and objective laws. "Der Positivismus und der reine Rationalismus sind die Grundlagen für bestimmte Fehlentwicklungen, die heute bis zu der ungeheuren Kriegsgefahr führen, in der wir uns befinden" (DiA2 906), she argues. In her view, both capitalist and socialist societies promote an idea of progress based on a one-sided rationality that results in "die absolute Ausschaltung alles Nicht-Rationalen" (DiA2 906). The definition of scientific knowledge as the only valid type of knowledge precludes alternative epistemologies and ontologies.

Claus Träger relates the anti-Enlightenment theories of Romanticism advanced by Western literary critics to the "Versuch der Kritischen Theorie Marcusescher Provienz, die 'repressive' Funktion des prometheischen 'Leistungsprinzip' mit einer Freisetzung der Arbeit durch das 'Lustprinzip' jenseits des Antagonimus der Klassen und Gesellschaftsordungen zu überwinden."[7] In his conversations with Silvia Bovenschen and Marianne Schuller (1977), Herbert Marcuse argued that "feminine" qualities such as the pleasure principle can function as a critique of the dominant "masculine" principle, as a protest "gegen destruktive Produktivität, gegen Aggression, Leistungsprinzip."[8] Marcuse states:

> Rettung der Umwelt, Freiheit in den Lebenszusammenhängen, in den Lebensweisen, vor allem aber Stillegung destruktiver Produktivität, sind emanzipierende und emanzipatorische Projekte. Und sie sind verknüpft mit den femininen Qualitäten, wie sie sich in der Geschichte der Zivilisation herausgebildet haben und zur zweiten Natur geworden sind. (78)

Like Wolf, Marcuse emphasizes the sociohistoric basis of gender: if women held public positions of power, they would in his view reproduce aggressive, competitive, "masculine" behavior. Marcuse locates the "feminine" at society's margins, a position from which change can be effected. Both Marcuse and Wolf attempt to break down the symbolic opposition of masculinity/reason and femininity/emotion. Like Wolf, Marcuse contends, "daß die *wirklichen* Bedürfnisse *menschliche* Bedürfnisse sind und nicht männliche oder weibliche. Sie müssen in gemeinsamer Arbeit und in gemeinsamer Freude von Männern *und* von Frauen entdeckt *und* erfüllt werden" (87). Overcoming these entrenched roles requires dismantling the traditional division of labor that frees men of important social obligations and fosters their singular devotion to such areas as science, technology, economics and politics.

In attributing positive value to those symbolically "feminine" traits devalued in the process of Enlightenment, the Romantic's critique of Enlightenment merges with a critique of the symbolic masculine. In their illuminating essay on "Romanticism as a feminist vision," Robert Sayre and Michael Löwy classify Wolf as a quintessential "Romantic writer" because of her recourse to the German Romantic tradition in texts such as *Neue Lebensansichten eines Katers* and *Kein Ort. Nirgends* and because of her decidedly Romantic worldview.[9] Sayre and Löwy characterize Wolf's worldview as "a form of cultural criticism of 'modernity'—the capitalist/industrial/technological civilisation born in the eighteenth century and still predominant—which is inspired by *premodern* values" (105). The "elective affinity" between Wolf's "feminist" worldview and the "Romantic" worldview comes to light in Sayre and Löwy's delineation of those aspects of civilization discredited by the Romantics: "the disenchantment of the world, the quantification and reification of social relations, the destructive force of machinization, the reign of abstract rationality, and the dissolution of communitarian bonds" (105). In place of these features of modernity, the Romantics advocated such "feminine" values as "imagination, subjective experience, fantasy, community, and reintegration with nature" (105-106). In *Kein Ort. Nirgends*, Wolf lays bare how the growing oppositions between object and subject, reason and emotion, man and woman, science and art have led to the further subordination of the subject, emotion, women and art, to the further supression of the symbolic "feminine" and of individual women.

For the French feminist writer Hélène Cixous, Kleist's literary style exemplifies "feminine writing," as does the writing of Kafka and Proust. Feminine writing, in her view, is produced by "subjects who are breakers of automatisms, by peripheral figures."[10] For Cixious, "feminine" becomes a metaphor for transgression and subversion, for a metonymical, avant-garde writing style divorced from the sex of the author. In her text "Sorties," Cixious highlights woman's symbolic location in Western culture and illuminates the binaries that operate in a symbolic system that locates woman on the side of the heart, passivity, nature and Pathos and man on the side of the mind, activity, culture and Logos. Whereas man is associated with advancement and progress, he is "step, advance, seed, progress," woman upholds and perpetuates the system, she is "ground—which supports the step, receptacle."

Similarly defining the "feminine" in terms of positionality, Bulgarian-French feminist philosopher Julia Kristeva draws attention to the subversive potential of marginalization: "Call it 'woman' or the oppressed classes of society," Kristeva asserts, "it is the same struggle, and never the one without the other."[11] In "A New Type of Intellectual: The Dissident," Kristeva underscores the need to analyze women's position within the symbolic order and to break that order's laws. For Kristeva, dissidents are those exiled on account of their intellectual stance (e.g., dissident writers in the East bloc), political or religious orientations, or gender (e.g., women). In her view, the radical potential of dissidence lies in thought; dissidence, in other words, is not necessarily tied to action. She contends that "through the efforts of thought in language [...] one can attempt to bring about multiple sublations of the unnameable, the unrepresentable, the void. This is the real cutting edge of dissidence."[12] In its traversal of boundaries, including those between man and woman, this sublation can be termed "feminine."[13] Divorcing the "feminine" from gender and locating it in language, Cixous and Kristeva avoided implications of essentialism or ontological arguments. Heavily indebted to the poststructuralist theories of Derrida and Lacan, they attempt to deconstruct the hierarchical thinking on which the division between "masculinity" and "femininity" is based.

In a speech honoring GDR writer Thomas Brasch with the 1987 Kleist-Preis, Wolf characterizes as quintessentially "Kleistian" the "Riß der Zeit" that runs through the author, his works, and his country, the tragic predicament, "zwischen zwei Wertsystemen [zu] stehen, die ihn beide vor falsche Alternativen stellen."[14] In addition, Wolf accentuates Kleist's marginalization and his need to be recognized. She applauds the radical nature of Kleist's works for their time, his inability neatly to conform to the dominant binaries of good and bad, healthy and sick, and his "'weibliche' Sehnsucht nach einer Vernunft-ordnung, in der Gefühle Geltung haben sollten" (68). For Wolf, then, Kleist is also a "feminine" writer. Unable to divide the world into crass polarities, he expresses the desire, "jene Wand zu durchbrechen, die zwischen die Phantasien der Literaten und die Realitäten der Welt gesetzt ist" (KON 14). More distinctly than in her other works, in her texts focusing on the early Romantics Wolf explicitly distinguishes "masculine" and "feminine" qualities, i.e., gender, from sex. In characterizing Günderrode, Wolf stresses that she too is marked by the Kleistian "Riß der Zeit": "Der Riß der Zeit geht durch sie. Sie spaltet sich in mehrere Personen, darunter einen Mann" Wolf writes in "Der Schatten eines Traumes" (DiA2 569).

The two quotes with which Wolf prefaces Kein Ort. Nirgends, one by the historical Kleist, the other by the historical Günderrode, highlight the inability of these poets to reconcile the disparate parts of themselves—their inability to live in their time. In nuce, these citations relate the internal split of the early Romantic writers, their futile struggles "als ganzer Mensch zu leben." Kleist's statement, "Ich trage ein Herz mit mir herum, wie ein nördliches Land den Keim einer Südfrucht. Es treibt und treibt, und es kann nicht reifen" (KON 5), highlights the division between reason and emotion that contributes to self-alienation. Wolf juxtaposes this quote with a statement taken from Günderrode's correspondence. By associating these two quotes, Wolf reveals the shared pre-dicament of these two historical figures. Prefiguring her own suicide, as well as Kleist's, Günderrode takes the Kleistian division to its inevitable conclusion when she contends: "Deswegen kömmt es mir aber vor, als sähe ich mich im Sarg liegen und meine beiden Ichs starren sich ganz verwundert an" (KON 5). Both writers suffer the consequences of the limited possibilities for self-actualization in their society. Similar to Christa T., they view conformity as the only means of survival. Kleist recognizes that to survive he must suppress the most vital part of his self: "Er hat die Wahl—falls das eine Wahl zu nennen ist—, das verzehrende Ungenügen, sein bestes Teil, planvoll in sich abzutöten oder ihm freien Lauf zu lassen und am irdischen Elend zugrunde zu gehn" (KON 31).

Kleist's failure to adapt is interpreted by his personal physician, Wedekind, as a "Krankheitszeichen" (KON 7). Kleist's "illness," like Christa T.'s, is a sign of his inability to conform to the austerity that epitomizes the age of Enlightenment: "Strenge, Pflichterfüllung, Selbstzucht" (KON 32). Akin to Christa T., Kleist recognizes the shortcomings of his time, the divergence of the ideal from the real, and reacts by turning inward. This introspection, Wedekind acknowledges, only exacerbates Kleist's condition. Wedekind suggests to Kleist: "Es ist nicht gut, daß der Mensch zu tief in sich hineinblickt" (KON 15). Survival means silencing his inner voice, "die Stimme in sich knebeln, die da reizt und höhnt und weitertreibt, auf den wunden Punkt hin" (KON 12). As was the case with Christa T., subduing this voice at the same time extinguishes "diese zügellose Hoffnung [...], was ihn zu dem macht, der er ist" (KON 97). It constitutes an act of conformity that likewise leads to death.

Günderrode similarly recognizes assimilation as the price for survival, and lacks the desire to conform to a world gone awry. She proclaims: "Doch zu Verstellung und Entgegenkommen fehlt mir ein für allemal die Lust. Ich fühle zu nichts Neigung, was die Welt behauptet. Ihre Forderungen, ihre Gesetze und Zwecke kommen mir allesamt so verkehrt vor" (KON 8). In her Büchner speech Wolf again employs the word "verkehrt" to describe the vulgar scientism of her time: "Der Zustand der Welt ist verkehrt, sagen wir probeweise und merken: es stimmt" (LS 322). As in Wolf's time, the laws and goals of Günderrode's society, the rising Industrial Age, demanded reason and scientific-technological progress. Echoing these laws, Merten posits the dominance of reason as a major accomplishment: "Sei es nicht grade die Größe dieses Zeitalters, daß es die niederen Leidenschaften gebändigt, die Vernunft an die Macht gehoben habe?" (KON 78) In Merten's view, literature should conform to the Enlightenment paradigm in which reason, objectivity and order govern the imagination. By contrast, Kleist ponders: "Ordnung! Ja: Ordentlich ist heute die Welt. Aber sagen Sie mir: Ist sie noch schön?" (KON 78) In a period in which science is viewed as the only access to truth, or even as truth itself, Wolf's Kleist insists on literature's unique ability to relate "die Abtrennung eines jenen von sich selbst, vom anderen, von der sie umgebenden" (KON 102). In full support of Kleist's position, Bettine goes further in declaring "den freien, uneingeschränkten—

nicht verantwortungslosen!— Lebensgenuß" (KON 79) as the only law to which one should subjugate oneself. Highly skeptical of science's potential to create a more humane society and enhance individual freedoms, she sees the negative consequences of the "iron age" for emotions and for the artist. "Die Wissenschaften? Die sich daran machen, uns eiserne Reifen um Herz und Stirn zu schmieden? Die uns ein eisernes Jahrhundert vorbereiten, in dem die Kunst vor fest verschlossenen Türen steht, der Künstler ein Fremdling wird?" (KON 79) Kleist likewise bemoans literature's fate in view of the polarization of the "two cultures": "Die Wege von Wissenschaft und Kunst haben sich getrennt [...]. Der Gang unsrer heutigen Kultur geht dahin, das Gebiet des Verstandes mehr und mehr zu erweitern, das Gebiet der Einbildung mehr und mehr zu verengen. Fast kann man das Ende der Künste errechnen" (KON 80). The progess of science, the "spirit of the times," von Esenbeck responds, transcends the "begreifliche, doch hypochondrische Lamento" expressed by Kleist (KON 80). Through her recurrent emphasis on literature's significance in a scientific age, Wolf continues the artist's lament.

In his review of *Kein Ort. Nirgends*, Jürgen Engler argues that Wolf remains caught in unproductive binaries such as those between reason and emotion, science and art noted above. Engler states: "Christa Wolf hält, scheint mir, fest am dualistischen Schema von Innerlichkeit und Äußerlichkeit, Authenzität und Anpassung, Idealischem und Pragmatischem, unwirksamen menschlichen Anspruch und wirksamer 'Hopp-hopp Philosophie.'"[15] To be sure, Wolf frequently represents social contradictions in terms of seemingly inextricable antagonisms. Christa T.'s unwavering demand for wholeness, for the absolute in the face of fragmentation as well as the use of clichés and stereotypes in "Selbstversuch" point to this tendency. Yet in representing the binaries informing Western culture, binaries that sanction only the masculine dimension of human experience, Wolf seeks to draw attention to how these oppositions continue to inform institutional structures, patterns of thought and interpersonal relationships.

Failing to conform to the masculine norm, both Kleist and Günderrode feel imprisoned by their gender. In conversation with Günderrode, Kleist figures himself as a victim of a society that forces men to define themselves through a public sphere of action, a realm in which subjectivity and emotions have no place. He asserts, "Sehn Sie nicht, wie unsre männliche Pflicht, zu handeln, uns unerfüllbar gemacht wird, daß wir nur falsch handeln können oder gar nicht! Während Sie wenigstens im Reich der Ideen schalten können, das man Ihnen zugeteilt hat" (KON 113). Like Kleist, Günderrode strives for access to the realm occupied by the other sex, as evident in her lament: "warum ward ich kein Mann! Ich habe keinen Sinn für weibliche Tugenden, für Weiberglück-seeligkeit" (LS 225). Countering Kleist's idealized view of women's access to the realm of ideas, she underscores that the ideas women are allowed to entertain in the private realm remain inconsequential in the public sphere and hence only perpetuate the division between action and thought. The early Romantics, regardless of their gender, strove to synthesize these two realms and, through their poetry, to transcend established boundaries. Their ideal, like Wolf's, is a unity of the masculine and the feminine, the full development of both genders. As Günderrode states: "Bis auf den Grund verschieden. Vom Grund her einander ähnlich. Frau. Mann. Unbrauchbare Wörter. Wir, jeder gefangen in seinem Geschlecht" (KON 109).

In *Kein Ort. Nirgends*, Wolf casts Kleist as an androgenous figure who opposes the masculine, patriarchal norm. Although clearly "feminine," Kleist's position is far from "feminist." Unable to recognize women as his equals, he ultimately affirms patriarchal images of women and shows himself unwilling to surrender his male privilege. Confronted with Günderrode's transgressions of typical female behavior, he is at once compelled—"Soll eine Frau so blicken?" (KON 10)—and taken aback, admittingly preferring women, "die im Rahmen bleiben" (KON 18). Envious that women are allowed to work with ideas, he nonetheless sees them as incapable of complex thought or any deeper understanding of the contradictions of their time: "Die Frau. Als habe sie eine Ahnung von dem entsetzlichen Widerspruch, auf dessen Grund das Verderben der Menschheit liegt. Und als brächte sie die Kraft auf, den Riß nicht zu leugnen, sondern zu ertragen" (KON 81).

Wolf represents Kleist's and Günderrode's self-identification with traditional gender roles through dreams. In his dream, Kleist casts himself as a man of action and aggression who chases down and kills a wild boar (KON 30). Günderrode's dream reverses the roles: she sees herself as a deer that is tracked down and killed by Savigny, and, reflecting on this dream, concedes that she finds it only natural that she bleed to death like the animal (KON 8). Even in her dreams, then, she cannot escape her "feminine" role.

In contrast to the poets Kleist, Günderrode and von Arnim, Wolf casts Wedekind, Merten, von Esenbeck and Savigny—men of business, science and law—in consonance with the rationalist "masculine" paradigm. The natural scientist Nees von Esenbeck professes his complete faith in the positive advances wrought by science and technology. He proclaims: "Ich gäbe mein Alles dafür, wenn ich in ein, zwei Jahrhunderten noch einmal auf dieser Welt leben und an den paradiesischen Zuständigkeiten teilhaben dürfte, welche die Menschheit—dank der Entfaltung der Wissenschaften!—dann genießt" (KON 80). Read against the contemporary backdrop of ecological crisis and nuclear proliferation, von Esenbeck's statement takes on an ironic undertone. In von Esenbeck's view, one consonant with that of Pawel in *Moskauer Novelle* and the philistine tomcat of "Neue Lebensansichten," scientific-technological progress will undoubtedly bring about heaven on earth: it is the new messiah of the Enlightenment age. Von Esenbeck's blind faith in the future diverts attention from present-day contradictions and obviates the need for individual self-determination. Unlike von Esenbeck, Kleist, like Christa T., is greatly disturbed by his society's "zyklopische Einseitigkeit" (KON 80) and asks with disbelief: "Muß die Menschheit durch diese Einöde, um ins Gelobte Land zu kommen?" (KON 80) At the time Wolf wrote *Kein Ort. Nirgends*, the GDR had not progressed much further toward the promised land. Underscoring the dearth of real human progress, Herminghouse speaks of the "Wüste des real existierenden Sozialismus" (246).

In her Günderrode essay, Wolf explicitly links the "sterile rationalism" of the early 1800s to the "vulgar materialism" of her own time, identifying with the early Romantics' attempt to defend themselves against "die eiskalte Abstraktion, diese ganze schauerliche Unbeirrbarkeit auf falsche, nicht mehr befragte Ziele hin, gegen die unaufhaltsame Verfestigung der zerstörerischen Strukturen, gegen das erbarmungslose Zweckmäßigkeitsdenken" (LS 231). In this regard Anna Kuhn remarks that the reactionary political context of the early Romantics' time "constitutes a perversion of Enlightenment ideals," while Wolf's society presents a "perversion of Marxist ideals."[16] In both societies actual conditions diverged significantly from the proclaimed ideal: on the one hand a truly enlightened society, on the other a truly socialist one. Situating Marx firmly within the Enlightenment tradition expands on Kuhn's model and draws attention to the common ideological tenets of Marxism and the Enlightenment: their humanist goals, emancipatory tendencies, longing for a better society, and the belief in an ultimate "realm of freedom." While they reproof the instrumentalization of Enlightenment thought, the early Romantics and Critical Theorists continue to ground their beliefs in these fundamental tenets.

In attempt to justify the inclusion of the Romantic writers in their country's literary canon, GDR critics turned their attention to the principles shared by Romanticism and Marxism. In this vein Claus Träger underscores the Romantics' anti-capitalist stance: "Die Romantik war [...] vor allem Opposition gegen die Grundtendenzen der bürgerlich-kapitalistischen Epoche, gegen das inhumane Wesen der sich kapitalisierenden Gesellschaftsbeziehungen" (46). This focus on common anti-capitalist tenets shifts attention away from the negative dialectic of enlightenment expressed in progressive GDR literature since the late 1960s: rather than attribute negative social consequences to the shared and unqualified belief in progress through science and technology, through industrialization, negative contradictions were attributed solely to capitalist mode of production. While the official reevaluation of Romanticism sought to account for societal contradictions, then, it at the same time obscured certain parallels and analogies associated with the dialectic of enlightenment.

In her acceptance speech for the 1980 Büchner Prize, Wolf makes explicit the contemporary political relevance of her critique of instrumental reason. Illuminating the global context that resonates in *Kein Ort. Nirgends*, Wolf characterizes the insanity of a nuclear age marked by the "Konstruktion von Waffen-, Über- und Superwaffensystemen, die dem altmodischen einzelnen Tod das Handwerk legen in den Phantasien von nuklearen Planungsstäben, [die] jeden von uns schon sieben-, acht-, zwanzigmal zerstrahlt, zerascht, zerstäubt haben" (LS 327–328). More specifically, she addresses the escalating threat posed by the imminent stationing of American tactical nuclear missiles in the Federal Republic in response to the Warsaw Pact's stationing of nuclear missiles in the East.[17] Defending the ideals of the Enlightenment—reason, emancipation and self-determination—against their perversion, Wolf remarks: "Wir, ernüchtert bis auf die Knochen, stehn entgeistert vor den vergegenständlichten Träumen jenes instrumentalen Denkens, das sich immer noch Vernunft nennt, aber den aufklärerischen Ansatz auf Emanzipation, auf Mündigkeit hin, längst entglitt und als blanker Nützlichkeitswahn in das Industriezeitalter eingetreten ist" (LS 320). Like her Frankfurt School predecessors, she brings to light the negative contradictions resulting from an unreflected belief in reason and science, recognizing that progress and "progressive" thought contain the seeds of political and personal regression.

Both in the *Büchner-Preis-Rede* and in *Kein Ort. Nirgends*, Wolf sheds light on sociohistoric turning points by focusing on literary predecesors. "Wir sind die ersten nicht," Wolf states, "An den Bruchstellen zwischen den Zeiten wird gebrochen: der Mut, das Rückgrad, die Hoffnung, die Unmittelbarkeit" (LS 323). The grounds for Wolf's recourse to Georg Büchner (1813–1837) far exceed the fact that her speech was given in acceptance of the prize that carries his name. Büchner's works, specifically his *Woyzeck* (1835), as Richard Gray notes, in many ways express the dialectic of enlightenment. Gray points out that Büchner's own position as a natural scientist enabled him to view the "potentials and dangers of modern science" from a position within the scientific establishment.[18] Wolf similarly remarks that Büchner recognized the insanity of his time and in his politically-engaged writings sought to expose social contradictions. However, in Büchner's time few were willing to acknowledge his claim, "daß der Fortschritt, den man gerade im großen Stil anwarf, das Zeug zum neuen Mythos in sich hatte" (LS 324). Expressing this dialectic in greater detail, Horkheimer and Adorno argue that the Enlightenment claims of universal truth and the reign of reason constitute a totalizing system that creates a new mythology: "so verstrickt Aufklärung mit jedem ihrer Schritte tiefer sich in Mythologie" (DA 18). The grave consequences they associate with the instrumentalization of Enlightenment ideals, foremost the rise of fascism in Germany, have their roots in the instrumentalization of reason that leads to alienation. Büchner, Wolf remarks, showed a keen awareness of these ramifications: "Büchner hat so früh, und ich glaube, mit Grauen gesehen, daß die Lust, die das neue Zeitalter an sich selber fand, an ihrer Wurzel mit Zerstörungslust verquickt war" (LS 324). Like Wolf, Büchner must have felt the need to illuminate Western culture's blind spot (LS 325).

Both in her Büchner speech and in her essays on the early Romantics, Wolf draws attention to the paradoxical consequences for women of the industrial revolution and the Enlightenment. With its promises of "Freiheit" and "Persön-lichkeit," the Enlightenment heightened women's expectations of themselves and of their partners, encouraged them to explore suppressed aspects of their personalities and to become independent. In Günderrode's letter exchange with other women, Wolf recognizes women's expression of their own needs and desires: "Ursprünglichkeit, Natürlichkeit, Wahrhaftigkeit, Intimität gehören zu ihrem universalen Glücksanspruch; sie lehnen ab, was die Hierarchie verlangt: Kälte, Steifheit, Absonderung und Etikette" (LS 236). Demanding "Vollkom-menheit" of herself and of her partner, like her female predecesors in Wolf's works, Günderrode undertakes a type of "Selbstversuch" (LS 237). In *Kein Ort. Nirgends*, she shares Kleist's need to be recognized (KON 28) and understood (KON 58). The dialogic relationship between the narrator and Christa T. prefigures the friendship Wolf represents between Günderrode and Bettine. A relationship built on the "feminine" values of equality, reciprocity, recognition, it serves as a model for non-objectifying interpersonal relationships.

In opposition to the rational norm, Günderrode and Bettine advance an alternate epistemology, a "Weiberphilosophie" or "Schwebe-Religion" based on humanity, joy and sensual pleasure (LS 314). Stressing the Other of instrumental reason, namely the soul, longing, curiosity and fantasy, they envision counter-models of society: Günderrode speaks of "einer anderen Art Vernunft" (LS 271), Bettine of "[e]ine[r] andre[n] Art Fortschritt" (LS 315). Wolf characterizes this alternate philosophy as

> eine Spielart [...] aufklärerischen Denkens, die geschärfte Ratio und gesteigerte Empfindungsfähigkeit in einer Person zusammenbringen will; die [...] die Einseitigkeit des instrumentalen, sachbezogenen Denkens (eines anderen Irrationalismus!) fürchtet; die eine andre, persönliche Art, der Natur—auch der eignen—nahezukommen, den seelenlosen Mechanismen der 'geisttötenden' Philosophie entgegen-setzt. (LS 314)

This philosophy unites reason and emotion in one person, it unites the masculine and the feminine. Countering man's domination of and alienation from nature and human nature, the Romantic philosophy these women develop seeks to bring individuals closer to nature and to themselves. In this "feminine" alternative, Wolf recognizes a possibility to divert society's course that, paradoxically, arose at an historical crossroads at which "die Weichen gerade unwiderruflich auf Ausbeutung der Natur, auf die Verkehrung von Mittel und Zweck und auf die Unterdrückung eines jeden 'weiblichen' Elements in der neuen Zivilisation gestellt waren" (LS 314). At a time when women assert themselves as subjects in their relationships and in their poetry, then, the "spirit of the times" demands utilitarian thinking, rationality and objectivity, further entrenching men in the "citadel of reason" and fostering the "inability to love":

> Der gleiche Augenblick, der Frauen befähigt, zu Personen zu werden— was heißt, ihr "wirkliches Selbst" hervorzubringen, und sei es wenigstens im Gedicht—, dieser gleiche historische Augenblick zwingt die Männer zur Selbstaufgabe, zur Selbstzerstückelung, beschädigt ihre Fähigkeit, zu lieben, zwingt sie, die Ansprüche unabhängiger, zur Liebe fähiger Frauen als "unrealistisch" abzuweisen. Sachlichkeit wird ihnen abverlangt. [...] Frauen, auf ausschließliche Liebe, rückhaltlose Hingabe angewiesen, erfahren das Grauen, zu zweitrangigen Objekten gemacht zu werden: Hier sind die Wurzeln auswegloser Leiden- schaften. (LS 262)

The recognition of men's "inability to love" leads women to look for "livable alternatives" (LS 329), to transcend the growing divisions between science and the imagination, man and woman, reason and emotion. In Günderrode's case, it results in suffering and death. In *Kein Ort. Nirgends*, the utopian promises of human progress, freedom and brotherliness common to the Enlightenment and Marxist projects reveal themselves as empty: "Unlebares Leben. Kein Ort, nirgends" (KON 108). Yet in the face of dystopia, the early Romantics' expression of an alternative epistemology and ontology offers a sign of hope. Cognizant of the insanity of the past and present, Wolf, like her predecessor Bettine von Arnim, continues to make suggestions "für eine andre, nichttötende Art, auf der Welt zu sein" (LS 318). Without hope, Wolf reminds us at the close of *Kein Ort. Nirgends*, there is no chance for a different future: "Wenn wir zu hoffen aufhören, kommt, was wir befürchten, bestimmt" (KON 117).

Kassandra

In her third *Kassandra*-lecture, Wolf asks to what extent progress through science and technology can be termed "progressive" when it seems to serve primarily regressive social tendencies, "was ... 'Fortschritt' sein könnte, da [es] doch der männliche Weg [ist], alle Erfindungen und Gegensätze auf die Spitze zu treiben, bis sie ihren äußersten negativen Punkt erreicht haben" (VK 101). With skepticism, she contemplates the contributions to society made by Europeans like herself: "Daß wir selbst die Kräfte in die Welt gesetzt haben, die uns bedrohen? Daß die Mega-Maschine in ihrer zerstörerischen Irrationalität das

End-Produkt unsrer Kultur geworden ist?" (VK 123). In her speech in acceptance of the 1980 Büchner Prize, Wolf addressed the technical and political possibility of a limited nuclear war waged on the battlefield of Central Europe and asserted her unwavering faith in literature's ability to effect change and secure life on earth: "Literatur heute muß Friedensforschung sein," she exclaimed (LS 331). The *Kölner Begegnung* (1981), *Berliner Begegnung* (1981), *Haager Treffen* (1982) and *Interlit* (1982) conferences, meetings at which authors from the East and the West discussed war, peace and the future of humankind, attest to the primacy of these issues for politically-engaged writers. At the *Berliner Begegnung*, Wolf stressed that literature must express what no longer seems "true" or possible once the mental armament for war begins, namely "Freundlichkeit, Anmut, Duft, Klang, Würde, Poesie; Vertrauen, auch Spontanität—das eigentlich Menschliche" (DiA1 442). At the *Haager Treffen*, she similarly argued that peacefulness must be learned: "destructive fantasies," she urged, must be countered with the "creative fantasies" of concrete utopias. Working for peace, literature should contribute "zu jener Vernunft, in der beides beschlossen ist: Rationales und Emotionales" (DiA1 445). As the preamble of the *Interlit* conference report states: "Der Frieden ist eine zu lebenswichtige Voraussetzung jeder Existenz, als daß sein Schutz allein Politikern, Militärs und Friedensforschern überlassen werden kann. [...] Frieden als die große Utopie? Eine Ästhetik des Widerstands gegen die Interessen der Machtpolitik."[19] Not limited to the public sphere of the West, the immanent threat of nuclear war heightened literature's oppositional role in the GDR as well.

Delivered as part of the 1982 *Frankfurter Poetikvorlesungen*, Wolf's *Kassandra*-project consists of a series of five lectures, four introductory lectures (*Voraussetzungen einer Erzählung. Kassandra*) and the fictional narrative *Kassandra*, the fifth lecture. The *Voraussetzungen* incorporate various non-fictional genres: the first two lectures are travelogues, the third a work diary and the fourth an open letter. The lectures also interweave various threads: Wolf's growing fascination with the mythological figure Cassandra; Cassandra's representation by male poets; diary entries from a trip to Greece; scenes from daily life in Wolf's country home in the Mecklenburg village of Meteln; news reports documenting nuclear proliferation; statements on women's writing and interpretations of texts by the Austrian writer Ingeborg Bachmann. The autobiographical lectures set a contemporary interpretive frame for the narrative *Kassandra* which, reinterpreting the Cassandra myth from a feminist perspective, takes up and re-weaves many of these strands. Other than its opening and closing frames, *Kassandra* is narrated in the first-person voice by the figure Cassandra as she reflects on her life and the fall of Troy in the hours preceding her death at the hands of the Greeks. Both in her narration of the past (*Kassandra*) and the present (*Voraussetzungen*), Wolf illuminates the dialectic between everyday life and major political events. In her third lecture, she notes that Homer described only the masculine line of thought: "Nur in den Lücken zwischen den Schlachtbeschreibungen schimmert das Alltagsleben durch, die Welt der Frau" (VK 91-92). In her *Kassandra*-project, she writes into the recorded, monumental past, into *His*tory, the past of women excluded from politics and representation.

Wolf fashioned the five lectures as a complexly interwoven unit with the *Kassandra* narrative comprising the fifth lecture. However, only the GDR Aufbau-Verlag retained the original sequencing; it published the lectures and the narrative as a single volume, with the narrative following the lectures. In the Federal Republic the *Voraussetzungen* and narrative *Kassandra* were (profitably) published separately. The English translation by Jan von Heurck contains the narrative and the lectures in one volume, yet positions the narrative before the lectures. Read out of sequence and as separate entities, the introductory lectures' open narrative style and the multi-dimensional aesthetic Wolf advocates there appear at odds with the closed form of the *Kassandra* narrative.

Like all of Wolf's works, *Kassandra* was granted publication in the GDR.[20] However, as Peter Graves points out, the edition published by the GDR Aufbau-Verlag omitted eight passages from the third lecture, Wolf's work diary covering the period from May 1980 to August 1981. These censored passages were subsequently included in the editions published by Western presses.[21] Entitled "Ein Arbeitsbuch über den Stoff, aus dem das Leben und die Träume sind," the third lecture brings the contemporary political relevance of *Kassandra* to the fore. Most of the censored sections center on the convergence of capitalism and socialism which, as we saw in the discussion of Maron's *Flug-asche*, was a taboo topic in the GDR. One passage refers to the "delusional" idea of deterrence, the notion of arming for peace promoted by the supreme commands of the NATO and the Warsaw Pact (VK 84); another critiques the Soviet Union's "erpresserische Doktrin des Todrüstens" and advocates a policy of unilateral disarmament (VK 88). Elsewhere Wolf describes how "both sides" incite citizens to prepare for war in the name of self-defense (VK 97). In other cut sections, Wolf vehemently opposes the use of the cherished words "freedom" and "socialism" to justify armament (VK 108), and represents those in power as alienated from everyday life, isolated leaders, "[d]ie die Menschen nicht kennen, die sie da der Vernichtung preisgeben" (VK 112). Additional censored lines document Wolf's overwhelming sense of resignation and doubt—her "Hoffnungsmüdigkeit" (VK 94). For obvious reasons, passages addressing censorship and self-censorship, "Reden und Schreiben mit gespaltener Zunge" (VK 109), were also omitted in the GDR. However, because the critique Wolf articulates in these censored passages resonates elsewhere in the lectures and narrative, their omission scarcely diminished the work's overtly political tenor.

Although conceived for the annual "Frankfurt Lectures on Poetics," Wolf states in a disclaimer preceding the introductory lectures to *Kassandra* that she does not ascribe to a normative, systematic theory of aesthetic principles—in other words, that she has no poetics. Poetics, in her view, is always linked to objectification: "Es gibt keine Poetik, und es kann keine geben, die verhindert, daß die lebendige Erfahung ungezählter Subjekte in Kunst-Objekten ertötet und begraben wird" (VK 8). Connecting alienation in art and literature to self-aliena-tion, Wolf ponders: "Sind also diese Kunst-Objekte ('Werke') auch Produkte der Entfremdung innerhalb dieser Kultur, deren andere perfekte Produkte zum Zweck der Selbstvernichtung produziert werden?" (VK 8) In her *Kassandra*-project she writes against "das unheimliche Wirken von Entfremdungs-erscheinungen auch in der Ästhetik, auch in der Kunst" (VK 8). As in her earlier essays, she underscores the dimension of the author in the text, the "subjective authenticity" that works against alienation in art and life. Wolf's attempt to understand Christa T. and to figure her as a literary subject, rather than as an object, prefigures her captivation by the figure Cassandra: with Cassandra, Wolf similarly seeks to defy objectification.

Rejecting the classical poetics of Aristotle and Horace, Wolf argues that epic poetry's opposition of good and evil, its singular story line and focus on exemplary heros reflects a patriarchal value system. Literature informed by this value system, like science, presents the world in purportedly neutral and quantifiable terms. Wolf asserts, "daß das strikte einwegbessene Vorgehn, das Herauspräperieren eine 'Stranges' zu Erzähl- und Untersuchungszwecken das ganze Gewebe und auch diesen 'Strang' beschädigt" (VK 139). This process of abstraction in her view characterizes the course of Western thought, "den Weg der Sonderung, der Analyse, des Verzichts auf die Mannigfaltigkeit der Erscheinungen zugunsten des Dualismus, des Monismus, zugunsten der Geschlossenheit von Weltbildern und Systemen; des Verzichts auf Subjektivität zugunsten gesicherter 'Objektivität'" (VK 139). In her *Büchner-Preis-Rede*, Wolf underscores how scientific language fosters alienation and, by making the absurd seem rational, effectively safeguards against the interference of human emotion. Abstraction, the method and language of science—the "tool" of enlightenment—further separates object and subject, manipulates the masses and serves to solidify and uphold the power (DA 19). In turn, Wolf argues that women should not simply adopt aesthetic modes passed down by men, but must develop synthetic forms that reflect their engagement, multiplicity and interdependence. Like the aesthetics of the early Romantic women, the "poetics" Wolf advocates fails to conform to a neatly systematized set of principles. It resembles an intricate artistic weaving: in parts imperfect, tangled and irreducible to a single thread.

Wolf begins her third *Kassandra*-lecture with the pronouncement that the literature of Western civilization consists of white man's reflection on himself.

She consequently asks: "Soll nun die Reflexion der weißen Frau auf sich selbst dazukommen? Und weiter nichts?" (VK 84) Echoing the growing awareness in the 1980s that claims of a unified female position fails to account for the interplay of gender, race, class, ethnicity and sexual orientation, Wolf envisions an aesthetic that reflects a different way of being in the world. Rather than simply adding the perspective of white women to that of white men, she advocates a literature that weaves together diverse positional perspectives.

Discussing the relationship of poetics and gender, Wolf enters into the debate on the nature of women's literary production sparked by the rapid increase of texts by women. As elaborated in my third chapter, without a public sphere for addressing feminist issues, GDR authors expressed their "femininst" views primarily through literature. Initiated by Silvia Bovenschen's 1976 essay "Über die Frage: gibt es eine weibliche Ästhetik,?"[22] the debate on a "feminine aesthetic" raised an array of questions about the relationship of feminism and femininity to artistic production. A West German scholar, Bovenschen, like Wolf, argues that men have set the prevailing artistic standards. Measured against these norms, women's artistic works have been viewed as "exotic aberrations." With the growth in women's writing spurred by the feminist movement, Bovenschen asks if it is possible to distinguish a unique "feminine" aesthetic. More specifically, she responds to the issues raised by Verena Stefan's *Häutungen*, a novel that subverts the traditional masculine aesthetic paradigm through innovative syntax and wordplay. Closely interwoven with this new aesthetic is Stefan's affirmation of women's proximity to nature and her definition of women as essentially sensuous and emotional. While Bovenschen supports Stefan's aesthetic innovation, she cautions against reducing the question of "feminine aesthetics" to one of ontological difference:

> Gibt es eine weibliche Ästhetik? Ganz gewiß wenn die Frage *das ästhetische Sensorium* und die Formen *des sinnlichen Erkennens* betrifft; sicher nicht, wenn darunter eine aparte Variante der Kunstprodukion oder eine ausgeklügelete Kunsttheorie verstanden wird. Die Auseinandersetzung der Frauen mit den formalen Eigengesetzlichkeiten eines Mediums, die Freisetzung ihrer Phantasie haben einen ungewissen Ausgang in einer Kunst in feministischer Absicht. (74)

Relating a "feminine aesthetic" to art with *feminist* intentions, Bovenschen argues that women's socialization engenders a distinct "aesthetic awareness" and different "modes of sensory perception" than men's. In her view, minimizing difference again downplays women's own desires and perpetuates the male norm. Equality, then, cannot be equated with emancipation. In this vein, she criticizes the official definition of equality in the GDR and sheds light

on "[der] Wahnwitz der Behauptung: wenn nur eine ökonomische 'Gleich-
stellung' die Egalität in den Produktions- und Öffentlichkeitssbereichen erreicht
sei, glätteten sich die Wogen des Geschlechterkampfes von selber" (65).

In her *Kassandra*-lectures, Wolf approaches the question of a "feminine
aesthetic" from a Marxist perspective. Elsewhere in her lectures, she cites *Über
den Ursprung der Familie*, in which Engels argues that women and men
comprise different classes: "'Der erste Klassengegensatz, der in der Geschichte
auftritt, fällt zusammen mit der Entwicklung des Antagonismus von Mann und
Weib in der Einzelehe, und die erste Klassenunterdrückung mit der des
weiblichen Geschlechts durch das männliche'" (VK 89). Wolf extends this class
argument. Because women occupy a different position than men, she argues that
they have a different perception of reality, which they in turn express in their
writing. She states:

> Inwieweit gibt es wirklich "weibliches" Schreiben? Insoweit Frauen
> aus historischen und biologischen Gründen eine andre Wirklichkeit
> erleben als Männer. Wirklichkeit anders erleben als Männer, und dies
> ausdrücken. Insoweit Frauen nicht zu den Herrschenden, sondern zu
> den Beherrschten gehören, jahrhundertelang, zu den Objekten der
> Objekte, Objekte zweiten Grades, oft genug Objekte von Männern, die
> selbst Objekte sind, also, ihrer sozialen Lage nach, unbedingt
> Angehörige der zweiten Kultur; insoweit sie aufhören, sich an dem
> Versuch abzuarbeiten, sich in die herrschenden Wahnsysteme zu
> integrieren. Insoweit sie, schreibend und lebend, auf Autonomie aus
> sind. Da begegnen sie dann den Männern, die auf Autonomie aus sind.
> Autonome Personen, Staaten und Systeme können sich gegenseitig
> fördern, müssen sich nicht bekämpfen wie solche, deren innere
> Unsicherheit und Unreife andauernd Abgrenzung und Imponier-
> gebärden verlangen. (VK 114–115)

Wolf acknowledges that historical and biological factors contribute to women's
perception of reality. While her recourse to biology may seem to affirm
women's essential difference from men, by linking the biological argument
closely to the historical one Wolf acknowledges and affirms that women's
biology is a significant factor in their historical subordination. She stresses,
moreover, that women's different perception is contingent upon their refusal to
integrate into the dominant "delusional systems." At the same time, she rejects
the separatist faction of Western feminists and warns that replacing a
"Männlichkeitswahn" with a "Weiblichkeitswahn" merely reverses and perpetuates the traditional gender paradigm (VK 115). The aim of both women and
men should be "autonomy," to become self-sufficienct, independent and to
pursue one's own goals. Wolf recognizes that autonomy, typically a masculine

trait opposed to feminine "attachment," is a prerequisite for relationships based on the personal strength and power of both partners. Bridging the gap between personal autonomy and the autonomy of states and political systems, moreover, she underscores the interdependence of the personal and the political.

Wolf's position echoes that of West German critic Hiltrud Gnüg, yet in contrasting Gnüg with Wolf some significant differences come to light. Gnüg and Wolf both approach the question of a feminine aesthetic by drawing on Marx's notion that being determines consciousness. Gnüg states, for example: "Die Gedanken der herrschenden Klasse sind in jeder Epoche die herrschenden Gedanken, d.h die Klasse, welche die herrschende materielle Macht der Gesellschaft ist, ist sogleich ihre herrschende geistige Macht."[23] Moreover, Gnüg similarly extends the Marxist model of class conflict to gender relations, arguing that because men have oppressed women for centuries, have curtailed their "political, creative and emancipatory possibilities," women can be seen as members of a separate class with distinct interests (131). Gnüg's acknowledgment that being determines consciousness, unlike Wolf's, does not lead her to argue for a unique "feminine aesthetic." In her view, the opposition of a "feminine" and a "masculine" aesthetic presupposes a fundamental and inherently essentialist difference between the two sexes. Theorists who argue for a "feminine aesthetic" by appropriating traits such as emotionality and sensitivity, she contends, only perpetuate existing gender ideologies that have historically been defined by men:

Dem jetzt verketzerten männlichen Prinzip wird nach wie vor seiner Rationalität, Begrifflichkeit, Zielgerichtetheit bescheinigt; auch die Aktivität wird nicht in Frage gestellt, nur wird sie jetzt als Aggression modifiziert. Und ebenso bereitwillig werden Emotionalität, Sinnlichkeit, Gefühl als weibliches Spezifikum angenommen. Logik, Systematik, Ratio, Abstraktionsvermögen werden dem männlichen Feindbild zuerkannt. (134)

Gnüg ultimately disaffirms a "feminine aesthetic" related to a specifically feminine mode of sensory perception or experience. Like Wolf and Bovenschen, she maintains that women's historical oppression has affected their consciousness, yet she reaches a different conclusion:

Indem die Frau aus ihre weiblichem Ghetto ausbricht ins Offene menschlicher Möglichkeiten, usurpiert sie nicht männliche Domäne, vermännlicht sie auch nicht, sie entdeckt die als männlich ausge-gebenen Qualitäten als eigentlich menschliche. Intellektualität, Produktivität, Kampfgeist sind keine männlichen Urphänomene, und auch der sich emanzipierende Mann heute verwahrt sich dagegen,

Emotionalität, Sensibilität, Sanftmut als weibliche Wesenszüge von sich zu weisen. (136)

For Gnüg, then, any new aesthetic forms created by women are not attributable to gender, but more generally represent the "new subjectivity" of the late 1970s, the "spirit of the times."

While these diverse writers and theorists vary in emphasis and reach different conclusions, they all attribute women's different mode of perception to women's socialization under patriarchy. Bovenschen suggests that women have developed a specific perception that may influence their literary production. Gnüg draws on Marx to argue that while women have developed a specific consciousness due to their oppression by men, no specific feminine aesthetic has resulted. Wolf also takes recourse to Marx and Engels, yet argues that women's oppression and objectification leads them to experience reality differently and to express this experience in their writings.

For Wolf, the Homeric epics exemplify the imbrication of a masculine aesthetic, masculine structures, and the dialectic of enlightenment: "die Literatur des Abendlandes [beginnt] mit der Verherrlichung eines Raubkrieges" (VK 19). In a central chapter of *Dialektik der Aufklärung,* Horkheimer and Adorno interpret Homer's *Odyssey,* the founding text of Western civilization, as a document of barbarism that exemplifies the entwinement of self-renunciation and self-preservation, regression and progress, myth and enlightenment. Like Wolf, they see the historical trajectory of imperialism and patriarchy as implicit in epic narration, positing that domination and exploitation inform both epic and myth (DA 52). In his struggles against the mythical powers that tempt him to divert from his course, Odysseus employs trickery and deceit. His attempts at self-preservation through the domination of nature result in self-renunciation and self-alienation: "Odysseus [...] wirft sich weg gleichsam, um sich zu gewinnen; die Entfremdung der Natur, die er leistet, vollzieht sich in der Preisgabe der Natur, mit der er in jedem Abenteuer sich mißt..." (DA 55).

For Horkheimer and Adorno, Odysseus's self-renunciation is paradigmatic for the course of Western civilization. On his journey, Odysseus employs reason as an instrument of domination over the natural world: he refuses to eat the Lotus blossoms, outwits the Cyclops and silences the seductive songs of the Sirens. Odysseus's encounter with the enchantress Circe illuminates his use of trickery and sheds light on women's position in patriarchal culture. As in their essay "Mensch und Tier," Horkheimer and Adorno depict women as complicit in their subordination. Although Circe possesses power over men, employing her power perpetuates her subjugation: "Es ist, als wiederhole die zaubernde Hetäre in dem Ritual, dem sie die Männer unterwirft, nochmals jenes, dem die patriarchal Gesellschaft sie selber immer auf neue unterwirft" (DA 79). Further pointing to women's position in the process of enlightenment, they continue:

"Gleich ihr (Kirke) sind unterm Druck der Zivilisation Frauen vorab geneigt, das zivilisatorische Urteil über die Frau sich zu eigen zu machen und den Sexus zu diffamieren" (DA 79). Odysseus is only able to resist Circe's magical powers by tricking her into giving an oath that prevents his mutilation and finally, after he sleeps with her, reduces her powers. For Horkheimer and Adorno, Odysseus represents the prototype of alienated, enlightened man: his thinking is nominalistic, his interests atomistic, he is "[d]er listige Einzelgänger," "homo oeconomicus" (DA 68–69).

In the *Voraussetzungen*, Wolf draws attention to this interplay of enlightenment and myth at the root of Western civilization and further articulates its consequences for women. She contends:

> "Lernen durch das Leid"—dies scheint das Gesetz der neuen Götter zu sein, der Weg des männlichen Denkens auch, das die Mutter Natur nicht lieben, sondern durchschauen will, um sie zu beherrschen und das erstaunliche Gebäude einer naturfernen Geiseswelt zu errichten, aus der Frauen von nun an ausgeschlossen sind [...]. Weisheit wider Willen. Kulturgewinn durch Naturverlust. Fortschritt durch Leid: die Formeln [...] die der Kultur des Abendlands zugrunde liegen. (VK 75–76)

In her view, Western civilization's definition of "progress" as the domination of nature rests on women's subordination and their exclusion from defining progress.

In her "Büchner-Preis-Rede," Wolf further reflects on women's position vis-à-vis "das erstaunliche Gebäude einer naturfernen Geisteswelt." As in *Kein Ort. Nirgends*, she draws attention to the position of women at a more recent junction of Western civilizaiton, the historical Enlightenment. Citing the retreat of Büchner's Danton into the "Zitadelle der Vernunft," Wolf turns her eye to Büchner's female figures:

> Wo bleiben Rosetta, Marie, Marion, Lena, Julie, Lucille? Außerhalb der Zitadelle, selbstverständlich. Ungeschützt im Vorfeld. Kein Denk-Gebäude nimmt sie auf. Man macht sie glauben: anders als auf diese Art—verschanzt!—könne kein Mensch vernünftig denken [...]. Von unten, von außen blicken sie auf die angestrengte Geistestätigkeit des Mannes, die, je länger, je mehr darauf gerichtet ist, seine Festung durch Messungen, Berechnungen, ausgeklügelte Zahlen- und Plansysteme abzusichern. (LS 323)

The apocalyptic aura of the early 1980s led Wolf to search further back in time for the genesis of this destruction. In her *Kassandra*-lectures and narrative, she pursues the following questions:

Wann hat es angefangen? [...] War dieser Verlauf unausweichlich?
Gab es Kreuz- und Wendepunkte, an denen die Menschheit, will sagen:
die europäische und nordamerikanische Menschheit, Erfinder und
Träger der technischen Zivilisation, andere Erscheidungen hätte treffen
können, deren Verlauf nicht selbstzerstörerisch gewesen wäre? War
denn, fragen wir uns, mit der Erfindung der ersten Waffen—zur
Jagd—, mit ihrer Anwendung gegen um Nahrung rivalisierende
Gruppen, mit den Übergang matriarchalische strukturierter, wenig
effektiver Gruppen zu patriarchalischen, ökonmisch effektiveren, der
Grund für die weitere Entwicklung gelegt? (VK 108)

For Wolf, the "crossroads and turning points" of Western civilization are
inextricably linked to technical progress, to the development and use of
weapons to dominate others that arose at the time of transition from matriarchal
to patriarchal society. Weaving together threads of technological progress,
utilitarian thinking and women's subordination visible throughout her oeuvre,
the *Kassandra*-project reveals intricate patterns and connections: Wolf herself
has termed *Kassandra* a "Schlüsselerzählung" (VK 119).

In the GDR, reviews of *Kassandra* were mixed. The most scathing,
polemical and personal attack came from Wilhelm Girnus upon the pre-
publication of excerpts of *Kassandra* in *Sinn und Form* (1/83).[24] Although he
dwells primarily on Wolf's use of sources and translations, Girnus also takes
issue with the text's political intent, bluntly referring to Wolf's focus on gender
issues as "blühender Unsinn" (442). In his review, Girnus argues in terms of
"Wer-wen," capitalism or communism, the "Ausbeuterbande" versus the
"Weltfriedensfront," and thus exhibits precisely the binary mode of thought
Wolf writes against in her *Kassandra*-project. He claims, for example, "Wer
aber gegen den Kommunismus Sturm läuft, wählt den Krieg" (445). The
polemic tone of Girnus's review should not be seen as representative of the
work's critical reception in the GDR. In fact, Girnus's review provoked a series
of public responses that uphold the fundamental tenets of Wolf's text. Literary
critics supported Wolf's indictment of Western, patriarchal thinking that
perpetuates the oppression of women (Gebhard Engelmann); her insistence that
the course of history be changed, and that women figure significantly in
charting a new course (Melitta Waligora); her argument for writing women into
history (Heinz Berg).[25] The diverse reviews published in *Weimarer Beiträge*
further documents the range of interpretations of Wolf's text in the GDR.[26]

Analogous to the reception of Wolf's other texts, some critics have read the
pacifist tone of the *Kassandra* narrative and lectures as a naive rejection of all
scientific projects. Girnus, for example, strongly criticizes as bourgeois
irrationality Wolf's rejection of a scientific worldview based on objectivity and
reason—one that he sees as fundamental to communism.[27] Anticipating such

criticism, Wolf reflects in the *Voraussetzungen*: "Bedenkenswert, auch heute: wie die Kritik an der Einseitigkeit des männlichen Rationalismus Gefahr läuft, als Irrationalismus, Wissenschaftsfeindlichkeit mißverstanden, auch mißbraucht zu werden" (VK 101). In a discussion with young scientists noted in the *Voraussetzungen*, she suggests that with the abuse of scientific discoveries in her age, scientists should be required to take a Hippocratic oath forbidding them to pursue research for military purposes, a suggestion which the scientists discredit as unrealistic, as "Wissenschaftsfeindlichkeit" (VK 136). Yet Wolf explicitly rejects a "back to nature" approach (VK 145) that would again be based on an all-or-nothing mentality. Fundamental to Wolf's indictment of scientific-technological progress is a critique of instrumental reason, of a specific mode of scientific and mathematical thinking through which science becomes divorced from its ends and consequently viewed as "ein selbständiges Gebilde [...], dessen Gesetze auf andre Gebilde zu übertragen sind und dort beweisen oder gar erzeugen, was eine der größten Lebensabwehrmythen dieser Zeit ist: 'Wissenschaftlichkeit'" (VK 87).

Wolf's interest in the Trojan War revolves less around the details of war itself than around the question when the "pre-war" begins (VK 78), that is, how a way of thinking that leads to war originates. In the *Voraussetzungen*, Wolf comments on the early socialization of males into a war mentality upon observing a group of young boys at the airport who battle each other with toy weapons. In *Kassandra*, the Greeks epitomize the mentality of war—the new mode of objective, binary thought that arose with patriarchy: "Für die Griechen gibt es nur entweder Wahrheit oder Lüge, richtig oder falsch, Sieg oder Niederlage, Freund oder Feind, Leben oder Tod. Was nicht sichtbar, riechbar, hörbar, tastbar ist, ist nicht vorhanden" (VK 124). Although they initially sustain remnants of matriarchy and its values, the Trojans eventually internalize and reproduce this mode of thinking. In place of subjectivity and a valuation of self-knowledge and intersubjective knowledge, they adopt a rationalist mentality based on objectivity and utilitarianism.

Cassandra slowly recognizes that in wartime Greek and Trojan leaders employ tactics of deceit and trickery not only against the enemy, but against their own people. As a war mentality develops, the original grounds for battle—gold and free access to the Dardanelles—retreat. To legitimate war preparation in Troy, Eumulos employs the following strategy: "Er setzt voraus, was er erst schaffen mußte: Krieg. Ist er soweit gekommen, nimmt er diesen Krieg als das Normale und setzt voraus, aus ihm führt nur ein Weg, der heißt: der Sieg" (K 123). The creation of an enemy leads to mental armament, and victory becomes rationalized at any cost. Cassandra recognizes that the Trojans have become like the Greeks, yet is alone in wanting to learn more about the enemy, "[d]a man den Feind schlagen, nicht aber kennen sollte" (K 16)

In Wolf's text the Greek "hero" Achilles embodies the barbarian war

mentality: he is savagely aggressive and unable to love. Not only does he ruth-
lessly attack Cassandra's brother Troilus and strangle him once he is rendered
defenseless, but proceeds to decapitate Troilus like a sacrificial lamb. After
killing Penthesilea, he rapes her corpse. Designated "das Vieh" by Cassandra,
Achilles shows a blatant disregard for moral values and human dignity.

The spread of the utilitarian war mentality exacerbates women's objectification and their marginalization. Infiltrating family structures, it renders the
personal and political inseparable: Priam bars his wife Hecube from the war
council; Agamennon sacrifices his daughter Clytamnesta; Polyxena becomes the
object of barter for her father, is traded to Achilles and used to lure him into the
caves; Cassandra is married off to her father's potential ally, Eurpylos. In the
Voraussetzungen, Wolf asserts: "In Kassandra ist eine der ersten Frauengestalten
überliefert, deren Schicksal vorformt, was dann, dreitausend Jahre lang, den
Frauen geschehen soll: daß sie zum Objekt gemacht werden" (VK 86). Wolf
highlights the continuity between women's objectification past and present in
the first lecture, a travelogue, noting the socialized subservience of a group of
Syrian women she observes at the airport and of the Greek women she
encounters during her travels.

Those directly implicated in the structures of power are blind to their
mechanisms and to the consequences of their actions. Western Christian
civilization, Wolf remarks, is founded on a double standard that acknowledges
the commandment, "Du sollst nicht töten," while it simultaneously rescinds this
commandment for practical action. This results in what Wolf terms society's
"blind spot," "jener dunkle blinde Fleck, der ihr das Wichtigste, ihr
mörderisches Doppelleben, verbirgt: ein Defizit das leider [...] mit Notwendig-
keit auch jene Prozesse, die zur Selbstvernichtung führen, vor den treibenden
Kräften dieser Zivilisations unsichtbar macht" (VK 40).

Cassandra's transition from "blindness" to "vision" exemplifies Wolf's
standpoint epistemology. Cassandra is given the gift of prophesy by Apollo,
under the condition that no one would believe her predictions, and only
develops "vision" once she distances herself from the power structures of the
palace world. Initially, she is blind to the reality behind the palace facade. "Ich
sah nichts," she states, "Mit der Sehergabe überfordert, war ich blind. [...]
Durch den Jahreslauf des Gottes und die Forderungen des Palastes wurde mein
Leben bestimmt. Man könnte auch sagen: erdrückt" (K 33). Once outside the
palace world, Cassandra recognizes the link between its machinations and the
move toward war: "der in den Kampf bedingungslos Verstrickte sieht ja nichts"
(VK 17), Wolf asserts in her lectures. Although initially incapable of reconciling
her inclination to conform with her thirst for knowledge, Cassandra comes to
reject the insignias of her class when she realizes that assimilation reproduces
the dominant mode of thought (K 33). Moving from a position within the power
structures to a position outside the citadel, Cassandra reverses the historical

trajectory of woman's entrance into the public sphere. In her "Büchner-Preis-Rede," Wolf illuminate the self-sacrifice associated with the freedoms that come with power and self-determination: "mit ihrem Eintritt in die Zitadelle unterliegt sie auch deren Gesetzen! [...] Um frei zu werden, ist sie neue Verstrickungen eingegangen. Um zu sich selbst zu kommen, wurden ihr neue Arten der Selbstverleugnung abverlangt" (LS 327). In both instances, "vision" hinges on a positional perspective.

Cassandra's clearest "visions" occur during bouts of madness that come about when Cassandra's realizes the (self-)deception underlying the Trojans' war tactics. The first attack occurs when Cassandra recognizes the deceit and failure of the second ship's mission; speaking with a voice foreign to her, she states: "ich hab es gewußt, ich hab es gewußt" (K 47). During her second attack, she screams out prior to the launch that the third ship should not sail (K 70). The third bout of madness sets in when Cassandra recognizes that Helen is a mere phantom, that the mission of the third ship was also predicated on deception and that, consequently, the Trojans were lost (K 158). Pointing out the rise in delusional thinking and deceitful actions on the part of the Trojans, Anna Kuhn aptly interprets the three ships as symbolizing "distinct levels of moral decay.[28] In all three instances, Cassandra recognizes the truth behind the deceitful façade and reacts to an increasingly rationalized world with a bout of "irrationality." While those near to Cassandra interpret her madness as a sign of illness or insanity, Cassandra, like her predecessors Christa T., Kleist, Günderrode, Josefa and Rosalind, recognizes "die listigen Bündnisse zwischen unseren unterdrückten Äußerungen und den Krankheiten" (K 47).

The palace world, marked in Cassandra's childhood by rejection, abhorrence and estrangement, continues to revolve around silence and secrecy (K 60): "Hekabe, Priamos, Panthoos. So viele Namen für Täuschung. Für Zurücksetzung. Verkennung" (K 74–75). In an attempt to counter the delusional thinking on which war is predicated, Cassandra pragmatically suggests to the Trojan war council that they end the war "[d]urch die Wahrheit über Helena. Durch Gold und Waren, und was sie wollen" (K 88). In the council's view, Cassandra's insistence on the truth further substantiates her madness. While Cassandra bases her notion of victory on knowledge, self-knowledge and interpersonal relationships, the council's considerations rest solely on objective principles. Thinking in binaries of victory or defeat, friend or foe, its members allow neither negotiations nor concessions to effect their decision to enter into battle.

In her third lecture, Wolf links the past and the present by underscoring how the peace rhetoric of the super powers reflects the binaries dominant in Troy. In the name of peace, the supreme commands of the NATO and Warsaw pact countries confer only to escalate the arms race, "um der angenommenen waffentechnischen Überlegenheit des jeweiligen 'Gegners' etwas Gleichwertiges entgegensetzen zu können" (VK 84). Like Cassandra, Wolf forsees the probable consequences and advocates a "third way": "Es ist das andere, das sie zwischen ihren scharfen Unterscheidungen zerquetschen, das Dritte, das es nach ihrer Meinung nicht gibt, das lächelnde Lebendige, das imstande ist, sich immer wieder aus sich selbst hervorzubringen, das Ungetrennte, Geist im Leben, Leben im Geist" (K 124–125), Cassandra recognizes. This third, synthetic dimension takes on concrete form in the cave community depicted in the *Kassandra*-narrative. Situated on the foot of the Ida mountains, the margins of society, this non-heirarchical community includes men and women of all social classes and nationalities who seek an alternative way of living. Despite their differences, they work together to create "einen schmalen Streifen Zukunft" (K 156). Melding the sensual and the rational, the cave provides a meeting place to discuss the war and debate alternatives, but also to cook, eat, laugh, dance, play and learn (K 138). Cassandra stresses the vital role of Anchises in the caves— the value of his keen understanding and sincere belief in human goodness. In fact, Anchises in many respects exemplifies the utopian aspect of life in the caves: "Anchises war es, glaube ich, der von ganzem Herzen unser Leben in den Höhlen liebte, ohne Vorbehalt, ohne Trauer und Bedenken. Der sich einen Traum erfüllte und uns Jüngere lehrte, wie man mit beiden Beinen auf der Erde träumt" (K 156), she stresses. Echoing Bloch's concept of concrete utopia, the cave's inhabitants explore a "third way" "[z]wischen Töten und Sterben [...]: Leben" (K 138).

Affirming the utopian life of the cave community, Wolf advocates an ontology based on shared values of community, equality and respect. In her work diary of 1980 and 1981, she interweaves descriptions of her everyday life in Meteln, of baking, eating, wine-drinking and chatting with friends and family, with the news reports documenting the absurdity and danger of the contemporary political situation. We read that the U.S. computer that controls the launching of missiles by detecting a Soviet first strike repeatedly sounds a false alarm; three tons of TNT exist for each of our planet's inhabitants; researchers in Groningen predict that unless the super powers completely alter their current policies, Europe has only three to four years left; the Federal Republic stores American poison gasses to be deployed during wartime.

The culture of the caves reflects the principles informing the matriarchal culture of the Minoens. As Wolf remarks, for some feminists Minoen culture takes on a symbolic function: "Feministinnen [...] sahen in den Königreichen der Minoer *die* Gemeinwesen, an die ihr sehnsüchtiges utopisches Denken [...] als an ein Konkretum anknüpfen konnte. Es *gab* es doch einmal, das Land, in dem die Frauen frei und den Männern gleichgestellt waren" (VK 61). In the *Voraussetzungen*, Wolf highlights the Minoens' peacefulness, sense of community and their ability to derive meaning from their work. In essence, she represents Minoen culture as "eine Insel der Vollkommenheit" (VK 59).

Although her view of matriarchal culture is glorified, Wolf is not blind to its imperfections. She notes, for example, that Minoean men and women held slaves. Wolf explicitly distances herself from the cultural feminist views of the two American feminists, Sue and Helen, whom she encounters in Greece. Sue and Helen categorically reject "alle männliche Kunst, alle Abbilder des Mannes" (VK 64). For Wolf, emancipation can only emerge if men and women work together toward a common goal. In Wolf's view, Sue and Helen's complete rejection of all things masculine runs the risk of replacing the irrational and exclusionary masculine paradigm with an equally irrational and exclusionary feminine paradigm.

Wolf's critique of the Amazon leader Penthesilea underlines her approach to women and war. Particularly when theorizing women's relationship to the historically male realms of war and militarism, sex role stereotypes of man as warrior and solidier and woman as wife and mother are often employed to uphold women's "natural" difference from men: while she is naturally peaceful, he is naturally aggressive. Taken to its logical conclusion, this line of reasoning implies that a feminine or feminist society would be free of war. The violence of the Amazons, however, shows that both genders have a potential for aggression and provides an argument against women's "natural" pacifity. In taking up arms, Wolf argues that the Amazons replicate male violence and a dualistic war mentality. She implies in *Kassandra*, moreover, that these women do not limit their battle to the Greeks; they go so far as to murder their own husbands (K 137). For Cassandra, the Amazon's edict, "Lieber kämpfend sterben, als versklavt sein," presents an unviable alternative (K 136–137). In Wolf's view Penthesilea, in rejecting Killa's offer to join the cave community and to explore a third, pacifist way of living, upholds false antinomies of life or death, men or women, us or them. Penthesilea ultimately chooses death.

A counter-argument to Wolf's feminist pacifism would be that rejecting weapons means rejecting power. Convinced that women are not more peaceable by nature than men, West German feminist theorist Alice Schwarzer argues that "feminine pacifity" is a negative by-product of a socialization process that keeps women from positions of power and hence from positions from which they can effect change. Schwarzer argues: "Ich glaube nicht, daß es in einer Gesellschaft, in der Frauen die (oder mehr) Macht hätten, automatisch auch friedfertiger umgehen würde!"[29] Rejecting the moral or ethical superiority that cultural feminists, in reversing the value attributed to "masculine" and "feminine" characteristics, attribute to women's nature, Schwarzer argues that women are "bestenfalls aufgrund ihrer Prägungen und Lebensumstände menschlicher und schlimmstenfalls nur gut, weil sie nicht die Macht zum Bösen haben" (89). She therefore questions whether women can succeed in changing the world from a position that solidifies rather than dismantles traditional gender stereotypes.

Wolf's position occupies a middle ground between Schwarzer's liberal (equality) feminism and cultural feminism. Like Schwarzer, Wolf attributes women's difference from men to structural gender differences ("Lebens-umstände") and their relation to power. Like cultural feminists, she ascribes positive value to feminine characteristics. However, rather than argue that women should conform to the masculine paradigm (liberal feminism) or are essentially different from men (cultural feminism), Wolf suggest that the difference in women's structural position in society can make visible the irrationality of dominant masculine paradigms and provide an understanding of social relations that could potentially divert the destructive teleology of Western civilization.

Wolf's perspective resonates with the feminist-pacifist engagement of many Western women's groups of the 1970s and early 1980s which had as their goal, as Herrad Schenk underscores, "immer den Zusammenhang zwischen Krieg, Militärismus, Gewalt einerseits, geschlechtsspezifischer Arbeitsteilung und Rolle der Frau andererseits herzustellen und zu problematisieren."[30] Wolf's feminist-pacifism emphasizes the personal consequences of the instrumentalization of reason and the domination of abstract, scientific thought. Stressing the alternative epistemology advocated by Wolf and her Cassandra figure, both of whom search for the limits of and grounds for women's knowledge claims, W. D. McDonald asserts: "This new grounding must place in relation the intuitive, imaginative insights of literature and the literary artist with the factual observations and logical arguments of the political thinker and activist. Neither are sufficient alone."[31] In *Voraussetzungen einer Erzählung. Kassandra*, Wolf cites Leonardo da Vinci's eloquent expression of the need for a unity of reason and emotion: "Die Erkenntnis, die nicht durch die Sinne gegangen ist, kann keine andere Wahrheit erzeugen als das Schädliche" (VK 122). Given the instrumentalization of reason and its consequences, Wolf asserts the importance of a fundamentally different perception of reality: she asserts a feminist way of knowing that unifies the mind and the senses.

Störfall

In her speech at the *Berliner Begegnung* in 1981, Wolf argued that the destructive trajectory of human civilization was far from a coincidental by-product of evolution: "Eine Zivilisation die imstande war, derartig exakt ihren eigenen Untergang zu planen [...]—eine solche Zivilisation ist krank, wahrscheinlich geisteskrank, vielleicht todkrank" (DiA1 440). In *Störfall*, Wolf further develops this metaphor of social illness as the first-person narrator interweaves the breaking news of the nuclear meltdown in Chernobyl with updates on the progress of her brother's brain surgery, which occurs the day she hears of the nuclear "accident." Like the scientists who attempt to detect the burning reactor core, the neurosurgeons who try to locate and remove the brother's brain tumor search for the "glühenden, pulsierenden Kern" (S 10), the "Kern des Übels" (S 25). This two-stranded narration, as Kuhn remarks, is a metaphorical inference "that the overly developed brain of homo technicus is diseased and that our runaway technology is like a cancer that takes over our bodies, incessantly, abnormally reproducing itself" (219). Wolf elaborates on the psychsomatic dimensions of "illness" in her essays "Krankheit als Liebesentzug" (1984) and "Krebs und Gesellschaft"(1991). In the former essay, Wolf remarks how the natural sciences continue to be regarded as "männlich [...] unbeirrt vom Störfaktor 'Emotionen'" (DiA2 729), and underlines how the supression of emotions, of the "feminine," has a recognizable effect on the health of individuals and societies (DiA2 729). In the latter essay, she critically questions the heirarchical structures of modern industrial societies and relates these to prevalent mental structures. Echoing the narrator's search for the "core" of society's ills, Wolf poses the question of "illness" she pursues in *Störfall*: "Was blockiert den direkten Weg zwischen unseren Einsichten und unseren Handlungen? Was hindert uns zum Beispiel, wenigstens jene Schadstoffe entscheidend zu vermindern, die direkt Krebs erzeugen? Was, Alternative zum Atomstrom schneller zu entwickeln?"[32]

The two quotes that preface *Störfall*, the first by the astronomer Carl Sagan, the second by the animal behaviorist Konrad Lorenz, give insight into Wolf's response to this question. Both Sagan and Lorenz approach the dialectic of progress and regression from the standpoint of evolution. Since the beginning of civilization, Sagan argues, invention has been inextricably linked with murder: "Die Verbindung zwischen Töten und Erfinden hat uns nie verlassen. Beide entstammen dem Ackerbau und der Zivilisation." Wolf draws this quote from the chapter "Eden as Metaphor: The Evolution of Man" in Sagan's *The Dragons of Eden*. There, Sagan contends that after its exile from Eden, "mankind was condemned to death; [...] the domination of men over women; the domestication of plants (Cain); the domination of animals (Abel); and murder (Cain and Abel)."[33] In Sagan's view civilization has developed from man's murder of his fellow man, of his brother: civilization has developed not from Abel, but from Cain. Sagan links the domination of humans over the natural world to the relatively large size and rapid growth of the human brain. A particular feature of humans, Sagan notes, is the rapid development of the neocortex, the area of the brain responsible for abstract reasoning and language. These human attributes figure prominently in *Störfall*.

Wolf's narrator ponders, for example, if in the evolution of the human brain, "des Guten ein wenig zuviel getan wurde" (S 47):

Hat unser übergroßer unbeschäftigter Gehirnteil sich in eine manisch-destruktive Hyperaktivität geflüchtet und, schneller und schneller,

schließlich—heute—in   rasender   Geschwindigkeit   immer   neue
Phantasien herausgeschleudert, die wir, unfähig, uns zu bremsen, in
Wunschziele umgewandelt und unserer Maschinenwelt als Produk-
tionsaufgaben übertragen haben? (S 80)

Wolf poses this question to her readers and suggests an affirmative answer when
she relates the brain's "hyperactivity" to humankind's destructive "fantasies."
Echoing the dialectic of enlightenment, she recognizes: "Der intelligente
Mensch schafft sich die Mittel zur Unterwerfung der Natur und seiner
Artgenossen. Die Regeln und Normen, die er sich selbst auferlegt hat, sucht er,
und sei es um den Preis der Selbstvernichtung, unter Anwendung offener oder
versteckter Gewalt zu durchbrechen ..." (S 52). Drawing on Sagan, Wolf also
calls attention to the R-complex or Reptilian-complex, a feature of the human
brain associated with aggressive, ritualistic and hierarchical behavior (S 60–62).
In addition, she takes up Sagan's argument that language evinces the superiority
of humans over animals and contributes to domination. Historically used to
delimit one tribe from another, language served to mark as foreign and Other
those who spoke a different tongue. This Otherness in turn led to objectification:
"Der Andersprechende war der Fremde, war kein Mensch, unterlag nicht dem
Tötungstabu" (S 91). In this way, paradoxically, language became a tool of
domination: "Sprache, die Identität schafft, [trägt] zugleich aber entscheidend
dazu bei [...], die Tötungshemmung gegen den anderssprechenden Artgenossen
abzubauen" (S 91). Wolf depicts how scientific language and statistical thinking
similarly compound the anonymity of the victims of progress. Following the
Chernobyl disaster, the threat of radiation is conveyed in a language "foreign" to
the narrator, a language with words such as "Nukleide," "Halbwertszeit,"
"Caesium," "Becquerel," and "Jod 131." The narrator also recognizes how
scientists downplay the grave human costs when they assert, "Jede relativ neue
Technologie [...] fordere zunächst auch Opfer" (S 49). Although conceding that
all new technologies entail risks, they fail to address the enormity of the risk
associated with nuclear energy. Instead, they detail the security precautions
taken to preclude reactor breakdowns and relay the numerous "peaceful" uses
that make nuclear energy seem essential (S 111–112).

Unlike the scientists, Wolf's narrator illuminates the lethal use of nuclear
energy and focuses her attention on the victims of progress. She relates the fate
of Chernobyl's victims to the predicament of the Japanese fishermen killed by
American H-bomb tests on the Bikini atoll. Recollecting the fate of the Japanese
fishermen, the narrator states: "Ja, habe ich eine Person in mir denken hören,
warum immer nur die japanischen Fischer. Warum nicht einmal wir?" (S 11)
Her question alludes to Anna Seghers's short story "Der japanische Fischer"
(1954), which centers on the human consequences of scientific "progress" and
the need to empathize with the victims overlooked in the relentless flow of

history. Regarding the perversion of human reason exemplified by the American H-bomb tests, Seghers's narrator states: "Nichts nützt mehr dem Menschen sein Bewußtsein, das er allein unter allen Lebewesen nach Millionen Jahren Entwicklung auf unserm Erdball erreicht hat, wenn er zuläßt, daß dieses Bewußtsein zur Erfindung einiger Bomben dient, die wieder alles bewußte Leben in einer Sekunde zerstört."[34] Although Segher's narrator admittedly knows little more about the Japanese fisherman than his nationality and occupation, a news correspondent's description of a fisher's empty eyes indelibly etches a human face into her memory that contrasts with the seemingly anonymous and "faceless" victims of the H-bomb tests. "So wenig, wie ich gefürchtet hatte, war gar nicht über den Japaner bekannt. Durchaus nicht so wenig, wie es die Wasserstoffbomben-Amerikaner hofften, die die Inseln verschwinden ließen," Seghers writes (165). Like Wolf, Seghers draws her readers' attention to the objectification and annihilation of the individual in the name of progress.

Wolf's representation of scientific-technological progress, as we have seen, grew increasingly critical. In *Der geteilte Himmel*, the successful Soviet space mission still served as a visible sign that so-called scientific-technological revolution would bring about a fundamental transformation of human relations: "Dadurch bekam alles, was bisher geschehen ist, seinen Sinn..." (GH 143). Wolf depicted the ideological significance of Juri Gargarin's successful space mission not only through her characters' jubilation, but by means of frequent textual repetition of the impending "news" and its rendering in capital letters as "DIE NACHRICHT." In *Störfall*, Wolf again employs the techniques of repetition and capitalization, yet in this text "DIE NACHRICHT" refers to the Chernobyl nuclear catastrophe. Through this use of self-citation, Wolf explicitly links the meltdown in Chernobyl to the dissipation of her previously held beliefs. *Störfall*'s narrator disavows the potential of "real existing socialism" to usher in a truly humane society, stating: "Jenes Ziel in einer sehr fernen Zukunft, auf das sich bis jetzt alle Linien zubewegt hatten, war weggesprengt worden, gemeinsam mit dem spaltbaren Material in einem Reaktorgehäuse ist es dabeigewesen zu verglühen" (S 9). While she rejects orthodox Marxism's objective and mechanistic means, she also recognizes that she cannot live without goals. "Wie aber könnte ich gehen ohne Ziel?" (S 30) she asks. She thus echoes Bloch's insistence on a concrete utopia, on the importance of sustaining hope for a better and more humane society.

Wolf's explicit dismissal of the party line did not go unnoticed by orthodox critics. In his review of *Störfall*, Soviet literary critic Alexander Kosorukow continues to predicate the Marxist goal of a humane society on scientific-technological progress, retaining the conviction that the former is inextricably linked to the latter.[35] Without differentiating between means and ends, Kosorukow asserts: "Das Ziel, das da [in *Störfall*] verglühte, ist [...] 'Gerechtigkeit, Gleichheit, Menschlichkeit für alle'" (295). While Kosorukow maintains that Wolf's text fails to make any new goal explicit, he recognizes an implicit goal in the narrative's subtext, namely "die Heilung des BRUDERS—mit der unerläßlichen Unterstützung durch die SCHWESTER—und in der Vervollkommung ihres eigenen Lebens, ihres Denkens, ihres Bewußtseins" (296). Ironically, this new goal is based on the subjective qualities of sisterliness, on "Anteilnahme, Selbstachtung, Vertrauen und Freundlichkeit" (LS 209), precisely those factors that in Kosorukow's view undermine the emancipatory potential of objective historical processes.

Sounding her focus on the cleft between humans and the "truly human," Wolf prefaces *Störfall* with an additional quote: "Das langgesuchte Zwischenglied zwischen dem Tier und dem wahrhaft humanen Menschen sind wir." Similar to the quote by Carl Sagan that precedes it, this statement by animal behaviorist Konrad Lorenz points to the evolutionary distinction between humans and animals. Lorenz negates the equation of humans with the truly humane, yet like Wolf he leaves open the possibility of attaining that goal. Offering further insight into Wolf's recourse to Lorenz, Kuhn notes that Wolf excerpts this passage from the chapter "On the Virtue of Humility" in Lorenz's *On Aggression*, a chapter in which Lorenz criticizes androcentricity (222–223). Like Wolf, Lorenz underlines the importance of self-knowledge and responsibility if we are to work "'against the pathological disintegration of our social structure, and if, armed with atomic weapons, we cannot control our aggressive behavior any more sensibly than any animal species.'"[36]

From the perspective of human evolution, Wolf sheds light on issues of gender. Men's "inability to love," a dominant theme in Wolf's work, finds its most extreme manifestation in the representation of the Lawrence Livermore Laboratory scientists working on the Strategic Defense Initiative (SDI). Wolf casts these young Star Warriors as solely devoted to developing an atomically-driven x-ray laser designed to protect the United States from an eventual nuclear attack (S 70). Upon reading an article about these scientists, she reflects: "Sie kennen, habe ich gelesen, nicht Vater noch Mutter. Nicht Bruder noch Schwester. Nicht Frau noch Kind [...] Was sie kennen, diese halben Kinder mit den hochtrainierten Gehirnen [...] ist ihre Maschine. Ihr lieber geliebter Computer" (S 70). In "Neue Lebensansichten eines Katers," Wolf satirically prefigures the image of the scientist who is unable to love, detached from others yet wholly dedicated to his computer, what Wolf terms an "Ersatzbefriedigung," an "Ersatzleben," an "Ersatz für Liebe" (S 70). In *Störfall*, it seems, reality has indeed become "phantastischer als jedes Phantasieprodukt" (LS 17).

Störfall highlights the importance of subjectivity, responsibility, self-knowledge and intersubjective knowledge for building a communist society. As I noted earlier, the disparate responses of Blasing and Christa T. to the question of what is necessary for humankind's survival reflect the divergence between the officially heralded belief in scientific-technological progress and a concept of progress based on a valuation of personal and intersubjective factors. A similar contrast informs the representation of progress in *Störfall*, as Wolf reveals the "utopia" of the male scientists, "genug Energie für alle und auf ewig" (S 37), as incompatible with the overriding socialist utopia of "Gerechtigkeit, Gleichheit, Menschlichkeit für alle" (S 37). Wolf's narrator incessantly questions whether the means justify the ends and ponders with incredulity the ideological claim, "[d]aß die Wissenschaft, der neue Gott, uns alle Lösungen liefern werde, um die wir ihn angehen würden" (S 37). She explictly rejects the mechanistic view that scientific-technological progress necessarily results in social progress.

Regarding the Star Wars scientists, the narrator ponders: "Was sind sie: legitime Nachfahren des von 'der Wahrheit' besessenen Wissenschaftlers, ein Mythos, der uns allen vertraut ist?" (S 71) Wolf ascribes to these men of science those "masculine" qualities that in her view have led our society to the brink of destruction: greed, endless striving and the inability to love. Through the association of the young scientist Peter Hagelstein with Frankenstein (S 72), she goes so far as to attribute monster-like qualities to them. While Wolf prefaces *Störfall* with a disclaimer that none of the text's characters is identical with a living person, she bases her "fictional" Hagelstein on an actual figure. In addition to the name Peter Hagelstein, other sources document this scientist's career path, eventual resignation from Livermore due to a "crisis of conscience," as well details such as his piano-playing.[37] The actual Hagelstein, we learn, joined the Livermore Lab in the mid-1970s to pursue research in the development of the X-ray laser that later proved central to the Strategic Defense Initiative (SDI) project. Originally, he foresaw humanistic, peaceful applications for the technology he ultimately rejected, such as the imaging of cells to track clues for cancer and other diseases. Yet despite his expressed anti-militarism, Hagelstein eventually succumbed to political pressure and participated in the X-ray laser's application in the defense industry. For Wolf, Hagelstein represents a modern-day Faust driven less by the Faustian thirst for knowledge than by the desire for fame: his goal, she points out, is the Nobel Prize. As Kuhn underscores, this perversion of humanistic goals into destructive political ends reflects the dialectic of enlightenment: "Originally liberating, the concept of reason as thirst for knowledge in the service of the community is perverted into instrumental rationality" (221).

In her modern-day version of *Faust*, Wolf casts Gretchen, Hagelstein's partner Josephine Stein, not as the passive victim of Goethe's drama, but as a political activist who joins demonstrations outside the gates of Livermore and eventually leaves Hagelstein when he decides to colloborate on the SDI project. Rather than let herself be destroyed by Hagelstein-Faust, Josie-Gretchen seeks to redeem him (S 73). For Kuhn, Wolf's reinterpretation of Goethe's *Faust* substantiates Wolf's "belief that women, because they are marginalized and excluded from existing patriarchal structures, can better withstand the pressures to conform and often become a force of resistance and a catalyst for peace" (221). Hagelstein-Faust's pact with a false god no doubt confirms Wolf's skepticism about science and scientists. Nonetheless, she chooses to document the suprisingly optimistic turn that his story takes. Five months after the narrator first reads about Hagelstein, he resigns from his position at Livermore. This resignation, in turn, gives her hope: "Einer hat es geschafft. Nichts ist endgültig" (S 102).

Wolf's representation of the one-dimensional lives of the male Star Warriors stands in stark opposition to her depiction of women's everyday lives. The narrator makes a list of activities and pleasures she believes to be foreign to these men, such as caring for infants, cooking, cleaning, sewing and knitting, singing and telling stories to a sick child (S 38). As in her previous texts, Wolf suggests that the roles into which women have historically been socialized engender epistemologies and ontologies that differ from men's. In *Störfall*, the narrator questions whether "eine Frau, die monatelang ihren Säugling stillt, eine Hemmung [...] verbieten würde, mit Wort und Tat diejenigen zu unterstützen, die ihre Milch vergiften können" (S 27).

Wolf's focus on structural factors in her representation of gender and science resonates with the work of standpoint theorists Nancy Hartsock and Hilary Rose. Like Wolf, Rose locates the roots of society's telos in the sexual division of labor, the division between manual and mental labor and the claims that although theorists both within, e.g. Thomas Kuhn, and outside of science have successfully shown that science is not a neutral enterprise, they continue to be blind to the fact that not only capitalism, but also patriarchy stuctures science.[38] Rose focuses on the exclusion of reproduction, of caring labor, in the production of science, asserting that "a theoretical recognition of caring labor [...] is necessary for any adequate materialist analysis of science and is a crucial precondition for an alternative epistemology..." (275). In her view, "the attitudes dominant in science and technology must be transformed, for their telos is nuclear annihilation" (265). Like Wolf, Rose sees the integration of "hand, brain and heart" as essential for the construction of a new science and a new technology that will help to divert society from its destructive course.

Imploding science and technology into everyday life, the Chernobyl disaster radically transformed the everyday and gave common words ominous new meanings. The narrator can no longer innocently think "[d]as Grün explodiert" (S 9) when she sees the first signs of spring or speak naively of a "strahlender Himmel" or a "Wolke." In addition to the contamination of language, she relates how the radioactive cloud tainted her vegetables, the milk, even the children's sandboxes. Wolf's focus on such quotidian details has come under harsh attack. For example, West German critic Uwe Wittstock bluntly asserts "[n]ichts ist so banal, als daß es nicht doch für mitteilenswert erachtete...."[39] Invalidating the dialectic between history and History at play in Wolf's text, Wittstock asserts that *Störfall* conveys little that factual accounts of the Chernobyl disaster did not state as well or better: "Das meiste hat man im Sommer 1986 knapper und treffender formuliert in Zeitungen und Zeitschriften lesen können," he contends (139). For Wittstock, Wolf's prose since the mid-1970s is predicated on strict gender polarity (139). To be sure, Wolf accentauates that the *masculine* line of thought has led society to the brink of destruction. She asks in her *Kassandra*-lectures, for example, if "'das Denken,' hätten Frauen seit über zweitausend Jahren an ihm mitgedacht, heute ein andres Leben führen würde" (VK 145). Wittstock supports his claim that Wolf holds to a dualistic worldview by recalling former British Prime Minister Margaret Thatcher's dispatchment of troops to the Falkland Islands, a line of reasoning that fails to account for the explicit connections Wolf makes between power and positionality. Citing Thatcher to counter the idea that women are "kinder and gentler by nature, [...] and that they will indeed transform the world when they get the power to do so," Carol Tarvis echoes Wolf's project.[40] Tarvis underscores that "if we instead see women's daily behavior, like men's, as more influenced by the roles they play, the ideologies they believe in, and the work they do than by anything fundamental to their gender, then we need to transform roles, ideologies, and work so that humane qualities can be encouraged in both sexes" (62).

In *Störfall*, Wolf's focus on socialized behavior is further exemplified in the representation of the narrator's one-and-a-half-year-old grandson who, not yet socialized to suppress his emotions, weeps when his sister knocks down the broomstick doll with which he is playing. When her daughter relates this story, the narrator reflects: "Die kleinen Jungs [...]. Was sie mit denen anstellen müssen, um sie hart zu kriegen" (S 24). Her daughter, in turn, responds that the boys' revenge will come later: "Wem man die Liebesfähigkeit austreibe, der müsse dann andere hindern, zu lieben" (S 24).

Men's socialized thirst for (scientific) knowledge is also allegorized in the intertextual reference to the Grimm fairy tale "Brüderchen und Schwesterchen." In that tale, the sister warns the brother not to drink from the stream, yet he fails to obey her and is consequently transformed into a deer. The narrator considers: "Es war ein Verhängnis, daß man entweder verdursten oder sich in ein wildes Tier verwandeln sollte, und ich habe dir, Brüderchen, oft und oft vorgehalten, daß ich, Schwesterchen, doch auch bezähmen konnte; daß ich, obwohl so durstig wie du, doch auch nicht unbedingt trinken mußte" (S 81). This intertext draws attention to the unquestioned and unlimited thirst for knowledge, objectivity and "truth" against which Wolf writes. It also suggests that harmony and brotherliness may ultimately prevail, as in the fairy tale in which brother and sister live happily ever after.

Elsewhere in *Störfall*, Wolf questions the concept of "brotherliness" at the heart of socialist ideology. While she refers to her brother with such terms of endearment as "Bruderherz" and "Brüderchen," the narrator also invokes the perversions of brotherliness in war: "Brüderlich verbunden, brüderlich geeinigt, brüderliche Kampfesgrüße" (S 98). On a more personal level, she recounts her own aggressive behavior in childhood fights with her brother, whose arm she once twisted with such force that it was at risk of remaining stiff. In a self-critical tone, then, she also searches for the "blind spot" within herself. Like Sagan, she underscores that aggression is not only a male trait, but a human one.

In *Störfall*, Wolf attributes the proliferation of nuclear weapons to the instrumentalization of reason in patriarchal society. In her illuminating discussion of supernatural elements in Wolf's prose, Myra Love sheds light on Wolf's exploration of alternatives beyond the "citadel of reason," stressing that Wolf's search for alternatives does not necessarily constitute a negation of reason, of which some critics have accused Wolf, but rather functions as a means of transcending "the fortresslike and prisonlike limitations on the rational mind as ego-mind."[41] In *Störfall*, the narrator transmits psychic energy to her brother during his brain surgery, sending him messages to encourage and comfort him, and to give him strength: she tells him that all will go well (S 10); concentrates on the surgeon's hands (S 13); compels the brother to perservere when she senses that his will to live is dwindling (S 20). The process of psychic healing in which the narrator engages cannot be rationalized in scientific terms; it goes beyond Western culture's accepted concepts of time and space. Both the telepathic transfer of thought from sister to brother and the sister's clairvoyant awareness of the moment at which his surgery successfully ends undermine rational categories of knowledge and understanding. As Love emphasizes, these paranormal events represent "a refusal to accept the limits of perception that our various intellectual frameworks establish as final" (7). Opposing such a reading, Wittstock discredits Wolf's invocation of psychic powers, her so-called "Ausflüge in magische oder okkulte Bereiche" (141). In reference to lines that conjure up the supernatural, Wittstock exclaims: "Solche Zeilen kann man, auch wenn man kein bornierter Verfechter unserer maschinen- und zahlengläubigen Zivilisation ist, nur mit Kopfschütteln lesen" (141). Just as these "non-rational" elements go hand in hand with Wolf's representation of gender, Wittstock's wholesale dismissal of these mystical elements corresponds to his discreditation of Wolf's representation of gender discussed earlier.

In addition to the two examples of the paranormal cited by Love, Wolf weaves into *Störfall* other non-rational elements that substantiate the paranormal's subversive function. While furtively weeding her garden, the narrator speaks to a "Herrn der Brennesseln oder einem für größere Zusammen-hänge zuständigen Naturgeist" (S 32). Moreover, she conveys her awareness of "einen anderen Gott, der die Welt nicht geschaffen hat und sie nicht regiert. Einen fremden, unbekannten Gott" (S 46), a god she becomes aware of by intensely focusing her psychic energy. The mediation of this god takes on a mystical, spiritual form. Regarding this god's felt presence, the narrator contends: "unter einer unerhörten, mich womöglich zerreißenden Anstrengung könnte ich die mich plötzlich umgebende Macht oder Kraft oder Energie oder Potenz (bis zum Schmerzhaften verdichtete Atmosphäre) auch dazu bringen, sich zu materialisieren: ihr Gesicht zu zeigen" (S 46).

Textual references to hand reading represent another intriguing invocation of the supernatural. Wolf's narrator mentions that she is reading a book by Charlotte Wolff, presumably Wolff's *The Human Hand*.[42] In this work, Wolff theorizes the correspondence of personality to the shape and lines of the human hand. In *Störfall*, the narrator recalls the many times she and her brother compared their hands, and recounts: "An Größe sind deine Hände den meinen allmählich nachgekommen, aber ihre Umrisse sind so verschieden geblieben, daß man keinen Fachmann dazu brauchte, uns unsere unterschiedlichen Charaktere und Neigungen aus der Hand zu lesen..." (S 90). Although Wolff devised a sophisticated typology of the human hand based on clinical studies, such means of personality assessment and prediction are generally rejected as "unscientific." The narrator also expresses her fascination with the evolution of the human hand, an additional feature discussed by Wolff. Intrigued by the distinctions between simian and human hands, the narrator contemplates the differences between primates and humans. In *The Story of the Human Hand*, Walter Sorell contends that the development of a third line on the human hand, in contrast to the two lines on the simian hand, "symbolized the clear separation of man's brain function from his emotional reactions, or, in other words, his growing ability to control his emotions through the process of thinking."[43] As we have seen, a critique of the suppression of emotions through reason is a dominant theme in Wolf's oeuvre. In *Störfall*, the narrator expresses her surprise that in Greek the word "A-tom" means the same as "In-dividuum," in Latin "indivisible" ("unspaltbar") (S 35). This etymology underscores her holistic belief in the essential unity of the individual. As in her earlier texts, then, Wolf seeks a synthesis of emotion and reason.

In her essay "Krebs und Gesellschaft," Wolf expresses her interest in the "new thinking" emerging in and about the natural sciences. Characterized by such works as Chopra Keepak's *Quantum Healing*, this thinking is anti-hierarchical and seeks to make connections among the disciplines. Closing her essay, Wolf quotes from *Die heilende Kraft der Imagination. Heilung durch Gedankenkraft*, a text by the American physician Jeanne Achterberg, as follows: "Nun, da sich die schwer faßbaren Geheimnisse des menschlichen Geistes zu enthüllen beginnen, spielt sich vor unseren Augen ein faszienierendes, noch nie dagewesenes Drama ab: Das wissenschaftliche Paradigma wechselt, die Metaphern vermischen sich. Es ist ein guter Augenblick zu leben" (136). In light of the instrumentalization of reason and its consequences, Wolf asserts the importance of a fundamentally different perception of reality: she asserts a feminist epistemology that unifies the mind and the senses.

Notes

1 Wolfgang Emmerich, "'Dialektik der Aufklärung' in der jüngeren DDR-Literatur," *Die Literatur der DDR. 1976–1986. Akten der internationalen Konferenz. Pisa. Mai 1987*, ed. Anna Chiarloni, Gemma Sartori and Fabrizio Cambi (Pisa: Giardini, 1988) 415.

2 Georgina Paul notes that Wolf's initial composition of *Was bleibt* (June/July 1979) is also a reaction to the expulsion of GDR writers following a meeting of the Berlin Writer's Union on June 7, 1979. In May 1979, the SED had levied a fine of 9000 Marks on Stefan Heym for publishing his novel *Colin* in the West without proper authorization from GDR authorities. At that time, the government also modified the penal code, implementing clauses that made such actions subject to criminal prosecution and imprisonment. See: "'Ich meine nichts, was könnte gestrichen werden': Christa Wolf's 'Brief über die Bettine,'" *Christa Wolf in Perspective* (German Monitor 30), ed. Ian Wallace (Amsterdam: Rodopi, 1994) 26–28. See also: Joachim Walter, ed., *Protokoll eines Tribunals. Die Ausschlüsse aus dem DDR-Schriftstellerverband 1979* (Reinbek bei Hamburg: Rowohlt, 1991).

3 Anna K. Kuhn, "'Zweige vom selben Stamm'? Christa Wolf's *Was bleibt, Kein Ort. Nirgends*, and *Sommerstück*," *Christa Wolf in Perspective* 194. As the article's title indicates, Kuhn also compares these two works with *Sommerstück*, a text that Wolf also began in 1979 but only attemped to publish (in revised form) ten years later.

4 See Patricia Herminghouse, "Die Wiederentdeckung der Romantik: Zur Funktion der Dicherfiguren in der neuren DDR-Literatur," *Amsterdamer Beiträge zur neueren Germanistik 11/12*, ed. Jos Hoogeveen and Gerd Labroisse (Amsterdam: Rodopi, 1981) 222–223.

5 Han-Dietrich Dahnke, "Literarische Prozesse in der Periode von 1789 bis 1806," *Weimarer Beiträge* 1 (1971): 63.

6 Han-Dietrich Dahnke, "Zur Stellung und Leistung der deutschen romantishen Literatur," *Weimarer Beiträge* 4 (1978): 5.

7 Claus Träger, "Ursprünge und Stellung der Romantik," *Weimarer Beiträge* 21.2 (1975): 44. Also quoted by Herminghouse, 223.

8 Herbert Marcuse et al., "'Weiblichkeitsbilder.' Gesprächsteilnehmer Herbert Marcuse, Silvia Bovenschen und Marianne Schuller," *Gespräche mit Herbert Marcuse* (Frankfurt a. M.: Suhrkamp, 1978) 65.

9 Robert Sayre and Michael Löwy, "Romanticism as a Feminist Vision: The

Quest for Christa Wolf," *New German Critique* 64 (Winter 1995): 105–134.

10 Hélène Cixous, "The Laugh of the Medusa," *New French Feminisms. An Anthology*, ed. Elaine Marks and Isabelle de Courtivron (New York: Schocken, 1981) 253.

11 Julia Kristeva, "La femme, ce n'est jamais ca," *Tel Quel* 59 (Autumn 1974): 19–24. Quoted in Toril Moi, *Sexual/Textual Politics. Feminist Literary Theory* (London: Routledge, 1988) 164.

12 Julia Kristeva, "A New Type of Intellectual: The Dissident," *The Kristeva Reader*, ed. Toril Moi (New York: Columbia University Press, 1986) 300.

13 Julia Kristeva, "Julia Kristeva," *New French Feminisms,* 167.

14 Chista Wolf, "Laudatio für Thomas Brasch," *Ansprachen* (Darmstadt: Luchterhand, 1988) 64.

15 Jürgen Engler, "Herrschaft der Analogie," *Kritik 79. Rezensionen zur DDR-Literatur*, ed. Eberhard Günter et al. (Halle: Mitteldeutscher Verlag, 1980): 233

16 Anna Kuhn, *Christa Wolf's Utopian Vision: From Marxism to Feminism* (Cambridge: Cambridge University Press, 1988) 147.

17 Although the NATO "double-track" decision to position these weapons was made in December 1979, i.e., followed the writing of *Kein Ort. Nirgends*, its conception and broader implications coincide with Wolf's writing.

18 Richard Gray, "The Dialectic of Enlightenment in Büchner's *Woyzeck*," *German Quarterly* 4.1 (1988): 80.

19 Reprinted in Bernt Engelmann et al., *Es geht, es geht* (München: Goldmann, 1982) 148.

20 Here the title *Kassandra* applies to both the lectures and the narrative, since they were published as a unit in the GDR.

21 See Peter J. Graves, "Christa Wolf's *Kassandra*: The Censoring of the GDR Edition," *Modern Language Review* 81.4 (1986): 944–956. The 6th edition of *Kassandra*, published shortly before the GDR's collapse, included the previously censored passages.

22 Silvia Bovenschen, "Über die Frage: gibt es eine weibliche Ästhetik?" *Ästhetik und Kommunikation* 25 (1976): 60–75.

23 Hiltrud Gnüg, "Gibt es eine weibliche Ästhetik?" *Kürbiskern* 1 (1978): 131.

24 Wilhelm Girnus, "Wer baute das siebentorige Theben?" *Sinn und Form* 34.2 (1983): 439–447.

25 Gebhard Engelmann et al. "Zuschriften an Wilhelm Girnus," *Sinn und Form* 34.5 (1983): 1087–1105.

26 Sigrid Bock et al., "Für und Wider: 'Kassandra' von Christa Wolf," *Weimarer Beiträge* 30.8 (1984): 1353–1381.

27 Wilhelm Girnus, "... Kein 'Wenn und Aber' und das poetische Licht Sapphos. Noch einmal zu Christa Wolf," *Sinn und Form* 34.5 (1983): 1102.

28 Kuhn, *Christa Wolf's Utopian Vision* 198.

29 Quoted in Herrad Schenk, *Frauen kommen ohne Waffen. Feminismus und Pazifismus* (München: Beck, 1983) 89.

30 Schenk, *Frauen kommen ohne Waffen* 168.

31 W. D. McDonald, "Who's Afraid of Wolf's Cassandra—or Cassandra's Wolf?: Male Tradition and Women's Knowledge in *Cassandra*," *The Journal of Narrative Technique* 23.2 (1990): 274.

32 Chista Wolf, "Krebs und Gesellschaft," *Auf dem Weg nach Tabou. Texte 1990–1994* (Köln: Kiepenheuer & Witsch, 1994) 116.

33 Carl Sagan, *The Dragons of Eden* (New York: Random House, 1977) 94.

34 Anna Seghers, "Der japanishe Fischer," *Das Leben im Atomzeitalter: Schriftsteller und Dichter zum Thema unserer Zeit*, ed. Walter Jens (Gräfelfing: Moos & Partner, 1987) 165.

35 Alexander Kosorukow, "Auf der Such nach der Wahrheit. Über Christa Wolf's Erzählung *Störfall*," *Christa Wolf. Ein Arbeitsbuch. Studien—Dokumente—Bibliographie*, ed. Angela Drescher (Berlin/Weimar: Aufbau, 1989) 292–308.

36 Lorenz, quoted in Kuhn, 223.

37 See for example Sharon Begley et al., "A Crisis of Conscience. Objections to Star Wars," *Newsweek* (22 September 1986): 88.

38 Hilary Rose, "Hand, Brain, and Heart: A Feminist Epistemology for the Natural Sciences," *Sex and Scientific Inquiry*, ed. Sandra Harding and Jean F. O'Barr (Chicago: University of Chicago Press, 1987) 273.

39 Uwe Wittstock, Von der Stalinallee zum Prenzlauer Berg. Wege der DDR-Literatur 1949–1989 (München: Piper, 1989) 138.

40 Carol Tarvis, *The Mismeasure of Woman* (New York: Simon and Schuster, 1992) 62.

41 Myra Love, "'A Little Susceptible to the Supernatural?': On Christa Wolf," *Women in German Yearbook 7* (1991) 9.

42 In addition to her novel *Hindsight*, from which Wolf quotes in *Störfall*, pg. 92, Wolff also published extensively on hand reading.

43 Walter Sorell, *The Story of the Human Hand* (Indianapolis: Bobb-Merrill Co., 1967) 78.

CHAPTER SEVEN

An Insider's View on Gender and Science:
Helga Königsdorf's *Respektloser Umgang*
and *Ungelegener Befund*

> Denn was ist Geschichte denn, wenn
> nicht ein sich ständig korrigierender
> Irrweg.
>
> Helga Königsdorf, 1990

Unlike Christa Wolf, who studied German literature and began publishing literary texts in the early 1960s, Helga Königsdorf, born in 1936, was trained as a physicist and mathematician. After twenty years working as a professor of mathematics at the *Akademie der Wissenschaften*, Königsdorf published her first literary work, a collection of short stories entitled *Meine ungehörigen Träume* (1978). Her pre-*Wende* publications include additional short story collections, *Der Lauf der Dinge* (1982), *Lichtverhältnisse* (1988) and *Ein sehr exakter Schein. Satiren und Geschichten aus dem Gebiet der Wissenschaft* (1990), as well as two longer narratives, *Respektloser Umgang* (1986) and *Ungelegener Befund* (1989).[1] Even after making a name for herself as a fiction writer—she was the recipient of the 1985 Heinrich Mann Prize—Königsdorf continued her work as a mathematician. From a position within the scientific establishment, she offers an "insider's" perspective on the interplay of gender and science.

As highlighted in the first chapter, Königsdorf was among those GDR writers who responded to the immanent collapse of their country by articulating their firm belief that the GDR could still become a truly socialist society. At a meeting between party members and the Central Committee on November 8, 1989, one day before the opening of the Wall, Königsdorf argued that in placing the consolidation and fortification of power above humanistic values, the GDR's "feudalistic" variant of socialism constituted a misuse of the term socialism.[2] In her literary texts, Königsdorf asserts the need for a fundamental change in GDR society, calls attention to the regimentation of everyday life and, like Wolf, bases social change on humanistic values and individual responsibility.

In her early interviews, Königsdorf explains why she turned to writing fiction after a long career as an internationally acclaimed mathematician. She attributes this decision in part to the nature of the discipline of mathematics: "Mathematik ist eine Wissenschaft, die sehr viel rationale Disziplin erfordert, in der man sich also reduzieren muß und zugleich allgemeine Probleme des Lebens auf die Dauer doch stärker ausklammert. Vielleicht war es dieses Gefühl, darüber einige Dinge vernachlässigt zu haben, das mich wieder zum Schreiben brachte."[3] While noting that mathematics demands creativity, she highlights how it demands mental processes that exclude subjective concerns and lead to "einer sehr starken Einengung der Persönlichkeit" (10). To address the problems and issues with which she grappled, Königsdorf turned to literature.

At the X. Writers' Congress in 1987, Königsdorf addressed literature's function at a time of global threat. In light of the shortage of natural resources, irreversible environmental degradation and the massive destructive potential of the world's nuclear arsenal, she maintains: "Die Gattung Mensch ist dabei, die Grundlagen ihrer Existenz zu erschüttern."[4] This awareness echoes Wolf's insistence that in the scientific age literature's primary function must be to strengthen the self and foster the courage to say "I." Speaking of literature's new "Cassandra function," Königsdorf is optimistic that the warnings of the new Cassandra will not fall on deaf ears, that people will heed Cassandra's warnings.

Königsdorf relates the difficulty of saying "I" to an authoritarian ideology that rewards conformity and subordination and encourages individuals to define themselves through institutions, organizations or their country. Recognizing the tendency towards complacency in the GDR, she contends: "Aber wir, die wir scheinbar die Dialektik mit der Muttermilch eingeflößt bekommen haben, vergessen das Dialektische nur allzugern" (58). In her view, blind faith in objective historical processes has exacerbated the lack of engagement and contributed to the precarious state of humankind. "Unsere Welt braucht das 'Ich' bei Strafe des Untergangs," Königsdorf warns (58–59). Rather than look to objective forces to work against society's (self-)destruction, she focuses on the need for personal engagement and sense of moral responsibility. The pre-*Wende* narratives *Respektloser Umgang* (1986) and *Ungelegener Befund* (1989) develop these themes and reflect the tense global political climate.

Through sarcasm, irony, dreams and fantasy, Königsdorf short stories highlight gender issues and illuminate the rationalistic thought characteristic of the scientific establishment. The stories revolve around two major themes: gender relations and the rituals and behaviors of the scientific realm. For example, the female protagonists in *Meine ungehörigen Träume* undertake radical measures in their personal struggles for fulfillment and their efforts to escape the stiflingly and ritualized routines of their daily lives. In recognition of her protagonists' unorthodox attempts at emancipation, Königsdorf closes the volume with an authorial note exclaiming: "[I]ch [...] sehe meinem unvermeindlichen Schicksal, nach Erscheinen dieser Geschichten ein unbemanntes Dasein fristen zu müssen, gefaßt ins Auge" (MT 133). In one of her best-known stories from that volume, "Bolero," the highly educated, lonely and bored female protagonist laconically describes her affair with a man she met at an academic lecture. She repeatedly mentions his ordinariness, claiming "es war nichts, aber auch gar nichts Besonderes an ihn" (MT 8). Only through his diligent note taking at the tedious and predictable lecture did he catch her eye.

While the affair remains both sexually and emotionally unsatisfying, the man pleases only himself and faithfully returns to his family after their rendezvous, she willing plays by his rules. Available at his every beck and call, she prepares exotic dishes, dresses seductively, pampers him endlessly and, despite her reservations and the ensuing nausea, heeds his demand that she use oral contraceptives. Noting the woman's willing subordination, Eva Kaufmann is right to contend: "Königsdorfs Darstellung schließt aus, die Frau lediglich als Opfer zu sehen."[5] At the narrative's close, following an evening in which the woman feels particularly close to her lover, she shoves him off the balcony of her twelfth floor apartment, tossing his shoes and jacket after him. She then proceeds with her regular routine: she cleans the apartment, takes a bath and listens to Ravel's "Bolero" as they often had together. The murder, then, fails to disrupt the woman's daily routine; it has no emotional impact. The only concern she expresses is "wie diejenigen, die seinen Nachruf verfassen, die Tatsache, daß er ohne Schuhe Selbstmord beging, damit in Einklang bringen, daß er der korrekteste Mensch war, den sie oder irgend jemand anders kannten" (MT 14).

A similar attempt to escape a stultifying routine characterizes the narrative "Der unangemessene Aufstand des Zahlographen Karl-Egon Kuller" from the collection *Ein sehr exakter Schein*. Kuller, a highly respected and internationally acclaimed mathematician, seeks to alter the heretofore all too predictable and orderly course of his life: "Zum erstenmal in seinem Leben würde er den Erwartungen, die man in ihn setzte, nicht entsprechen" (ES 71). Unlike the first-person narrator of "Bolero," Kuller had long suppressed his desire to break free from societal restrictions: "Es kam ihm vor, als hätte er im Laufe seines Lebens eine Unmenge Sprengstoff akkumuliert, der nun zur Explosion drängte" (ES 72). Then, at a major scientific conference he presents an utterly absurd and unfounded theory about "pyromantische Astralistik." Yet he follows the expected protocol: his lecture title sounds scientific and significant; he dutifully thanks those who aided him with this project; he attaches an impressive bibliography. His goal in presenting this preposterous theory is described as follows: "Er wollte mit diesen Phantaprojekoren die verlogene Konstruktion seines Lebens niederreißen. Er wußte nicht, wie es danach weitergehen würde. Auf jeden Fall ganz anders, und das war gut" (ES 83). Although his theory is completely unfounded, absurd, and supported by meaningless drawings and figures, the audience reacts as usual. Even the question session proceeds smoothly. In fact, rather than the rebuke he expected, Kuller receives praise and is even encouraged to pursue his fascinating line of inquiry. His attempt to disrupt the routine thus fails completely. Utterly disillusioned after the session, he suffers a fatal heart attack. In this and other short stories set in the scientific realm, Königsdorf successfully unmasks the world of science as "Ein sehr exakter Schein": she reveals that which reputes to be scientific and accountable as governed by blind adherence to ritual, protocol and the illusion of objectivity.

Respektloser Umgang

Like *Störfall*, Königsdorf's *Respektloser Umgang* appeared in the wake of the 1986 Chernobyl disaster. Both texts interweave the personal and political and bring subjective concerns and ethical and moral questions to bear on global issues. Moreover, both narratives are documentary in nature, interspersing fictionalized passages with excepts and summaries of political accounts, historical documents and biographical information. Both texts are also highly autobiographical and narrated in the first person. Like her narrator, Königsdorf is a successful scientist, suffers from Parkinson's disease and has two children: at the time she wrote the novel, Königsdorf's son was an aspiring physicist, her daughter a professional dancer. Although Königsdorf was born in 1936 and her narrator in 1938, this age difference can be interpreted as an attempt to rationalize the narrator's inexplicable encounters with the atomic physicist Lise Meitner. As if a matter of fate, the narrator's date of birth coincides with the date that Meitner, an Austrian Jew, was forced into exile.

Like Wolf and Maron, Königsdorf employs "non-rational" elements to illuminate the limiting strictures of the "citadel of reason." At times going beyond conventional parameters of time and space, Königsdorf calls these boundaries into question and disrupts rational discourse. In *Respektloser Umgang*, it becomes increasingly difficult for the narrator (and the reader) to distinguish fantasy and reality, illusion and fact. At first, the narrator rationalizes the appearance of Lise Meitner, who had been dead nearly twenty years, as a sign of her own illness, "ein Krankheitszeichen" (RU 8), attributing her mental confusion to the green pills she takes to control the symptoms of her chronic illness (RU 9). Meitner's presence thus appears to be a product of the narrator's drug-induced hallucinations. Critics have generally accepted this justification and probed neither the changing nature of Meitner's presence in the text nor the broader implications of Königsdorf's use of the fantastic.

When Meitner first appears, the narrator states with conviction that she will be able to separate reality from illusion. Yet from the beginning Meitner insists on her independence and autonomy: she denies that she is a mere by-product of the narrator's hallucinations and demands to be recognized as an equal. In contrast to the narrator, Meitner justifies her meeting with the narrator as an unlikely yet possible "Kollision zweier Traumwelten, die den Gesetzen von Raum und Zeit nicht unterworfen seien" (RU 10). The narrator counters this hypothesis with the rational statement that one can only dream about the past, not about the future, and that Meitner can therefore only be a product of her (the narrator's) dream. In this way, she denies Meitner's existence outside her hallucinations. Eventually, however, Meitner's appearances become independent from the narrator's imagination. Initially, Meitner appears in the narrator's room, and in her imagination, only to disappear again as the hallucination ends. Yet as the narrative progresses, Meitner exits the room through the door (RU 35). She also arrives on her own accord at the Institute where the narrator is employed (RU 38). For the narrator, these occurrences reveal that she is no longer able to distinguish the border between hallucination and reality. Yet she concludes, "Dann kann doch nur die Grenze falsch gesetzt sein" (RU 39).

The boundaries between fiction and reality, between the inexplicable and that which the narrator can explain in terms of the natural laws of time, space and matter, thus become fluid. Further on, the narrator herself travels back in time to Meitner's days at the Kaiser-Wilhelm-Institut. Elsewhere, when Meitner reappears at the Institute in the present, the narrator wonders how to introduce Meitner to her colleagues. These considerations attest to Meitner's independent existence and reveal that the narrator comes to consider Meitner as more than a simple by-product of her hallucinations. At another point, the narrator travels back in time to October 1933 and claims that she herself is Lise Meitner: "Ich bin Lise Meitner. Es ist wie in meinen Träumen, in denen ich immer mehr Beobachter werde" (RU 71), she contends. Moreover, the young assistants at the Institute see a figure fitting Meitner's description leave the room, an occurrence that further supports Meitner's actual and independent existence in the narrator's reality (RU 107). Acting on her own volition, Meitner also announces that she will soon depart, that she will no longer appear.

Meitner's diverse manifestations induce the narrator to reconsider her explanation for her dialogues with the dead. She comes to justify Meitner's appearances as follows: "Sie gleichen keinenfalls den Ausgeburten eines psychotischen Gehirns. War meine Erklärung also voreilig. Verbirgt sich etwas ganz andres dahinter" (RU 80). Although she rescinds her initial, rational explanations, she is slow to divulge the hidden meaning of Meitner's presence.

In his classic study *The Fantastic* (1970), Tzvetan Todorov explains the ambiguity that lies at the heart of the fantastic:

In a world which is indeed our world, the one we know, [...] there occurs an event which cannot be explained by the laws of this same familiar world. The person who experiences the event must opt for one of two possible solutions: either he is the victim of an illusion of the senses, of a product of the imagination—and laws of the world remain what they are; or else the event has indeed taken place, it is an integral part of reality—but then this reality is controlled by laws unknown to us.[6]

The fantastic, Todorov asserts, resides in this uncertainty: "The fantastic is the hesitation experienced by a person who knows only the laws of nature, confronting an apparently supernatural event" (25). We either adapt the fantastic occurrence to our reality or we accept a change in our reality. In this way, the fantastic can transcend the laws of nature as we know them.

A mathematician, the narrator holds firmly to the laws of nature, the laws of objective reality. The opening scene of *Respektloser Umgang* underscores the clarity offered by mathematical formulae and constructions, yet also links the narrator's breakdowns to this pursuit. Meitner first appears precisely when the narrator's curiosity for the truth that lies beyond mathematical formulae, for the transgression of the limits set by its rational thought structures, is aroused: "Die Verlockung des verbotenen Zimmers. Habe ich das Verbot nicht immer als Zumutung empfunden" (RU 8), the narrator asks.

Todorov lays out three conditions for the genre of the fantastic, all of which are met by Königsdorf's text (33). First, the reader must consider the world of the text a "real" world and hesitate between explanations of occurrences in natural and supernatural terms. Secondly, the reader's hesitation must also be experienced by one of the literary characters; most commonly this character is a first-person narrator. Thirdly, the reader must reject allegorical and "poetic" readings of the text, that is s/he must be able to relate the fantastic occurrence to his/her real world experience. Todorov mentions drug-induced madness as one tool of the fantastic, and underscores that the character often interprets the fantastic event ambiguously: "Sometimes he too believes in his own madness, but never to the point of certainty" (37). This madness, Todorov adds, may also be considered a "higher reason" (40).

As in *Störfall*, the invocation of the supernatural transcends the limiting strictures of reason and supports the critique of abstract rationality. Königsdorf's Lise Meitner similarly asserts:

> Die Rettung der Menschheit kann nur noch aus dem Bereich der Überwelt kommen. [...] zwischen Himmel und Erde läge so manches. Die Welt der Vorstellungen, Erinnerungen, Bilder, Träume, Erfahrungen. Von Generation zu Generation überliefert. Die Welt der unendlichen Möglichkeiten neben dieser einen Realität. Die Welt der Mythen und Märchen. (RU 48)

Both Wolf and Königsdorf situate their critiques of science and technology within a context of global nuclear threat. Moreover, they examine women's roles and positions in relation to the scientific establishment and patriarchal structures. In *Störfall*, Wolf focuses on the one-dimensional lives of the Star Warriors at Lawrence Livermore Laboratory. For Wolf, the "masculine qualities" these scientists embody, their abstract rationality, greed and endless striving, have brought society to the brink of destruction. *Respektloser Umgang* centers on the scientists who discovered the possibility of splitting the uranium atom, a discovery which set the stage for the building of the atomic bomb. Königsdorf's focus is not on the men of science, but on Lise Meitner (1878–

1968), an atomic physicist instrumental in the discovery of nuclear fission. With the exception of "Selbstversuch," Wolf relegates scientific activity and categories of thought almost exclusively to men. Representing a woman in science, Königsdorf offers a differentiated perspective on the nexus of women and science. Through the figure of Lise Meitner, she accentuates the historical presence of women in science and the barriers these women confronted. She also offers further insight into women's marginalization and vision. Moreover, she calls into question women's unified position by depicting a woman oppressed on account of her gender and her race.

While she illuminates the historic and current abuses of science and questions current notions of "progress," Königsdorf also points to science's positive applications. Like Wolf, she employs personal illness as a metaphor for the "illness" of humankind. In *Störfall*, the nuclear reactor breakdown in Chernobyl and the "breakdown" resulting from the brother's brain tumor symbolize science's potential both to jeopardize and to prolong human life. Although medical science ultimately saves the brother, one can also attribute his recovery to the non-scientific means the sister employs to strengthen the brother's will to live.

In *Respektloser Umgang*, the narrator's illness goes unnamed, though her dependence on dopamine and progressive debilitation lead the reader to assume that, like Königsdorf, she suffers from Parkinson's disease. The narrator expresses her inability to accept her terminal illness in both personal and global terms: "Es kann doch nicht einfach so zu Ende gehen. Und ehe wir es begreifen, sind wir schon tot. Im Kleinen wie im Großen. Wir haben keinerlei Erfahrung mit Bedrohung, die der ganzen Menschheit gilt" (RU 52). She relates her tendency to deny her fate to the broader tendency to deny the apocalyptic prognoses for the future: "Man redet sich das Ganze von der Seele und ist erleichtert. Gefährlich erleichtert. Aber wirklich nur für einen Moment. Im Großen wie im Kleinen" (RU 61). The fear engendered by illness further entwines the personal and the political: "Das erste Krankheitszeichen war die Angst" (RU 70), the narrator contends. While the fear of death compels her to address vital questions, her fear turns to despair in the face of the potential devastation wrought by scientific-technological developments. Her diminished hope is evident in her recognition: "Und was noch? Ist nicht Neurüstung, Umrüstung, Nachrüstung längst profitträchtiger als ein Krieg? [...] Inzwischen arbeitet man an hochwirksamen, rassenspezifischen Giften. Gaskammern erübrigen sich in der Zukunft. Was Faschismus einst anrichten konnte, war ein Klacks" (RU 70). In her view this is the course of society "[w]enn Ökonomie alles dirigiert" (RU 70). While Horkheimer and Adorno see instrumental reason as culminating in fascism, Königsdorf suggests the chilling possibility that the sins of fascism may only be a smidgen in the history of humankind. Like the authors of *Dialektik der Aufklärung*, she writes at a time when the future appears dismal. The sense that time is running out incites the narrator's sense of personal responsibility. "Braucht es also eine Störung des chemischen Gleichgewichts im Hirnstamm, um die Frage nach einem eigenen, inneren Auftrag zu stellen?" she ponders (RU 52). Her illness leads her to set her own stake in humankind's survival.

Despite her pessimism, the narrator unambiguously links scientific progress to her survival: "Gäbe es die Institution Wissenschaft nicht, wäre ich schon tot" (RU 69), she asserts. The positive advances of scientific-technological progress are further reflected in the advice she would give her son, an aspiring physicist: "Keinesfalls werde ich ihm sagen: Seit Hiroshima und Nagasaki verbietet sich Physik. Das wäre nichts als dumme Maschinenstürmerei" (RU 92). The narrator recognizes that the earth's limited resources increase the need for scientific research: "Gefährlich ist der Mythos, wir könnten mit ihrer Hilfe getrost jede Suppe auslöfeln, die wir uns einbrocken. Das Warten auf Wunder. Aber gefährlicher ist der Glaube, wir kämen ohne neue Kenntnis aus" (RU 93). Underscoring the importance of taking into account personal factors and consequences, she counters the notion of science's neutrality, of "science for science's sake" which, at least since the atomic bomb, has proven meaningless. Further contemplating the advice she will give her son, she reflects:

> Von der Würde des Menschen werde ich sprechen, die nicht aus naturwissenschaftlichen Kalkulationen folgt. Von der Verantwortung, die er übernehmen muß, weil es zwischen Verantwortung und Mitschuld in Zukunft nichts mehr gibt. Mitschuld am Mißbrauch von Erkenntnis. Mitschuld am Abstempeln zu Untermenschen. Zu Objekten. Zu Megatoten. (RU 94)

The narrator insists that silence and lack of engagement signify compliance. Merging past, present and future, Königsdorf illuminates the continuity between behavior patterns and thought structures. Relating the process of objectification to racism, fascism and atomic warfare, she warns against the lack of mediation between subject and object. In her *Kassandra*-lectures, Wolf likewise asks: "Das Objektmachen: Ist das nicht die Hauptquelle der Gewalt" (VK 114).

In her article "Gender and Science," Evelyn Fox Keller explores the relationship between science and feminism in light of the growing feminist critique of science. Writing as a feminist in science, Fox Keller emphasizes the dangers of the postmodern tendency to view science purely as a social product, stating that "science then dissolves into ideology and objectivity loses all intrinsic meaning."[7] What results is a complete cultural relativism that undermines science's potentially emancipatory function. Feminists, Fox Keller asserts, should not reject rationality and objectivity as masculine, since such a rejection leaves women outside the political realm and further perpetuates the opposition between male and female, objectivity and subjectivity. Like Wolf,

Königsdorf and Maron, she emphasizes: "The ideological ingredients of particular concern to feminists are found where objectivity is linked with autonomy and masculinity, and in turn, the goals of science with power and domination" (238).

Königsdorf underscores the growing cleft between scientific progress and humane values. In her theses on "Das Prinzip Menschenwürde" (1989) she states: "Im Erkenntnisrausch und Allmachtsdenken des wissenschaftlich-technischen Zeitalters ist das Nachdenken über Werte und Normen in den Hintergrund getreten. Alles scheint im Prinzip machbar."[8] Criticizing notions of science's omnipotence prevalent in the GDR, Königsdorf condemns the mentality fostered by the Cold War, namely "[e]rst einholen, dann über Risiken nachdenken" (8). On account of the immeasurable risks associated with today's technologies, she underscores: "Weder bedingungslose Fortschrittsgläubigkeit noch Handeln um einer utopischen Zukunft willen sind länger akzeptabel" (6). Not only must individuals take responsibility for the present and for the future, we must redefine our notions of progress: "Mit der Frage, was ist Fortschritt, wird sich die Frage, welche Wissenschaft brauchen wir, neu stellen" (6). In Königsdorf's view, a respect for human dignity must inform science. This position is evident in the categorical imperative she formulates as a guide for individual actions and, more specifically, for the actions of scientists: "*Prinzip Menschenwürde*: Handle so und trage Sorge, daß so gehandelt wird, daß die Wirkungen dieser Handlungen für gegenwärtiges und künftiges menschliches Leben, beträfen sie dich selbst, mit deiner Würde vereinbar wären" (7).

In *Respektloser Umgang*, the narrator's dialogues with Lise Meitner shed light on the the moral responsibility and accountability of scientists. As Joseph Pischel points out: "So wird Wissenschaft nicht zwischen Vergötzung und Verdammung dämonisiert, sondern als Ergebnis der Arbeit wie auch des gesellschaftlichen Versagens bestimmter Menschen mit ihrer materiellen und ideellen Motiven in bestimmten gesellschaftlichen Strukturen erfahrbar."[9] This subjective representation further deconstructs the myth that science is objective and "sacred." Similarly underscoring subjectivity and the individual, Sandra Harding contends in *The Science Question in Feminism*:

> If we are not willing to try to see the favored intellectual structures and practices of science as cultural artifacts rather than as sacred commandments handed down to humanity at the birth of modern science, then it will be hard to understand how [...] the masculine identities and behaviors or individual scientists have left their marks on the problematics, concepts, theories, methods, interpretations, ethics, meanings and goals of science.[10]

Like Harding, Königsdorf constructs science as a social product whose development and use is tied to specific individual and political goals. Königsdorf's narrator rejects all notions of science as "etwas Abstraktes. Nicht gebunden an ihre Träger" (RU 26). In the present age, she can no longer herald science as the fictionalized Meitner does in her claim: "Die Wissenschaft erzieht den Menschen zum wunschlosen Streben nach Wahrheit und Objektivität, sie lehrt den Menschen, Tatsachen anzuerkennen" (RU 111).

Both Königsdorf and Wolf draw on the lives of scientists to analyze the course of Western civilization and as a means to examine the relationship of the individual and society. In "Prinzip Menschenwürde," Königsdorf highlights this dialectic and maintains: "Verantwortliches Handeln kann sich nur als Prozeß im ständigen Wechselspiel zwischen politischen Strukturen und Wissen um Wertgefühlen des Einzelnen herausbilden" (10). In *Respektloser Umgang*, she breaks with traditional objective "histories." Her goal is not to construct a grand narrative about Lise Meitner and thereby to add the account of a great woman to the history of great men. Instead, she critiques this mode of historical representation. Regarding the official historiography of the GDR, the narrator laments: "Geschichte blieb ein von Heldensagen umrankter ökonomischer Pro- zeß, der mit mir wenig zu tun hatte" (RU 21). Rather than judge Meitner by traditional male standards of objectively definable success, Königsdorf approaches her from the standpoint of women's lives and relates personal concerns and sacrifices. Like Wolf's engagement with the figure of Cassandra, Königsdorf views Meitner subjectively, "from below."

By centering on an historical figure, *Respektloser Umgang* opens up a dialogue between women in science past (Lise Meitner) and present (the narrator). During a discussion following a reading by Königsdorf, critic Doris Berger asked the author why she chose Meitner as her subject. Berger postulates that Königsdorf's choice perhaps stemmed from a desire to represent a female predecessor in science, or constituted a response to the negative images of male scientists in texts of other GDR women writers such as Christa Wolf and Irmtraud Morgner. Berger implies that to represent a female atomic physicist would be anathema to Wolf and Morgner, "wo es immer heißt, die Männer haben ja die ganze schädliche Technik entwickelt, haben das ganze Selbstmord- programm entwickelt und wir [Frauen] sind auf der anderen Seite, haben nichts damit zu tun."[11] Though Berger's hypothesis seems plausible, Königsdorf's response to Berger reveals that her inspiration lies elsewhere: "Diese Interpretation ist sehr schön," she asserts, "[d]as ist aber ganz sicher bei meinem Schreibvorgang nicht so gewesen" (452). Lise Meitner, Königsdorf explains, was there first. In the early 1980s, Königsdorf was contracted to write a screenplay for a film on Meitner, yet found it difficult to express her current concerns in the form of the screenplay. This led her to turn to the genre of prose. Königsdorf goes on to relate what interested and irritated her in the historical depiction of Meitner:

Was mich ein bißchen gereizt hat, sind Darstellungen, wo es heißt, daß sie als Frau schlecht weggekommen ist. Ich glaube, dem wollte ich entgegentreten, da Lise Meitner eine stolze Person war. [...] Aus dem historischen Material geht hervor, daß diese Frau nicht nur gequält wurde, sondern durchaus ihren eigenen Willen hatte. Natürlich ist sie durch die Verhältnisse gebeutelt worden. Trotzdem war sie eine selbstbewußte und stolze Frau, mit der die Männer in ihrer Umgebung als ihre Kollegen ihre Mühe hatten. (452)

In her representation of Meitner not only as a victim of historical circumstances, but as a proud, successful and strong woman, Königsdorf goes further than Wolf in figuring women as historical subjects. This difference is illuminated in the divergent responses of Wolf and Königsdorf to the question of "feminine writing."

Confronted with Wolf's position on the question of a "feminine aesthetic" articulated in her *Kassandra*-lectures, namely that women are objects of history, second-degree objects of men who likewise lack autonomy, Königsdorf's narrator expresses skepticism. She is unwilling to accept Wolf's line of reasoning. Despite its apparent logic, she sees it as an affront against her female pride: "Wenn das wirklich so ist, möchte ich meinem weiblichen Dasein abschwören, denn es verletzt meinen Stolz. Da empfinde ich nicht einmal mehr Solidarität" (RU 54). Königsdorf acknowledges women's historical subordination and victimization, yet underlines the complexity of the process of objectification:

Bei diesem Geschehen gibt es immer zwei Seiten. Die eine, die den Angriff, das Objektemachen, als Machtmittel inszeniert, und die andere, die als Subjekt ihre Automomie bewahrt. Oder auch nicht. Sind die Mechnanismen tatsächlich so effektiv, daß es kein Entrinnen gibt? Lise Meitner etwa? [...] Und ich selbst? (RU 54)

This speculation about the impossibility of escaping the process of objectification evinces that Königsdorf does not completely disavow Wolf's position. Yet in her representation of Meitner, Königsdorf focuses less on the obstacles Meitner faced as a woman (in science) than on how Meitner could have or did resist her subordination as a woman and as a Jew. Moreover, she questions the documented view that Meitner intentionally deterred the discovery of atomic fission in order to keep its potential application from the Nazis.

In her focus on female complicity, Königsdorf echoes the concept of *Mittäterschaft* developed in the mid-1980s by feminist sociologist Christina Thürmer-Rohr. Thürmer-Rohr defines female complicity as follows: "Mittäter-schaft heißt Mit-dem-Täter: Loyalität mit dem Mann und seiner Gesellschaft,

Zustimmung zu seiner Herrschaft, auch noch in ihren abgetakelten Formen und in den Formen des Attentats auf alles, was tatsächlich oder vorübergehend zum Untertan gemacht werden kann."[12] Thürmer-Rohr underlines the importance of exploring women's involvement in societal processes despite the fact that women have largely been denied access to political power and have not participated directly in the production of knowledge or of the means of destruction. To examine how women have functioned and continue to function within patriarchy, the notion of woman as victim must be dismantled.

The narrator deals with Meitner and herself irreverently, without respect—hence the title *Respektloser Umgang*. The narrator's dialogues with Meitner serve as a vehicle for her to examine her own life, the lives of other scientists as well as of her parents and grandparents. Meitner therefore functions less as a role model, as Berger would like to believe, but as a "Bezugspunkt" (RU 107). As a point of reference, she allows the narrator to set herself in relation to the past and to gain a sense of continuity. This function comes to the fore in the trial scene in which both Meitner and the narrator's father are figured as judges. Trapped in a cabinet of mirrors, the narrator herself is forced to answer the questions she so incessantly asks both her father and Meitner. She thereby implicates herself as well:

> Wieviel kleinlicher Ehrgeiz und wieviel Geltungssucht bestimmen mein Leben. Habe ich nicht Menschen benutzt und weggeworfen, wie es mir gut dünkte! Wenn hier von Objektemachen die Rede ist: Ich war hervorragend auf dieser Strecke! Meinmann. Meinsohn. Meinmitarbeiter. [...] Ging es mir wirklich jemals um den Zustand der Welt, oder immer nur um mich? (RU 89)

In placing neither the narrator nor Meitner outside the process of objectification, Königsdorf dismantles traditional oppositions between inside and outside, perpetrators and victims.

In her theory of female complicity, Thürmer-Rohr underscores the negative consequences of perceiving women exclusively as objects or victims of history:

> Alle Schwächen und Insuffizienzen, alle Gedankenlosigkeit und Beschränktheiten, alle Ohnmacht sind wir gewohnt, als *Resultate* der Verhältnisse zu begreifen, die Frauen zwingen, so zu sein, wie sie sind: Frauen also Objekte der Geschichte, Frauen als Knetmasse, mit der man alles machen konnte, was Männern paßte.[13]

Without denying women's objectification and the necessity of bringing its many forms to light, Thürmer-Rohr stresses that an understanding of women as passive contributes to their powerlessness and in effect functions as a means of further discrimination. Shifting discussion away from women's oppression can be seen as detracting from the feminist cause, yet to recognize that women have contributed to or been complicit in their oppression is also to recognize that they can contribute to their emancipation. The unique contribution of feminist research, she argues, "ergibt sich nicht allein aus dem Bewußtsein und der Empörung des *Opfers* Frau, das seine *Ausgrenzug* aus der patriarchalischen Kultur und aus dem 'Subjekt' der Geschichte erkennt, sondern ebenso aus dem Bewußtsein der *Mittäterin* Frau, die von ihrem *Einschluß*, ihrer *Eingrenzung* in diese gleiche Kultur weiß" (146). In approaching Meitner, the narrator illuminates Meitner's objectification as a woman within patriarchal society, in the realm of science, and as a Jew in Nazi Germany. While she remarks that Meitner was "doppelt gedemütigt. Als Jüdin. Und als Frau" (RU 44), she also examines the opportunities Meitner possibly had to resist objectification.

A look at how biographers, contemporaries and Königsdorf document Meitner's life provides further insight into issues of gender and science. The composite picture of Meitner that emerges illuminates many aspects of the feminist empiricist approach identified by historian Londa Schiebinger in her discussion of the history of women in science.[14] One goal of feminist empiricism is to research and recuperate women's past achievements in science and thereby to write female scientists into history. Evelyn Fox Keller's book *A Feeling for the Organism* exemplifies this type of endeavor. Keller's work centers on the life of Barbara McClintock, a geneticist whose research on the mechanisms of genetic transposition in corn went unrecognized until parallel discoveries were made by men decades later. Only in 1983, forty years after her groundbreaking finding, was McClintock awarded the Nobel Prize. A second empiricist approach seeks to unveil the social biases that have historically prevented women from pursuing careers in science by focusing on women's limited access to education and employment in that discipline. In Germany, for example, women were granted permission to study at the university in 1908; only in 1920 did they gain the right to earn a doctorate degree and to teach at the university. Although this type of legal discrimination ended, discrimination continues in other forms: women still receive little recognition, earn less than men in equal positions, remain in the lower ranks of employment and are generally not socialized to achieve in science.

Tracing the life of Lise Meitner, Königsdorf highlights such issues. Parental constraint and social norms regarding "appropriate" fields of study for women kept Meitner from immediately pursuing her strong interest in physics. Although she expressed an early desire to study physics, her father insisted she first pass the state exam in French so, if the need arose, she would be able to support herself as a teacher. Only after she successfully passed this exam was she permitted to prepare for the entrance exam for physics at the University of Vienna. She received her doctorate there in 1905, the second woman at that institution to receive this degree in this discipline.

In 1907, Meitner went to Berlin to conduct postdoctoral research. There she attended lectures by Max Planck, through whom she gained access to the Berlin circle of physicists. Planck's own comments pertaining to women's position in science expose the dominant attitudes at that time—and one must consider that in his time Planck was sure to have been considered progressive. Planck's remarks reflect an additional approach to gender and science noted by Schiebinger, namely how gender bias in the biological sciences has misdefined and misrepresented women (27). Feminist research seeks to debunk claims of women's "natural" inability to do science, which have historically been upheld by purportedly scientific arguments. Theories of women's natural inferiority and weakness date back to Aristotle, and continue today in studies which, based on hormone research, brain lateralization and sociobiology, point to women's "different," i.e., inferior nature. The distinct social and political agendas of such studies repudiate the supposed neutrality of science. In *Respektloser Umgang*, the narrator quotes an excerpt from a text by Planck, in which he refers to the possibility of allowing women to sit in on his lectures and discussions:

> Wenn eine Frau, was nicht häufig, aber doch bisweilen vorkommt, für die Aufgaben der theoretischen Physik besondere Begabung besitzt und außerdem den Trieb in sich fühlt, ihr Talent zur Entfaltung zu bringen, so halte ich es, in persönlicher wie auch in sachlicher Hinsicht, für unrecht, ihr aus prinzipiellen Rücksichten die Mittel zum Studium von vornherein zu versagen; ich werde ihr gern, soweit es überhaupt mit der akademischen Ordnung verträglich ist, den probeweisen und stets widerruflichen Zutritt zu meinen Vorlesungen und Übungen gestatten und habe in dieser Beziehung auch bis jetzt nur gute Erfahrung gemacht.
>
> Andererseits muß ich aber daran festhalten, daß ein solcher Fall immer nur als Ausnahme betrachtet werden kann … im allgemeinen aber kann man nicht stark genug betonen, daß die Natur selbst der Frau ihren Beruf als Mutter und Hausfrau vorgeschrieben hat, und daß Naturgesetze unter keinen Umständen ohne schwere Schädigungen, welche sich im vorliegenden Fall besonders an dem nachwachsenden Geschlecht zeigen würden, ignoriert werden können. (RU 25)

According to Planck women should not categorically be denied the opportunity for advanced study. They should be allowed to attend his lectures, yet on a revocable basis. The study of theoretical physics by women, he points out, is a clear exception that goes against women's "natural" role as mother and housewife. Königsdorf's narrator admits Meitner's status as an exception: "Sie ist die Ausnahme. Sie ist nicht gegen weitere Ausnahmen. Soweit tritt sie für die

Gleichberechtigung ein" (RU 45), she contends.

While attending Planck's lecture in Berlin, Meitner met the chemist Otto Hahn, who sought a research assistant for his work on radioactivity. Hahn and Meitner began their collaborative research, which was to last thirty years, at the Chemical Institute headed by Emil Fischer. However, in keeping with the mores of the time, Fischer did not allow women to work in his laboratories or to have any contact with students. In Prussia, women had not yet been admitted to the university. Königsdorf highlights that Meitner was forced to carry out her experiments in a small room in the basement, the infamous "Holzwerkstatt."[15] This room had a separate entrance so that Meitner would not have to enter the Institute directly: "Hier durfte sie arbeiten" (RU 24), the narrator exclaims. Only when women were granted access to university study in Prussia two years later was the ban prohibiting women from working in laboratories lifted. Although Fischer then eliminated the physical restrictions on Meitner, Königsdorf represents how she continued to be treated like a second-class citizen by the (male) assistants, who demonstratively greeted only Hahn when they encountered Hahn and Meitner together (RU 24).

The autobiography of Otto Hahn includes anecdotes that magnify the difficulties Meitner encountered because of her gender.[16] Hahn remembers that in light of the excellent publications by Dr. Meitner in the *Naturwissenschaftliche Rundschau*, the editor of the Brockhaus encyclopedia contacted a Professor Skalerek to ask for the address of "Herr" Meitner, from whom he wanted to solicit an article for the encyclopedia. When Skalerek pointed out that the contributor he sought was female, the editor immediately and adamantly replied that he would in no way consider publishing an article by a woman.

In 1912 women were not yet allowed to teach at the university, and Meitner could therefore not be appointed as a *Privatdozentin*. Consequently, she became Max Planck's "assistant," albeit one of the first female science assistants at the Institute for Theoretical Physics at the University of Berlin. When after World War I women in Germany were allowed to pursue academic careers, Meitner became *Privatdozentin* for Physics at the University of Berlin. Hahn relates an additional anecdote that accentuates Meitner's status as an exception as a woman in academia and, to boot, in the sciences. Although the topic of Meitner's first lecture was "Problems of Cosmic Physics," a newspaper reported the lecture's title as "Problems in Cosmetic Physics," a topic that must have seemed more credible for a female *Dozentin* (66). In 1926, Lise Meitner became *Außerordentliche Professorin* at the University of Berlin, a position she retained until 1933, when Hitler's racial decrees prohibited Jews from teaching at the university.

Meitner spent thirty years conducting research in collaboration with Otto Hahn. Of the two, she was considered the theoretician. In addition to her nearly fifty joint publications with Hahn, she established herself in her own right as an expert in the field of atomic physics, particularly in the physics of beta and gamma rays. With the German annexation of Austria in 1938, Meitner, an Austrian citizen, was forced into exile at the age of sixty. Shortly thereafter, Hahn and Fritz Straßmann went on to provide conclusive experimental evidence of a phenomenon Meitner and her nephew Otto Frisch soon identified as the nuclear fission of the uranium atom. In 1946, Hahn received the Nobel Prize for this discovery.

Beyond the institutional and psychological obstacles Meitner confronted as a woman in science, Königsdorf's conjectures about Meitner's subjective opinions. "Dreißig Jahre gemeinsame Arbeit, und der Mann erhält den Nobelpreis allein" (RU 32), she has Meitner claim. In his autobiography, Hahn recounts a "rather unhappy" conversation in which Meitner argued that Hahn should not have sent her from Germany and expresses her discontent that Hahn alone received the Nobel Prize.[17] Hahn contends, however, that sending Meitner from Germany was in her own interests, and that he, with the aid of Straßmann, conducted the research that eventually earned him the Nobel Prize. Opposing Meitner's claim to the Nobel Prize, the narrator of *Respektloser Umgang* sides with Hahn. If anyone deserved the award along with Hahn, she suggests it was Straßmann, not Meitner: "Sie war ungerecht. Fakt ist, die Entdeckung, die gehörte dem Otto Hahn. Und dem Straßmann" (RU 32).

Renate Feyl begins her feminist biography of Meitner with the statement, "Ihre Arbeit ist gekrönt worden mit dem Nobelpreis für Otto Hahn,"[18] an obvious sign that Feyl's intentions differ from Königsdorf's. As Jeanette Clausen points out, Feyl portrays Meitner as a "superwoman-victim, her superior achievements subordinated to Hahn's, her modesty and devotion to her work saintly as a nun's."[19] Clausen argues that Königsdorf consciously writes against the idealized and sanitized representations of Meitner by feminist scholars such as Feyl, an approach based on "uncritical sympathy and an oversimplified woman-as-victim model" (179). In contrast to Feyl, Königsdorf paints a complex and contradictory picture of Meitner.

One point of ambiguity lies in Königsdorf's representation of Meitner's departure from Germany. As noted, in *Respektloser Umgang* the fictionalized Meitner contends that Hahn welcomed her departure. This assertion must be read with the knowledge that Meitner's presence at the Institute threatened its political neutrality. Moreover and more significantly, Meitner's presence as a Jew in Germany came to endanger her very existence. No longer protected by her Austrian citizenship after Austria's annexation and not permitted to leave Germany because of her status as a renowned scientist who, it was feared, would collaborate with the enemy and use her knowledge against Germany, Meitner's situation grew precarious. Although Hahn offered her refuge and helped to plan her escape through Holland, Meitner laments: "Sie waren froh, mich los zu sein. Auch Hähnchen" (RU 44). According to the narrator, Hahn was relieved to see

Meitner go because her "little triumphs" were a constant humiliation to him. For example, Meitner reportedly joked to Hahn on numerous occasions as he made his way from her laboratory to his on the second floor, "Geh nach oben, Hähnchen. Von Physik verstehst du nichts" (RU 45). Armin Hermann likewise documents this frequent exchange between Meitner and Hahn, yet unlike Königsdorf, sees it as part of the "spirited discussions" that resulted from their long collaborative endeavors.[20] For Hermann, this exchange exemplifies Meitner's growing self-confidence: it is more as a sign of Meitner and Hahn's equality than of any attempt on her part to subordinate or belittle him.

In *Respektloser Umgang*, the fictionalized Meitner's use of the diminutive "Hähnchen" and her frequent reminders that theoretical physics was not Hahn's strong point lead the narrator to agree that Hahn must have been relieved by her departure, despite the fact that he would need Meitner to interpret his discovery. The narrator contends: "Er muß erleichtert gewesen sein. Anders ist es einfach nicht vorstellbar. Jeder, den ich kenne, wäre erleichtert gewesen" (RU 44). Yet it is doubtful that Hahn was seriously humiliated by Meitner's joking. In fact, in a documented tribute to Hahn on the occasion of his eightieth birthday, Meitner draws attention to Hahn's "natürliche Liebenswürdigkeit und Freude am Scherzen."[21]

In the narrator's opinion, other aspects of Hahn's life contributed to Meitner's humiliation: "Der Mann hatte seinen Anteil daran. Nicht wissentlich. Das nicht. Immer korrekt. [...] Hier die Arbeit. Dort die Braut. Immer korrekt" (RU 44). The narrator suggests that the fact that Hahn had both his career and a wife must have been degrading for Meitner, whose life remained defined by her career: "Das einzige, was sie vorweisen kann, ist ihre Physik" (RU 45), she claims. We must keep in mind, however, that this negative interpretation of Meitner's singular devotion to her work stems from the narrator. In *Respektloser Umgang*, Meitner herself never expresses or alludes to her lack of a husband or children as a deficit. This suggests that her definition of equality differs from the narrator's. Although she represents an exception as a woman in science, Meitner enjoys the recognition this status affords her. It is the narrator who sees women's status as exceptions in science as a sign of their continued devaluation. She points out, for example, that Albert Einstein's designation of Meitner as "*unsere Madame Curie*" (RU 40) lauded Meitner's exceptional talent as a physicist, but also accentuated her gender. Although others might have viewed this comparison as an honor, she claims that Meitner wanted to be recognized in her own right: "sie wollte Lise Meitner sein" (RU 40).

The juxtaposition of Meitner's sense of equality with the narrator's sheds light on changing notions of equality. For her time, Meitner had surely come a long way: for one, she attained an advanced degree in a male-dominated field and received international recognition for her groundbreaking work in atomic physics. Yet the narrator's contemporary standards lead her to assert that

Meitner should have been able to "have it all." This perspective causes her to focus on the limitations of Meitner's position. Meitner, she accentuates, was "Nie Geliebte. Nie Mutter" (RU 11). Unlike her research partner Hahn, Meitner was forced to choose between career and family. It appears, however, that Meitner readily accepted her choice. She shows little support for women who "want it all": "Geliebte, Mutter, Wissenschaftlerin. Für die nicht. Die macht sich verdächtig. Irène Curie etwa" (RU 45), Meitner claims.

The narrator considers what would have been different in Meitner's life had she been a man, and concludes that everything could have proceeded the same except that, had she been a man, no one outside the field would speak of her today. In this way, she points to the privileges Meitner garnered because of her gender. Yet she questions: "Hätte dieser Mann eine größere Chance gehabt, außerdem ein Familienleben zu führen? Der wissenschaftliche Ruhm wäre seinem Ansehen als Mann zugute gekommen. Für die Frau war er eher abträglich. Hohe Leistungen in Physik oder Mathematik steigern nicht ihren Wert als Frau. Auch heute nicht" (RU 84). Both in Meitner's and the narrator's time, a position in science is seen to reduce a woman's femininity.

Unmarried and childless, Meitner made the Institute her family. "Sie war mit ihrer ganzen Person in dem Institut verwurzelt. Es bildete ihre Familie" (RU 43). As the "soul" of the Institute, the one who empathized with the students and the one in whom they would confide, Meitner differed from her male colleagues. As a consequence, the notion that she, as a Jew, constituted a threat to the Institute proved particularly devastating. In *Respektloser Umgang*, Meitner equates her forced exile from the Institute and the country with death, claiming, in words that echo the fate of Ingeborg Bachmann's female protagonist in *Der Fall Franza*, "Es war Mord. [...] Da sind hundert Möglichkeiten, einen Menschen umzubringen" (RU 34). Although Meitner continued her research at the Siegbahnsche Institute in Sweden, she never again enjoyed the sense of family and collaboration she had known at the Kaiser-Wilhelm-Institut.

The narrator feels split between the roles of scientist and mother. She states: "Biologisch weiblich. [...] Als soziales Wesen wäre ich lieber ein Mann. [...] Sozial fühle ich mich aber unvollständig" (RU 22). To Meitner, by contrast, Königsdorf attributes a sense of wholeness: "Sie habe sich stets komplett gefühlt. Diese Lust des Denkens. Diese kleinen Siege. Diese Überlegenheit" (RU 22). Unable to comprehend such a lack of inner conflict, the narrator asserts that the claim to wholeness must have been Meitner's way of rationalizing the limitations she faced.

Unlike Wolf, who in *Störfall* casts both genders in conformity with traditional gender roles—the women are housewives, mothers and writers, the men are scientists—Königsdorf transgresses traditional boundaries. Both the narrator's and Meitner's socialization processes are "masculine." The narrator says of herself: "Meine Interessen und Neigungen, meine Kinderfreundschaften, meine Zukunftsvorstellungen—alles männlich" (RU 55). She was raised as her father's son, not as his daughter, although her father in time found it necessary to make her aware of her (subordinate) role as woman. She continues to see herself as split in two, torn between her conflicting roles as a mother and as a mathematician: "Der Riß geht mitten durch mich hindurch" (RU 55), she claims. "Sie werden gemeinsam zugrunde gehen. Der Mann in mir. Die Frau in mir" (RU 56). As shown in the previous chapters, this split, a dimension of the Kleistian "Riß der Zeit," characterizes Wolf's protagonists as well.

The fact that Meitner remained unmarried, childless and devoted solely to her work evidently irritates the narrator. While for Meitner the opportunity to enter a man's world and attain professional equality indeed signified progress, for the narrator equality does not mean acquiescence to the male norm. Meitner stayed within the bounds of what the male scientific community deemed acceptable; she figures as a "masculine" point of reference. By contrast, the narrator transgresses those boundaries. She asserts her femininity and pays the consequences. The narrator's first "actual" encounter with Lise Meitner illuminates their differences. They meet in 1958 at festivities in honor of Max Planck's hundredth birthday. The narrator, at that time a student of physics, has bleached platinum blond hair, which is cut in the "Marilyn-Monroe-Look," and dons a petticoat and tight sweater (RU 24). By contrast, Meitner's appearance is extremely conservative: she dresses in black and wears her hair knotted back tightly. This difference in physical appearance could be interpreted as generational; it nonetheless exemplifies Meitner's conformity to the male norm. Königsdorf suggests that the men in the profession are more comfortable with this masculine image: the narrator's feminine appearance leads her examiners to doubt her serious interest in physics and give her a lower exam grade.

The narrator's relationship both to femininity and to feminism remains ambiguous and contradictory. While she wants to "have it all" and be treated as an equal, she concedes that she at times longs to be protected and taken care of. She asserts, "Dafür hätte ich auf die ganze Emanzipation gepfiffen," but is quick to add, "Vielleicht. Die Wahrheit hat viele Schichten" (RU 56). Königsdorf's Meitner also actively questions the advances GDR society had made toward equality. For example, she prods the narrator by asking how many female Nobel Prize winners the GDR has had and how the division of labor in the home is regulated. Despite women's economic and legal equality, in these areas the GDR saw little progress. Moreover, although the narrator initially claims that she would prefer to be a man socially, she later maintains: "Jetzt bin ich lieber eine Frau" (RU 84).

A comparison with Wolf's texts, in which "feminine" characteristics are attributed almost exclusively to women, brings to light the complex relationship between gender and science. Although a traditional conflation of sex and gender (male and masculine, female and feminine) informs Wolf's texts, Wolf attributes gender differences to socialization processes detrimental to both sexes. She argues that were women in positions of power, they would not necessarily act differently than men. In other words, she sees no essential relationship between moral and ethical behavior and the female sex. Rather, she bases her argument on positionality: women's socialization process and their marginalization within patriarchal society provide them a particular perspective on society not afforded to most men.

Both Kleist in *Kein Ort. Nirgends* and Anchises in *Kassandra* exemplify Wolf's positional perspective. As social outsiders, they are better able to see the machinations of those in power. Moreover, like most of Wolf's female characters, these men seek to synthesize the masculine and feminine within themselves. In her literary texts and critical essays, Wolf attempts to deconstruct the binaries that inform patriarchal society and privilege the masculine. In her *Kassandra*-lectures, she asserts that both women and men should strive for autonomy, "und Frauen, die sich auf ihre Weiblichkeit als Wert zurückziehen, handeln im Grunde, wie es ihnen andressiert wurde: Sie reagieren mit einem großen Ausweichmanöver auf die Herausforderung der Realität an ihre ganze Person" (VK 116). Wolf argues that the exclusive valuation of the masculine has fostered society's self-destructiveness. This exclusiveness, in turn, finds one of its most extreme and detrimental manifestations in the realm of science.

In *Respektloser Umgang*, sex and gender fail to coincide as neatly as they do in Wolf's texts. Both Meitner and the narrator follow a "masculine" pattern of socialization. Women in science remain marginalized because of their gender. Regarding Meitner and the narrator, Berger asserts: "Da sie das männliche Denken genau kennen, ohne sich jedoch ungebrochen damit zu identifizieren, sollen sie die Katastrophe aufhalten. Auf welche Weise dies geschehen soll, weiß auch die Erzählerin nicht recht ...."[22] Berger's assumptions call attention to the need to look more closely at how Königsdorf represents the possibility of social change.

Königsdorf's (fictionalized) Meitner asserts that her "mission" was to delay the discovery of nuclear fission and thus to prevent the Nazis from developing an atomic bomb: "Mein Plan sah vor, das Ganze so lange wie möglich herauszustrecken" (RU 113), she reveals. She claims that by laying stake in Fermi's (false) thesis of the transuranium elements, she intentionally led other researchers down the wrong path. Moreover, she states that in 1934 she recognized the possible validity of Ida Noddack's thesis regarding nuclear reactions which, though largely discredited by the scientific community at that time, later proved to be valid. Furthermore, the narrator recounts the story that in 1936 Meitner convinced Straßmann to throw out research results that provided experimental evidence of nuclear fission. Königsdorf has Meitner play with the idea that she resisted, yet the narrator points out that the idea of resistance has no historical basis: "Die Szene ist überliefert," she asserts, "[a]llerdings nicht mit dem Hintergrund, daß Meitner die Entdeckung verzögern wollte" (RU 112). Although the narrator rejects the idea that Meitner resisted, such possibilities allow her to play with the potential for resistance. As Meitner suggests: "Ist es wirklich so wichtig. Ich meine, ob es den Tatsachen entspricht oder nicht. Ist nicht lediglich von Bedeutung, daß es wahr sein könnte" (RU 114).

For Königsdorf, it is not incidental that a woman receives and is to carry out the "Auftrag." Like Wolf, she attributes to women the role of saving humankind. Although Meitner's forced exile from Germany kept her from carrying out her plan to forestall the discovery of nuclear fission, Königsdorf's Meitner explains: "Die Menschheit war fürs erste gerettet. Hiroshima aber nicht mehr zu verhindern. Jemand würde das Kreuz aufnehmen müssen. Über das Geschlecht war man bald einig" (RU 48). Despite unanimous opinions that a woman must carry out the mission, the lack of consensus about the specific characteristics this woman should have undermines the notion of a unified female position:

> Nach dieser schnellen Übereinkunft, es müsse ein weibliches Wesen sein, begann der Streit. Die einen verlangten, es solle sich um eine Frau handeln, die zu ihren biologischen Rythmen steht. Andernfalls, wenn man sich auf eine Art Neutrum festlege, wäre dies ein ernster Fall von Sexismus. Dagegen wurde eingewendet, eine solche Person hätte keine Chance, Mitgefühl oder Gehör zu finden. Wenigstens sollte sie die Sache hinter sich haben und außerdem müsse ihr *männliches* Denkvermögen amtlich bescheinigt sein. (RU 49)

As such considerations evince, Königsdorf does not define woman exclusively in terms of feminine attributes; in fact, at the very least her intellectual abilities should be "masculine." Moreover, the fictionalized Meitner's resistance fails to free her from responsibility or scrutiny. The narrator contemplates Meitner's own ethics and morals when she notes that Meitner was named "Woman of the Year" by the American press only a year after the bomb was dropped on Hiroshima. Calling into question Meitner's motives and those of the other scientists who worked on this project, the narrator claims: "Wem wollten sie das Feuer in die Hand geben! [...] Es ist wahr, man darf ihnen nicht die gesamte Verantwortung aufbürden. Doch man kann sie auch nicht aus der Verantwortung entlassen. Denn sie allein wußten, welche furchtbaren Kräfte da in Szene gesetzt werden konnten" (RU 98). The fictionalized Meitner shows no regret for her role in the discovery of atomic fission.

Dorothee Schmitz-Köster underscores the complexity and contradictory nature of Königsdorf's "Weiblichkeitsbegriff."[23] On the one hand Königsdorf problematizes Wolf's notions of women's writing and with this the idea that women's historical subordination and socialization results in a unique standpoint. On the other hand, Königsdorf ascribes to Meitner qualities of resistance and the task of saving humanity. Regarding this ambiguous stance, Schmitz-Köster exclaims: "Daß sie diese Handlungsweise ausgerechnet einer Frauengestalt zuordnet, Frauen damit als Widerständige zeichnet, vergrößert die Widersprüchlichkeit noch, die Königsdorfs Weiblichkeitsbegriff in sich birgt" (140). For Clausen, Königsdorf's representation of Meitner is less ambiguous: in her view, Königdorf rejects Wolf's thesis that women have a different way of perceiving the world and different structures of thought (179). I would contend, however, that Königsdorf rejects Wolf's standpoint epistemology only in part. As I have argued, Königsdorf's purposely casts a woman to carry out the mission and to pass it on to the female narrator. After all, the date of Meitner's departure from Germany, the end of her "Auftrag," coincides precisely with the narrator's birth.

Of course Meitner is not alone in her attempt to prevent the wartime use of atomic energy by the Germans. Königsdorf also represents men who resisted or attempted to resist. For example, she notes that in conjunction with other scientists, Albert Einstein sent a letter to President Roosevelt recommending that Uranium research be promoted so that the United States could be armed against the German atom bomb. Ironically, the pacifist Einstein believed that the United States would utilize the new energy "*weise und menschlich*" (RU 67). Moreover, the Hungarian scientist Leo Szilard suggested in 1933 that, given the possible consequences of a nuclear chain reaction, scientists should remain silent rather than reveal their discoveries (RU 68).

In addition to possible acts of resistance performed by Meitner and other scientists, the narrator examines the complicity and resistance of her grandparents and parents. She interprets her Jewish grandmother's decision to starve herself to death as an act of resistance rather than a sign of madness as others had claimed. The narrator suggests that her grandmother, unlike those around her, recognized the insanity of Nazi Germany: "War ihr Entsetzen denn wirklich Wahnsinn? Ist sie nicht die einzige Hellsichtige gewesen, in einer tauben, blinden Umwelt, die nichts begreifen wollte?" (RU 36) she asks. Like Meitner, the grandmother was a Jew who posed a threat to her non-Jewish family: "Die Jüdin gefährdete die Familie" (RU 38). In describing her father, the narrator claims: "Der Gedanke an Widerstand gegen die Obrigkeit war in seinem logischen System überhaupt nicht vorgesehen" (RU 98). A half-Jew with great reverence for law and order, the father went so far as to greet the Nürnberg Racial Laws since they at least afforded him some rights: "Schlechtes Recht sei besser als gar kein Recht" (RU 38), he maintained. The father's acceptance of these limited rights, in the narrator's view, was completely self-serving. In fact, she contends that his wife attempted to poison his Jewish mother when he recognized the threat she posed to the family (RU 38). However, she also hypothesizes about her father's possibilities to resist. During the war, he was contacted by the Gestapo and struck a deal to guard some mysterious boxes marked "Reichspostminister." The narrator hints that they contained the raw materials for building atomic bombs. Her father never questioned the contents of the boxes or opened them. Could he have acted, fled or disposed of the contents? Ethical questions such as these concern the narrator.

Through these hypothetical accounts, the narrative emphasis shifts from actual acts of resistance (though these remain important) to possible acts of resistance: what could have been done in the past opens up the question of what can be done in the present and the future. As Clausen underscores, *Respektloser Umgang* is not devoid of hope; rather, "Königsdorf seems to ask readers to look to themselves and their own possibilities for moral behavior" (179). Through her encounters with Meitner and in working through her memories of her grandparents' and parents' actions, the narrator gains a sense of continuity with the past and assumes responsibility for the future: she takes on Lise Meitner's "Auftrag."

The global threat of the 1980s intensified the need to set a stake in the future. The narrator paints a dim picture of the political reality of the GDR. She also extends her critique beyond the GDR's borders. She characterizes the realms of science, politics and economics as dominated by instrumental rationality. The state's focus on the forces of production has discredited all notions of "Individualhumanismus": the state has become an "Ameisenstaat. Eine Zentrale. Ein Gehirn. Ein Organismus" (RU 20). Within this normativized structure, the individual becomes simply a cog in the wheel and loses all sense of responsibility for the course of history. Königsdorf illuminates that a purely pragmatic mode of thinking results in a deficit of moral and ethical considerations, the prerequisites for any real social progress.

Respektloser Umgang depicts Cold War politics as leading to the senseless proliferation of nuclear weapons in Central Europe: the narrator reports of the nuclear winter that would set in were forty-five percent of the available nuclear weapons employed (RU 99); describes the delusional politics of deterrence as "Sicherheit durch Abschreckung. Mehr Sprengköpfe. Mehr Raketen" (RU 12); tells of newly-developed, race-specific poisoned gases (RU 70). Moreover, unreflected "progress" has resulted in extensive and irreversible environmental degradation: toxic foam flows in the polluted rivers (RU 100); sulfur dioxide thickens the air (RU 107); the number of swallows has declined, "[i]rgend etwas ist ihnen zugestoßen" (RU 116). Socialism has evidently not brought about the promised changes. "Welche wesentliche neue Qualität zeichnet die Welt aus?" (RU 78-9) the narrator asks in clear recognition of the contradictions between self-realization and the demands of a society that measures success in terms of scientific-technological progress and economic productivity (RU 56).

Faced with the rationalization of all societal processes, Königsdorf, like Wolf and Maron, upholds the value of everyday life. "Die Gier nach den Dingen, nach Macht, nach Ruhm. Einmal wird alles verblassen, vor dem einfachen Wunsch zu leben" (RU 155). In response to a society based on greed, power and prestige, Königsdorf underscores the importance of interpersonal relationships, of caring, responsibility and human dignity. Her narrative closes with a tranquil image of everyday life: women chat, children play in the grass, men haul in crates of drinks, the aroma of coffee fills the air. Through her encounters with Meitner, and in the face of terminal illness and global threat, the narrator comes to recognize her own self-worth and the value of setting a personal stake in the future. Despite her progressing illness, the links she has forged with the past have strengthened her will to live, to pass on this will and to create a livable future.

Ungelegener Befund

In her next longer literary text, *Ungelegener Befund* (1989), Königsdorf takes up many of the themes she explores in *Respektloser Umgang*. She further illuminates historical continuities, the need for individual and collective responsibility, and the importance of ethical and moral imperatives in the realm of science. Yet here Königsdorf addresses these themes within the historical context of *Vergangenheitsbewältigung*, the coming to terms with the Nazi past. In the GDR, Christa Wolf's 1976 *Kindheitsmuster* marked a critical turn toward addressing the lack of *Vergangenheitsbewältigung*. Although the country's political system had undergone a radical transformation, both Wolf and Königsdorf suggest that the citizenry had not: past patterns of behavior continued in the present. Königsdorf describes the GDR's anti-fascism as "der verordnete, mißbrauchte Antifaschismus [...], [d]er gefährlich ist, weil er neuen Faschismus produziert."[24] She goes on to claim, "Antifaschismus kann nur etwas Inneres werden, wenn wir unsere Geschichte ganz annehmen." When anti-fascism becomes a decree from above, it obviates personal and subjective engagement with the past. In other words, ordained anti-fascism fosters complacency and denial. Founded explicitly as an "anti-fascist" state, the GDR disclaimed any continuity between fascist Germany and socialist Germany. Selectively excluding this period of German history from its heritage, it rapidly decreed its citizens to be the true "Sieger der Geschichte" and heralded as its leaders and heroes those communists active in the anti-fascist resistance.

Königsdorf explores both the personal and political consequences of the GDR's sovereign attitude toward history and its repercussions in the realm of science and personal relationships. In *Respektloser Umgang*, the narrator claims that the heroic images of anti-fascist resistance fighters, although admired and revered, did not offer her a means of identifying with the past: "als ihresgleichen konnte ich mich nicht verstehen" (RU 21), she contends. Unsure whether she would have endured or resisted, the narrator feels disconnected from the past, and claims, "Geschichte blieb ein von Heldensagen umrankter historischer Prozeß, der mit mir wenig zu tun hatte" (RU 21). Only through viewing her life in relation to Lise Meitner, her parents and her grandparents, does she gain a sense of personal and political continuity and begin to set a stake in society's future. In *Ungelegener Befund*, Königsdorf similarly reveals how the repression of Nazi atrocities and the concomitant glorification of resistance reified public memory of the Third Reich.

An epistolary narrative, *Ungelegener Befund* centers on Dieter Jhanz, a lecturer in biology in a small GDR university town. Jhanz is asked to give a speech in honor of his deceased father who, for twenty-five years, headed a home for mentally handicapped children, which is to be dedicated in his name. Remembering his father as a humanitarian, Jhanz agrees to hold the speech and begins to examine and reflect on his father's life. Although his father destroyed almost all his personal documents, Jhanz obtains a bundle of letters written between 1938 to 1945 from his long-time friend, Helmuth Paul, an archivist who aids Jhanz in his research into his family history. Based on the handwriting, Paul concluded that these letters were written by Jhanz's father. Through the letters, Jhanz comes to realize that his father was a "kleiner Karrierefaschist" (UB 44) who, as a soldier in Hitler's army, sought to be promoted to a position with a racial hygiene project in the concentration camps. Although he initially disavowed his father's association with the letters—the names had been crossed out—Jhanz begins to pursue questions that had remained unanswered throughout his father's lifetime. Why had his father burned the letters, along with a packet of letters from his wife, shortly before his death? Why did his mother, whom he initially thought had died shortly after childbirth, commit suicide when Jhanz was only one year of age? Jhanz's lack of answers points to a history shrouded in deceitful silence, and leads him to conclude that his father had indeed authored the incriminating letters.

Jhanz's decision to withdraw his initial offer to give the commemorative speech is seen by his father's friends and previous co-workers as unfounded and self-serving. Their attitudes regarding the older Jhanz's alleged fascist activities indicate a denial and an unwillingness to confront the past. For example, the former mayor relies on his keen "Menschenkenntnis" (UB 82) to assure him that the older Jhanz could not have been a Nazi. Yet the mayor reveals his lack of "Menschenkenntnis" in his assessment of the Neo-Nazi activities. He refuses to consider that such fascistic sentiments could have arisen within the socialist GDR, asserting that they must stem from the detrimental influences from the West. "Leider wurde der Faschismus nur in unserem Teil Deutschlands ausgerottet" (UB 83) he claims, "[w]ieso lassen wir zu, daß er sich durch die Hintertür wieder einschleicht?" (UB 83) Similarly, the author of an anonymous letter to Jhanz minimizes the significance of collaboration with the Nazis and condemns the presence of foreign guest workers in the GDR, nonetheless insisting, "Ich bin kein Rassist." (UB 77).

The denial and hypocrisy of his father's supporters demonstrate how the prevalent attitude toward history fostered complacency and kept the citizenry from recognizing how past attitudes and patterns of behavior continue to inform the present. Jhanz sees, "daß sich niemand wirklich für die Wahrheit interessierte. [...] Die Wahrheit müßte heißen: Unsere Väter brandschatzten, raubten, mordeten. Nur sehr wenige widerstanden" (UB 86). By acknowledging the probable "true" histories of his father's generation, Jhanz explicitly critiques official history. Further reflecting on the letters from his father's supporters, Jhanz asserts: "Mit ihnen hat es nie etwas zu tun gehabt. Entweder sie waren auf der richtigen Seite, oder sie kamen in der Geschichte nicht vor. Die Schuld blieb etwas Abstraktes, immer die von anderen. Nichts scheint mir so gefährlich wie mißbrauchte Wahrheit, weil sie der Lüge einen Tugendschein verleiht" (UB 81). The official perspective on history in his view serves to skew the truth. An emphasis on this limited aspect of Germany's Nazi past led to an identification with the victims, not the *Mitläufer* or perpetrators, and precluded the process of working though both individual and collective guilt.

Jhanz begins to pursue the vexing question Christa Wolf poses in *Kindheitsmuster*, "Wie sind wir geworden, wie wir heute sind?" He not only points to the denial on the part of his father's generation, but recognizes that he also feels no sense of responsibility for German history. He thus also implicates his own generation, and with this himself: "Indem wir uns der Verantwortung für die Geschichte entzogen, wir, die mittlere Generation, ließen wir die Väter im Stich und dann die Söhne. Wie sollen die, unsere Söhne, nun die Verant-wortung tragen können, für das, was kommen wird?" (UB 87) Recognizing the difficulty for those directly implicated to confront the past, Jhanz sees his generation, one too young to be held directly responsible for the wartime atrocities, as having a particular obligation to demand and to pass on a sense of moral responsibility. He realizes, then, that like his father, he has failed the younger generation. The representative of this generation is Jhanz's student, Felix K., who shows little understanding of the ethical norms and moral behavior. "Von uns aus der Geschichte entlassen" (UB 98), Jhanz asserts.

In addition to the actual correspondence that makes up *Ungelegener Befund*, Jhanz pens a series of letters that he does not intend to send. These unsent letters dairy his fears, dreams, and desires. In them, he reveals his homosexual desire for Felix, a fantasized lover who resembles Jhanz's student, Felix K.. Jhanz describes Felix as "[e]ine Erfindung aus Wirklichkeitsnot" (UB 14), an imagined partner who stands in for the confidant Jhanz lacks. This fantasized relationship brings to light the stale, small town conservatism that forces Jhanz to repress his homosexuality. The pressure to conform to traditional gender expectations further undermines the notion of a unified female or male standpoint.

The similar attitudes towards science exhibited by Dieter Jhanz, his father, and Felix K. suggest a generational continuity in the absence of moral memory. All three are biologists interested in the optimization of the human being through genetic engineering. Dieter Jhanz seeks promotion to the position of Professor through collaboration on a project to index the human genome. His father sought promotion to an army project focused on racial hygiene. Like his father, Dieter Jhanz is a conformist: "Auch mein Vater wäre nie auf die Idee gekommen, allgemein Anerkanntes zu hinterfragen" (UB 95), he contends. To be sure, before he received the letter documenting his father's involvement in the Nazi racial programs, Jhanz had not openly questioned his family history. All inquisitiveness was repressed on the political level through the discourse of anti-fascism and on the personal level through his father's silence about the past. Socialized to obey rather than to question, Jhanz embraced the official ideology of scientific-technological progress and had no moral scruples about the genome project.

Felix K.'s conformity to scientific norms is even more extreme than Jhanz's. Whereas Jhanz shows sensitivity and sentimentality, reveals his dreams and fantasies and gains an awareness of the consequences of instrumental rationality, Felix K.'s thoughts remain completely scientific. He unabashedly proclaims himself "Mittelpunkt der Welt" (UB 98) and, as master of the universe, plans to recreate the world: "Wir können die Welt neu schaffen" (UB 38), he claims. Lacking reverence for the beauty of nature—for him violets are simply an "Informationsstruktur" (UB 102)—he demonstrates an unwavering belief in the "Erhabenheit der Vernunft" (UB 102). According to Jhanz, Felix K.'s ideal is a completely rationalized, cybernetic society of perfected and optimized human beings. Like Wolf and Maron, who represent the inability to love as a consequence of abstract rationality, Königsdorf depicts Felix's complete devotion to science as a sign of his low self-esteem:

> Sein mangelndes Selbstgefühl wird er durch Schöpferrausch kompen-
> sieren. Er wird seine Biographie nach seiner Genomanalyse gestalten
> oder sich selbst reparieren. Er wird dies zum allgemeinen Gesetz
> erheben und dann mit der Optimierung der nächsten Generation
> beginnen. Das Ganze wird lautlos vor sich gehen, sehr einleuchtend
> sein und sich mit ökonomischen Kalkül und Machterhaltung verbinden.
> (UB 99)

For Jhanz, Felix K.'s vision of the future is horrific and will ultimately lead to self-destruction.

By drawing parallels to the legend of Icarus, Königsdorf accentuates the deadly consequences of this one-dimensional rationality. According to the legend, Icarus was the son of Daedalus, a skillful engineer and inventor.

Trapped in a tower by King Minos, Daedalus fabricated wings for himself and his son out of feathers, wax and string. Prepared for flight, Daedalus warned young Icarus to fly neither too low, so the dampness from the water would not clog his wings, nor too high, so that the wax would not be melted by the sun's heat. Reveling in the success of his flight, Icarus began to soar upwards and, as his father had warned, his wings melted and he came crashing down. Jhanz invokes this legend in his unsent letters. In a dream of winged flight, he expresses his love for Felix K. (UB 27). Characterizing Felix K., Jhanz stresses his drive for success: "Das einzig Wirkliche für ihn ist der Erfolg. Und eines Tages wird er abstürzen" (UB 37). In this statement, the similarities between Felix and Icarus become clear. Both strive for success and, as the myth suggests, both will come crashing down. The fine line between the idyll and the abyss, the synchronicity of flight and striving with catastrophic crash and demise, lies at the heart of the Icarus legend.

In Jhanz's dream of Icarus's birth, the analogy between Felix K. and Icarus is made more explicit (UB 103-104). In his dream, Jhanz sees a woman's body covered with mechanized, automated vermin that attempt to penetrate the woman's skin while they chant "Schneller. Stärker. Effektiver. Beständiger. Stärker. Unanfälliger" (UB 103). The woman then proceeds to give birth to a winged boy. Awakened from his dream out of fear and repulsion, Jhanz attempts to cry out the name Felix, yet his lips utter a different name: Icarus. The interweaving of sexuality and a nightmarish vision of a purely scientific society illuminates the complexity of Jhanz's relationship to Felix K., himself a product of a thoroughly rationalized society. Jhanz, moreover, can be seen as corresponding to Daedalus: although he is the one who gave Felix K. his wings, his role is also to warn him of the dangers of blindly striving for success. Echoing the notion of the "Auftrag" that Königsdorf develops in *Respektloser Umgang*, Jhanz asserts, "die menschliche Würde kann sich unmöglich in der Beherrschung von Techniken erschöpfen. Da muß etwas sein, das wir empfangen haben und weitergeben müssen. Etwas, gegen das unser ehrgeiziges Treiben bedeutungslos wird" (UB 23).

In *Ungelegener Befund*, Königsdorf further represents the loss of human dignity that has resulted from the domination over physical nature and inner nature. Jhanz ponders whether the price of such progress is the loss of the soul:

Der Mensch hat sich zur Herrschaft aufgeschwungen, und er muß sie wahrnehmen [...] Aber ist er dann noch, was der Mensch einst war? Oder löst sich alles auf in ein Raster von Informationsquanten und programmierbaren Algorithmen? Besteht nicht die Gefahr, daß bei diesem Zerfallen das Gefäß der Seele undicht wird? Daß ihm etwas verlorengeht, wodurch er zugleich unfähig wird, diesen Verlust zu bemerken? (UB 75)

Christa Wolf, terming this inability to perceive aspects of the past and present the "blind spot," contends: "Genau dieser Fleck bringt die Selbstzerstörung hervor. Ihn nicht nur zu umschreiben sondern in ihn hineinzugehen, sozusagen in den Mittelpunkt des *hurricanes*: das ist meiner Meinung nach Aufgabe der Literatur."[25] According to Wolf, the probing of one's own and society's blind spots is an individual process that requires subjectivity and introspection, not rationality and objectivity.

In *Ungelegener Befund*, Jhanz begins this process. To Helmuth Paul, he writes: "Ich denke, wir sind jetzt in einem Alter, in dem es höchste Zeit wird, sich mit den Vätern auseinanderzusetzen" (UB 34). Paul's failure to confront his own father's past suggests, however, that Jhanz's process of self-questioning remains an exception. The fate of Paul's father remains a mystery: Paul leads Jhanz to believe, perhaps in order to deter further inquiry, that his father could have been a communist who fell victim to the Nazis, rather than a collaborator or perpetrator. The text offers further explanations for Paul's refusal to delve more deeply into his father's past. For example, we learn that Jhanz's father became irate over Helmuth and Dieter's childhood plan to arrange a marriage between their two widowed parents. Moreover, the possibility remains that the incriminating letters were authored not by Jhanz's father, but instead by Paul's.

As in *Respektloser Umgang*, Königsdorf plays with possibilities of resistance and collaboration. At the end of the narrative, Jhanz receives a letter from Paul stating that Jhanz's father may not have authored the letters after all. Although this was initially Jhanz's impression as well, he is now unwilling facilely to accept Paul's latest theory: "Denn stellte sich heraus, mein Vater hätte mit den Briefen nichts zu tun, wozu wäre diese Wahrheit gut. Die von Anfang an jede Verantwortung ablehnten, diese trägen Kleinbürger, die ihre Ohren vor jeder unangenehmen Botschaft verschließen, würden sie sich [...] gerechtfertigt fühlen" (UB 108). In an age where society's potential for self-destruction is so immense, Königsdorf underlines the danger of forgetting. Jhanz fears, "daß durch die Gewalt der Technik auch Vergessen das Ende des Leben bedeuten kann" (UB 73).

Notes

1 Königsdorf has published the stories in these collections in other editions. *Mit Klitschmann im Regen* (1983) contains the stories from *Meine ungehörigen Träume* dealing with gender issues. *Die geschlossenen Türen am Abend* (1989) contains stories from *Meine ungehörigen Träume*, *Der Lauf der Dinge* and *Lichtverhältnisse*. The stories relating to science collected in *Ein sehr exakter Schein* also appeared in previous collections.

2 Helga Königsdorf, "Rede auf dem Meeting von Mitgliedern der SED vor

dem Haus der ZK," *neue deutsche literatur* 38.3 (1990): 181.

3 Helga Königsdorf, "Schreib-Auskunft: Helga Königsdorf," *neue deutsche literatur* 27.4 (1979): 9.

4 Königsdorf, "Rede auf dem X. Schriftstellerkongreß der DDR," *neue deutsche literatur* 36.3 (1998): 57.

5 Eva Kaufmann, "Spielarten des Komischen. Zur Schreibweise von Helga Königsdorf," *"Wen kümmert's, wer spricht": zur Literatur und Kulturgeschichte von Frauen aus Ost und West*, ed. Inge Stefan (Köln: Böhlau, 1991) 180.

6 Tzvetan Todorov, *The Fantastic. A Structural Approach to a Literary Genre*, trans. Richard Howard (Ithaca: Cornell University Press, 1975) 25.

7 Evelyn Fox Keller, "Gender and Science," *Sex and Scientific Inquiry*, ed. Sandra Harding and Jean F. O'Barr (Chicago: University of Chicago Press, 1987) 237.

8 Helga Königsdorf, "Das Prinzip Menschenwürde. Thesen für einen Vortrag," *neue deutsche Literatur* 37.10 (1989): 6.

9 Joseph Pischel et al., "*Respektloser Umgang* von Helga Königsdorf. Für und Wider," *Weimarer Beiträge* 33.8 (1987): 1355.

10 Sandra Harding, *The Science Question in Feminism* (Ithaca: Cornell University Press, 1986) 39.

11 Königsdorf, "Diskussion nach der Lesung von Helga Königsdorf," *Die Literatur der DDR. 1976–1986. Akten der internationalen Konferenz. Pisa. Mai 1987*, ed. Anna Chiarloni, Gemma Sartori and Fabrizio Cambi (Pisa: Giardini, 1988) 452.

12 Christina Thürmer-Rohr, "Einführung—Forschen heißt wühlen," *Mittäterschaft und Entdeckungslust* (Berlin: Orlanda Frauenverlag, 1989) 12–13.

13 Christina Thürmer-Rohr, *Vagabundinnen. Feministische Essays* (Berlin: Orlanda Frauenverlag, 1987) 50.

14 Londa Schiebinger, "The History and Philosophy of Women in Science: A Review Essay," *Sex and Scientific Inquiry.* 7–34.

15 The "Holzwerkstatt" was actually on the ground floor, not in the basement. It is unclear whether Königsdorf intentionally places it in the basement, perhaps to make Meitner's predicament appear more extreme. See for example Walter Gerlach, *Otto Hahn. Ein Forscherleben unserer Zeit*, ed. and rev. Dieter Hahn (Stuttgart: Wissenschaftliche Verlagsanstalt, 1984) 32.

16 Otto Hahn, *Otto Hahn: A Scientific Autobiography*, trans. and ed. Willy Ley (New York: Charles Scribner's Sons, 1966) 64–66.

17 Otto Hahn, *Otto Hahn: My Life. The Autobiography of a Scientist*, trans. Ernst Kaiser and Eithne Wilkens (New York: Herder & Herder, 1970) 199.

18 Renate Feyl, *Der lautlose Aufbruch. Frauen in der Wissenschaft* (Berlin: Neues Leben, 1981) 178.

19 Jeanette Clausen, "Resisting Objectification: Helga Königsdorf's Lise

Meitner," *Studies in GDR Culture and Society 10*, ed. Margy Gerber et al. (Lanham: University Press of America, 1991) 168.

20 Armin Hermann, *The New Physics. The Route into the Atomic Age* (Munich: Heinz Moos, 1979) 98.

21 Lise Meitner, "Otto Hahn zum 80. Geburtstag," *Naturwissenschaften* 46.5 (1959): 157–58. Quoted in Gerlach and Hahn, 186.

22 Doris Berger, "Vom schwierigen sprachlichen Umgang mit der Katastrophe. Texte von DDR-Autoren gegen die automare Bedrohung," *Die Literatur der DDR. 1976–1986* 181.

23 Dorothee Schmitz-Köster, *Troubadora und Kassandra. Weibliches Schreiben in der DDR* (Köln: Pahl-Rugenstein, 1989) 140.

24 Quoted in Carola Samlowsky, "Sperrige Gedankenprosa. Helga Königsdorfs Abrechnung mit dem Antifaschismus," *Tagesspiegel* 11 March 1990.

25 Christa Wolf, "Documentation Christa Wolf. Ein Gespräch über *Kassandra*," *German Quarterly* 57.1 (1984): 115.

CONCLUSION

Interpreting selected works by Wolf, Maron and Königsdorf, I have focused on the critique of science as part of a gendered discourse. Countering a "masculine" notion of enlightenment progress through science and reason that was furthered and intensified in GDR ideology, these writers assert those "feminine" values traditionally associated with women's roles and everyday lives. In this they go beyond the central tenets of the dialectic of enlightenment as theorized by Horkheimer and Adorno to reveal the complex interplay of Western notions of science and progress with symbolic, structural and individual gender. Often conflating science, technology and their political implementation, they represent how these forces are employed as tools of domination over the natural world, over human nature and over women. In tracing the critique of progress chronologically from the early 1960s to the late 1980s I have also shown how Wolf's texts resonate with global issues, cultural politics, aesthetic doctrine and feminist theory. Against the backdrop of her own time, Wolf probes historical and cultural turning points that have led Western civilization on a self-destructive course. Her perspective draws attention to the social repercussions of women's marginalization in the process of enlightenment.

Read with and against Wolf's works, Maron's texts illuminate further dimensions of the gendered critique of progress in East German women's literature. One such dimension is generational affiliation. While many writers of Wolf's generation long held to their initial conviction that they were living in and helping to build the "better" German state, the younger generation, represented here by Maron, lacked such an incipiently positive association with the state. Subverting fundamental tenets of Marxist ideology, Maron's direct indictment of socialist "progress" kept her works from being published in the GDR. While the pre-*Wende* works of Wolf and Königsdorf show a concrete utopian impulse, Maron's *Flugasche* and *Überläuferin* represent the deformities engendered by patriarchal social structures and an oppressive technocracy to be so extreme that her female protagonists' only recourse is to fantasy, dreams and the imagination. As in the texts of Wolf and Königsdorf, this other realm undermines mechanistic notions of progress and the scientific rationalization of society. The fantastic narrative forms these writers employ defy the rational world of science and subvert traditional notions of reason and reality.

From her position within the scientific establishment, Königsdorf brings to light an additional perspective on the interplay of gender and science. While Wolf represents the realm of science as dominated by men and by masculine thought patterns and behavioral norms, Königsdorf differentiates women's position in and vis-à-vis the realm of science. In *Respektloser Umgang*, she casts a woman scientist instrumental in the discovery of nuclear fission and, illuminating numerous facets of feminist empiricism, calls into question a unified female perspective on science. Nonetheless, she too ascribes to women a particular role in changing society's course, of carrying out what she terms the "mission." Likewise skeptical that scientific-technological progress will facilitate the development of a more humane society, Königsdorf suggests alternatives to the Western, patriarchal epistemologies that structure our world.

The texts of GDR writer Irmtraud Morgner (1933–1990) also focus on the instrumentalization of reason and women's marginalization within a global context, expressing a critique of enlightenment from a feminist perspective. To treat them in detail goes beyond the bounds of this project; an interpretation of gender and science in Morgner's dense and complex oeuvre demands a separate study.[1] In her 1974 montage novel *Leben und Abenteuer der Troubadora Beatriz nach Zeugnissen ihrer Spielfrau Laura*, Morgner presents a fantastic and utopian narrative that enmeshes the themes of women's emancipation, writing, history and sexuality. Asleep for 800 years, the troubadour Beatriz awakes to find herself in the GDR, "das gelobte Land." Her bizarre excursions there and in capitalist countries lay bare internal conflicts and contradictions, yet ultimately point to the GDR's significant progress towards emancipation. In *Amanda* (1984), her second novel of what was to be the "Troubadora" trilogy, Morgner mediates her earlier optimism towards women's status in the GDR and the ability of economic change to bring about revolutionary social change. Unlike *Leben und Abenteuer der Troubadora Beatriz*, which Morgner set in the revolutionary context of 1968, *Amanda*'s context is that of global nuclear threat. Much as Wolf's *Kassandra*, the novel warns of Western civilization's self-annihilative trajectory. With its feminist perspective on militarism and environmental destruction, use of myth and the supernatural, and its focus on women's marginality and vision, *Amanda* further echoes Wolf's narrative.

Like Wolf, Königsdorf, and Maron, Morgner thematizes the dialectic of enlightenment. Echoing Horkheimer and Adorno, she writes: "Der wissenschaftlich und technisch hochgezüchtete Kannibalismus der Gegenwart erlaubt absolute Perfektion: Vernichtung der Artgenossen plus Selbstvernichtung. Fortschritt und Kultur haben also den Menschen nicht von seinem kannibalischen Kern weggeführt, sondern auf den zu."[2] Relating the catastrophic state of society and the lack of significant emancipation, she further illuminates the importance of integrating into the public realm those values that women have been socialized to develop in the private sphere, that part of themselves "unused" in patriarchal society. In *Amanda*, she asserts:

Die Fähigkeit zu hegen, eine beiden Menschenarten von Natur mehr oder weniger gegebene Eigenschaft, hat die herrschende Spezialisten-

kultur seit einigen Jahrtausenden allein bei Frauen hochentwickelt [...].
Hegen als Weiberressort für private Zwecke. Plötzlich ist der historische Punkt erreicht, das diese Fähigkeit bei Strafe des Untergangs
für die größten öffentlichen Zwecken unentbehrlich wird. Alleinherr-
schendes Eroberungsdenken in Gesellschaft, Wissenschaft und Technik
haben die Erde an Abgründe geworfen. Eroberungsdenken von
Männern—eine Kulturzüchtung, nicht Männernatur .... Nur wenn die
andere Hälfte der Menschheit, die Frauen, bestimmte, bisher nur für
private Zwecke entwickelte Fähigkeiten und Tugenden in die große
Politik einbringen, können atomare und ökologische Katastrophen
abgewendet werden. (306)

Stressing the utopian potential of the values preserved by the marginalized half
of humanity, Morgner, like those writers discussed here, compels her readers to
reflect on society's course and ultimately to consider how it can be diverted.

This study highlights how the feminist critique of science in East German
literature is at once directed at the GDR and situated within a broader critique
that suggests symmetries between capitalist and communist ideologies of
progress. With the demise of socialism and the consequent reassessment of the
role of writers and intellectuals, Western critics have been quick to revise the
prevailing image of Christa Wolf as a critical writer by pointing to the extent to
which her critique of progress targeted the West. In their view, Wolf's
indictment of the West ultimately exculpated the GDR, a country in which
modernization occurred less rapidly than in the West, and thus allowed those
"feminine" values Wolf advocates to flourish more readily. A close reading of
Wolf's GDR works reveals, however, that she fails to construct simple oppositions between ideologies or between genders, but rather advocates a "third way,"
an alternative beyond socialism or capitalism.

A brief look at the theme of women, science and progress in select post-
Wall texts by Wolf (*Medea. Stimmen*, 1996), Königsdorf (*Die unverzügliche
Rettung der Welt*, 1994) and Maron (*Animal triste*, 1996) substantiates this
reading. In an interview held in 1996, Wolf remarked that her interest in the
mythic figure of Medea, like her interest in Cassandra, was motivated by her
search for the roots of Western civilization's self-destructiveness.[3] Attributing a
positional perspective to GDR citizens, Wolf expresses her continued focus on
the detriments of Western notions and manifestations of progress:

Der Zusammenbruch der DDR und des ganzen 'realsozialistischen'
Systems ist auch Ausdruck einer Krise der industriellen Zivilisation
überhaupt. Die Grenzen des Wachstums sind nun nicht mehr zu
leugnen, und mir scheint, Leute im Osten sehen die Schwachstellen des
Systems, mit dem sie konfrontiert sind, deutlicher als viele im Westen.

In her feminist revision of the Medea-myth, Wolf gives this thesis literary form. As in her *Kassandra* narrative, she rewrites the ancient myth to highlight the dialectic of enlightenment, suggesting alternatives to patriarchy and to the split between reason and emotion that informs Western civilization.

Königsdorf again sounds a critique of progress in her 1994 essay collection, *Die unverzügliche Rettung der Welt* (1994).[4] As in her previous works, she presents a somber assessment of the state of humankind, drawing attention to the growing division between rich and poor, to world hunger and to the deplorable exploitation of nature. Given this apocalyptic vision, she stresses the need to recognize immediate dangers and threats, to assume personal responsibility and collectively to mobilize humanity to create a livable future. She thus echoes the "mission" taken on by the narrator of *Respektloser Umgang*. In contrast to her pre-*Wende* narratives, which indict socialism and capitalism, *Über die unverzügliche Rettung der Welt* frames the negative consequences of scientific-technological progress, instrumental reason and individualism within a bitter critique of capitalism whose deficits became more glaring and bitterly felt after socialism's collapse. For example, in the essay entitled "Lieben Sie Schmetterlinge," she defines the next generation's heritage as "Disneyland und Giftmüll."[5] In "Laßt uns eine Pyramide bauen" she focuses on the relation of capital and politics and, while she admits to real existing socialism's unviability and to her initial belief in capitalism, she ultimately weighs the touted advantages of socialism—no unemployment, no homelessness, no bankruptcy—over the "free play of power," where power is equated with money and the few who have it. The materialism and lack of humanistic values Königsdorf sees in post-*Wende* Germany engender little faith in Western democratic institutions and leave her in search of viable alternatives.

Asked in 1987 about the GDR-specificity of the social critique she voices in the *Überläuferin*, Maron responded that the predicament of her female protagonist was not restricted to the GDR society. She asserted: "Ich gehe eher von Grenzen aus, die innerhalb unserer Zivilisation liegen [...]. Im Westen sind die Mechanismen gewiß anders, aber sie würden mich auf ähnliche Weise belasten."[6] Maron's novel *Animale triste* (1996) reflects this assertion.[7] In GDR times, Maron's female protagonist, like her predecessors in *Flugasche* and *Animale triste*, dreamed of freedom. Yet unification fails to fulfill this dream. *Animale triste* traces the continuity of gender hierarchies and of the female subject's containment. Maron continues to cast her female subjects within a patriarchal social reality that inscribes its subjects as gendered, shedding light on the interchange of sexual difference and a system of power and domination whose imprint remains even after the most palpable embodiment of that power, the GDR state, has ceased to exist.

In the early post-Wall works of Wolf, Königsdorf and Maron, then, the gendered critique of progress persists. Despite the significant social and cultural changes of unification, these writers continue to articulate a feminist dialectic of enlightenment predicated on fundamental social change. Progress, its seems, remains an illusion.

Notes

1 For a recent study that investigates Morgner's critique of progress within the context of her use of fantastic narrative forms, see Alison Lewis, *Subverting Patriarchy: Feminism and Fantasy in the Works of Irmtraud Morgner* (Oxford: Berg, 1995). See also Patricia Herminghouse's discussion of Morgner in "Phantasie oder Fanatismus? Zur feministischen Wissenschaftskritik in der Literatur der DDR," *Zwischen gestern und morgen: Schriftstellerinnen der DDR aus amerikanischer Sicht*, ed. Ute Brandes (Berlin: Peter Lang, 1992) 69–94.

2 Irmtraud Morgner, *Amanda. Ein Hexenroman* (Darmstadt/Neuwied: Luchterhand, 1984) 305.

3 She states: "Aber mich hat dann immer stärker interessiert, was auch bei Kasssandra ein Movens gewesen ist: die Frage nach den destruktiven Wurzeln unserer Zivilisation …." See the interview "Sind Sie noch eine Leitfigur, Frau Wolf? Christa Wolf über Medea, Sündenbocke, Zerstörungslust, Wahrnehmungsblockaden, die Krise unserer Zivilisation," *Der Tagesspiegel* 29 April 1996.

4 I develop the ideas presented here in greater detail in my review of this work in *GDR Bulletin* 23 (1996): 24–25.

5 Helga Königsdorf, *Über die unverzügliche Rettung der Welt. Essays* (Berlin: Aufbau, 1994) 9.

6 Wilfrid Schoeller, "Literatur, das nicht gelebte Leben. Gespräch mit der Ostberliner Schriftstellerin Monika Maron," *Süddeutsche Zeitung* 6 March 1987.

7 I compare *Animale triste* with *Flugasche* and *Die Überläuferin* in "The Status of State and Subject: Reading Monika Maron from *Flugasche* to *Animal Triste*." *Wendezeiten/Zeitenwenden. Posistionsbestimmungen zur deutschsprachigen Literatur 1945–1995*. Weninger, Robert and Brigitte Rossbacher, ed. (Tübingen: Stauffenburg, 1997) 193–214.

WORKS CITED

Abicht, Ludo. "Review of *Unter den Linden*." *New German Critique* 6 (1975): 164–169.

Adelson, Leslie A. *Making Bodies, Making History: Feminism & German Identity*. Lincoln and London: University of Nebraska Press, 1993.

Adorno, Theodor and Max W. Horkheimer. *Dialektik der Aufklärung*. Frankfurt a. M.: Fischer, 1988 (1969).

Alcoff, Linda. "Cultural Feminism versus Post-Structuralism: The Identity Crisis in Feminist Theory." *Signs* (Spring 1988): 405–436.

Allert, Dietrich and Hubert Wetzelt. "Die große Liebe." *"Der geteilte Himmel" und seine Kritiker; Dokumentation mit einem Nachwort des Herausgebers*. Ed. Martin Reso. Halle: Mitteldeutscher Verlag, 1965. 78–85.

Anderson, Susan C. "Creativity and Non-Conformity in Monika Maron's *Die Überläuferin*." *Women in German Yearbook* 10 (1995): 152.

Anz, Thomas. *Es geht nicht um Christa Wolf. Der Literaturstreit im vereinten Deutschland*. Erweiterte Neuausgabe. Ed. Thomas Anz. Frankfurt a. M: Fischer, 1995.

Auer, Alfons. "Darf der Mensch, was er kann?" *Wissenschaft, Technik, Humanität: Beiträge zu einer konkreten Ethik*. Ed. Alois Buch and Jörg Splett. Frankfurt a. M.: Verlag Josef Knecht, 1982. 11–35.

Auer, Anne Marie et al. "'Respektloser Umgang' von Helga Königsdorf. Für und Wider." *Weimarer Beiträge* 33.8 (1987): 1338–1357.

Bahr, Gisela. "Blitz aus heiterm Himmel. Ein Versuch zur Emanzipation in der DDR." *Die Frau als Heldin und Autorin. 10. Amsterdamer Kolloquium*. Ed. Wolfgang Paulsen. Bern: Franke, 1979. 223–236.

Bammer, Angelika. "Trobadora in Amerika." *Irmtraud Morgner. Texten, Daten, Bilder*. Ed. Marlis Gerhardt. Frankfurt a. M.: Luchterhand, 1990. 196–211.

Barr, Marleen and Nicolas Smith, *Women and Utopia*. Lanham: University Press of America, 1983.

Bathrick, David. *The Powers of Speech. The Politics of Culture in the GDR*. Lincoln and London: University of Nebraska Press, 1995.

———. "Productive Mis-reading: GDR Literature in the USA." *GDR Bulletin* 16.2 (Fall 1990): 1–6.

Begley, Sharon et al. "A Crisis of Conscience. Objections to Star Wars." *Newsweek* 22 September 1986. 88.

Behn, Manfred. "Einleitung." *Wirkungsgeschichte von Christa Wolfs "Nachdenken über Christa T."* Ed. Manfred Behn. Königstein/Ts.: Athenäum, 1978. 1–24.

Benjamin, Walter. "Über den Begriff der Geschichte." *Gesammelte Schriften*. Vol. I.2. Ed. R. Tiedemann and H. Schweppenhauser. Frankfurt a. M.:

Suhrkamp, 1980. 693–703.

Berger, Doris. "Vom schwierigen sprachlichen Umgang mit der Katastrophe. Texte von DDR-Autoren gegen die atomare Bedrohung." *Die Literatur der DDR. 1976–1986. Akten der internationalen Konferenz. Pisa. Mai 1987.* Ed. Anna Chiarloni, Gemma Sartori and Fabrizio Cambi. Pisa: Giardini, 1988. 177–186.

Beyer, Wilhelm Raimund. *Die Sünden der Frankfurter Schule.* Frankfurt a. M.: Verlag Marxistische Blätter, 1971.

Biermann, Wolf. "Verlogene Treue." *Der Spiegel* 43 (23. October 1995): 39–44.

Bilke, Jörg Bernhard. "Der erste Umwelt-Roman aus Ost-Berlin: Monika Marons *Flugasche.* Wo die Bronchien schmerzen." *Die Welt* 24. March 1981. 17.

"Bleibt die Avantgarde zurück?" *Der Spiegel* 49 (4. December 1989): 230–233.

Bloch, Ernst. "Abschied von der Utopie?" *Abschied von der Utopie.* Ed. Hanna Gekle. Frankfurt a. M.: Suhrkamp, 1980. 76–82.

———. *Das Prinzip Hoffnung.* Frankfurt a. M.: Suhrkamp, 1959.

———. "Topos utopia." *Abschied von der Utopie.* Ed. Hanna Gekle. Frankfurt a. M.: Suhrkamp, 1980. 43–64.

———. *Tübinger Einleitung in die Philosophie.* Frankfurt a. M.: Suhrkamp, 1970.

Boa, Elizabeth. "Schwierigkeiten mit der ersten Person: Ingeborg Bachmanns *Malina* und Monika Marons *Flugasche, Die Überläuferin* und *Stille Zeile Sechs.*" *Kritische Wege der Landnahme. Ingeborg Bachmann im Blickfeld der neunziger Jahre. Londoner Symposium 1993 zum 20. Todestag der Dichterin (17.10.1973).* Sonderpublikation der Grillparzergesellschaft. Vol. 2. Ed. Robert Pichl and Alexander Stillmark (Wien: Hora Verlag, 1994) 125–145.

Bock, Sigrid et al. "Für und Wider: 'Kassandra' von Christa Wolf." *Weimarer Beiträge* 30:8 (1984): 1353–1381.

Bovenschen, Silvia. "Über die Frage: gibt es eine weibliche Ästhetik?" *Ästhetik und Kommunikation* 25 (1976): 60–75.

Bressau, Fritz. "Eröffnung der Konferenz." *Greif zur Feder Kumpel. Protokoll der Autorenkonfenz des Mitteldeutschen Verlages Halle (Saale) am 24. April 1959 im Kulturpalast des elektrochemischen Kombinats Bitterfeld.* Halle: Mitteldeutscher Verlag, 1959.

Buhr, M. and G. Kröber. *Mensch—Wissenschaft—Technik. Versuch einer marxistischen Analyse der wissenschaflich-technischen Revolution.* Köln: Pahl-Rugenstein, 1977.

Chodorow, Nancy. *The Reproduction of Mothering. Psychoanalysis and the Sociology of Gender.* Berkeley: University of California Press, 1978.

Cixous, Hélène. "Sorties." *New French Feminisms. An Anthology.* Ed. Elaine

Marks and Isabelle de Courtivron. New York: Schocken, 1981. 90–98.

———. "The Laugh of the Medusa." *New French Feminisms. An Anthology.* Ed. Elaine Marks and Isabelle de Courtivron. New York: Schocken, 1981. 245–264.

Clausen, Jeanette. "Resisting Objectification: Helga Königsdorf's Lise Meitner." *Studies in GDR Culture and Society 10.* Ed. Margy Gerber et al. Lanham: University Press of America, 1991. 165–180.

Corino, Karl. "Die verfolgende Unschuld. Der Fall Maron alias Mitsu." *Neue Zürcher Zeitung* 19 October 1995.

Dahnke, Hans Dietrich. "Literarische Prozesse in der Periode von 1789 bis 1806." *Weimarer Beiträge* 1 (1971): 46–71.

———. "Zur Stellung und Leistung der deutschen romantischen Literatur." *Weimarer Beiträge* 4 (1978): 5–19.

Damm, Sigrid and Jürgen Engler, "Notate des Zwiespalts und Allegorien der Vollendung." *Weimarer Beiträge* 7 (1975): 37–69.

De Bruyn, Günter. "Jubelschreie, Trauergesänge." *Die Zeit* 14 September 1990.

De Lauretis, Teresa. "Feminist Studies/Critical Studies: Issues, Terms, Contexts." *Feminist Studies/Critical Studies.* Ed. Teresa de Lauretis. Bloomington: Indiana University Press, 1986. 1–19.

De Lauretis, Teresa, Andreas Huyssen and Kathleen M. Woodward, ed. *The Technological Imagination.* Milwaukee/Madison: Univeristy of Wisconsin Press, 1980.

Derning, C. D., ed. *Marxism, Communism and Western Society. A Comparative Encyclopedia.* New York: Herder & Herder, 1972.

Dietz, Karl and Hannes Krauss, ed. *Der deutsch-deutsche Literaturstreit oder "Freund, es spricht sich leicht mit gebundener Zunge."* Frankfurt a. M.: Luchterhand, 1991.

Dölling, Irene. "Alte und neue Dilemmata: Frauen in der ehemaligen DDR." *Women in German Yearbook* 7 (1991): 121–136.

Drescher, Angela, ed. *Dokumentation zu Christa Wolfs "Nachdenken über Christa T."* Hamburg: Luchterhand, 1991.

Emmerich, Wolfgang. "'Dialektik der Aufklärung' in der jüngeren DDR-Literatur." *Die Literatur der DDR. 1976–1986. Akten der internationalen Konferenz. Pisa. Mai 1987.* Ed. Anna Chiarloni, Gemma Sartori and Fabrizio Cambi. Pisa: Giardini, 1988. 407–422.

———. *Kleine Literaturgeschichte der DDR.* Frankfurt a. M.: Luchterhand, 1989.

Engelmann, Bernt. et al. *Es geht, es geht.* München: Goldmann, 1982.

Engelmann, Gebhard et al. "Zuschriften an Wilhelm Girnus." *Sinn und Form* 34.5 (1983): 1087–1105.

Engler, Jürgen. "Herrschaft der Analogie." *Kritik 79. Rezensionen zur DDR-Literatur.* Ed. Eberhard Günter et al. Halle/Leipzig: Mitteldeutscher Verlag,

1980. 227–234.

Federico, Joseph. *Confronting Modernity. Rationality, Science, and Communication in German Literature of the 1980s.* Columbia, S.C.: Camden House, 1992.

Fehervary, Helen. "Prometheus Rebound: Technology and the Dialectic of Myth." *The Technological Imagination.* Ed. Teresa de Lauretis, Andreas Huyssen and Kathleen M. Woodward. Milwaukee/Madison: University of Wisconsin Press, 1980. 95–105.

Fehervary, Helen and Sara Lennox. "Introduction to translation of 'Selbstversuch.'" *New German Critique* 13 (1978): 109–112.

Felski, Rita. *Beyond Feminist Aesthetics. Feminist Literature and Social Change.* Cambridge: Harvard University Press, 1989.

Fest, Joachim. *Der zerstörte Traum. Vom Ende des utopischen Zeitalters.* Berlin: Corso bei Siedler, 1991.

Feyl, Renate. *Der lautlose Aufbruch. Frauen in der Wissenschaft.* Berlin: Neues Leben, 1981.

Flax, Jane. "Postmodernism in Gender Relations and Feminist Theory." *Feminism/Postmodernism.* Ed. Linda Nicholson. New York: Routedge, 1990.

———. *Thinking Fragments. Psychoanalysis, Feminism, and Postmodernism in the Contemporary West.* Berkeley/Los Angeles: University of California Press, 1990.

Fox Keller, Evelyn. "Gender and Science." *Sex and Scientific Inquiry. Sex and Scientific Inquiry.* Ed. Sandra Harding and Jean F. O'Barr. Chicago: University of Chicago Press, 1987. 233–246.

Förtsch, Eckart. "Fragen menschheitsgeschichtlichen Ausmaßes. Wissenschaft, Technik, Umwelt." *Die DDR Gesellschaft im Spiegel ihrer Literatur.* Ed. Gisela Helwig. Köln: Verlag Wissenschaft und Politik, 1986. 85–112.

Frank, Helmar. *Kybernetik und Philosophie.* Berlin: Dunker & Humblot, 1969.

Fries, Marilyn Sibley, ed. *Response to Christa Wolf. Critical Essays.* Detroit: Wayne State University Press, 1989.

Frisch, Otto Robert. "Lise Meitner." *Biographical Memoirs of the Fellows of the Royal Society* 16 (1970): 405–416.

Gedö, Andras. "Dialektik der Negation oder Negation der Dialekik." *Die "Frankfurter Schule" im Lichte des Marxismus.* Ed. Heinrich von Heiseler et al. Frankfurt a. M.: Verlag Marxistische Blätter, 1974. 7–25.

Gerber, Margy. "Impertinence, Productive Fear and Hope: The Writings of Helga Königsdorf." *Socialism and the Literary Imagination. Essays on East German Writers.* Ed. Martin Kane. Oxford: Berg, 1991. 179–194.

Gerlach, Walter. *Otto Hahn. Ein Forscherleben unserer Zeit.* Ed. and Rev. Dieter Hahn. Stuttgart: Wissenschaftliche Verlagsanstalt, 1984.

Girnus, Wilhelm. "Anläßlich Ritso. Ein Briefwechsel zwischen Günter Kunert und Wilhelm Girnus. *Sinn und Form* 31.4 (1979): 850–864.

———. "Noch einmal zu Christa Wolf." *Sinn und Form* 34.5 (1983): 1096–1105.

———. "Wer baute das siebentorige Theben? Kritische Bemerkungen zu Christa Wolfs Beitrag in *Sinn und Form* 1/83." *Sinn und Form* 34.2 (1983): 439–447.

Gnüg, Hiltrud. "Gibt es eine weibliche Ästhetik?" *Kürbiskern* 1 (1978): 131–140.

Grant, Colin B. "Öffentlichkeit—Diskurs—Kommunikation. Ein Interview mit Robert Weimann." *Weimarer Beiträge* 37.8 (1991) 1154. 1153–1162.

Graves, Peter J. "Christa Wolf's *Kassandra*: The Censoring of the GDR Edition." *Modern Language Review* 81.4 (1986): 944–956.

Gray, Richard. "The Dialectic of Enlightenment in Büchners *Woyzeck*." *German Quarterly* 61.1 (1988): 78–96.

Greiner, Ulrich. "Mangel an Feingefühl. Eine *ZEIT*kontroverse über Christa Wolf und ihre neue Erzählung." *Die Zeit* 1 June 1990.

Haase, Horst. "Nachdenken über ein Buch." *neue deutsche literatur* 4 (1969): 174–185.

Habermas, Jürgen. *Der philosophische Diskurs der Moderne. Zwölf Vorlesungen*. Frankfurt a. M.: Suhrkamp, 1986.

———. "Die Verschlingung von Mythos und Aufklärung. Bemerkungen zur *Dialektik der Aufklärung*—nach einer erneuten Lektüre." *Mythos und Moderne: Begriff und Bild einer Rekonstruktion*. Ed. Karl Heinz Bohrer. Frankfurt a. M.: Suhrkamp, 1983. 405–431.

Hager, Kurt. "Der X. Parteitag und die Kultur." *Sinn und Form* 33.3 (1981): 941–954.

Hahn, Otto. *Otto Hahn: A Scientific Autobiography*. Trans. and Ed. Willy Ley. New York: Charles Scribner's Sons, 1966.

———. *Otto Hahn: My Life. The Autobiography of a Scientist*. Trans. Ernst Kaiser and Eithne Wilkens. New York: Herder & Herder, 1970.

Hammer, Klaus. "Mobilisierung der Humanität. Helga Königsdorfs *Respektloser Umgang*." *neue deutsche literatur* 35.8 (1987): 138–142.

Hammerstein, Katarina von. "Warum nicht Christian T.? Christa Wolf zur Frauenfrage, untersucht an einem frühen Beispiel: *Nachdenken über Christa T.*" *New German Review* 1 (1985): 17–29.

Hanke, Irma. "Vom neuen Menschen zur sozialistischen Persönlichkeit. Zum Menschenbild der SED." *Deutschland Archiv* 9.5 (1976): 492–515.

Harding, Sandra. "The Instabililty of the Analytical Categories of Feminist Theory." *Sex and Scientific Inquiry*. Ed. Sandra Harding and Jean F. O'Barr. Chicago: University of Chicago Press, 1987. 283–302.

———. *The Science Question in Feminism*. Ithica: Cornell University Press, 1986.

————. *Whose Science? Whose Knowledge? Thinking from Women's Lives*. Ithaca: Cornell University Press, 1991.

Hartsock, Nancy. "The Feminist Standpoint: Developing the Ground for a Specifically Feminist Historical Materialism." *Discovering Reality*. Ed. Sandra Harding and Merrill B. Hintikka. Dordrecht, Holland: D. Reidel Publishing Co., 1983. 283–310.

Hein, Christoph, "Die Vernunft der Straße." *TAZ: DDR Journal zur Novemberrevolution* (1990): 73.

————. "Die Zensur ist überlebt, nutzlos, paradox, menschenfeindlich, volksfeindlich, ungesetzlich und strafbar." *Als Kind habe ich Stalin gesehen*. Berlin/Weimar: Aufbau, 1990. 77–104.

Heiseler, Heinrich et al. *Die "Frankfurter Schule" im Lichte des Marxismus*. Frankfurt a. M.: Verlag Marxistische Blätter, 1974.

Heisenberg, Werner. *Physics and Philosophy. The Revolution in Modern Science*. New York: Harper & Brothers Publishers, 1958.

Hermann, Armin. *The New Physics. The Route into the Atomic Age*. Munich: Heinz Moos, 1979.

Herminghouse, Patricia. "Die Wiederentdeckung der Romantik: Zur Funktion der Dicherfiguren in der neuren DDR-Literatur." *Amsterdamer Beiträge zur neueren Germanistik 11/12*. Ed. Jos Hoogeeven and Gerd Labroisse. Amsterdam: Rodopi, 1981. 217–248.

————. "Phantasie oder Fanatismus? Zur feministischen Wissenschaftskritik in der Literatur der DDR." *Zwischen gestern und morgen: Schriftstellerin der DDR aus amerikanischer Sicht*. Ed. Ute Brandes. Berlin: Peter Lang, 1992.

Herzinger, Richard and Heinz-Peter Preußer. "Vom Äußersten zum Ersten. DDR Literatur in der Tradition deutscher Zivilisationskritik." *Text und Kritik. Literatur in der DDR. Rückblicke*. München: text + kritik, 1991. 195–209.

Heuser, Magdalene. "Literatur von Frauen/Frauen in der Literatur." *Feminismus. Inspektion der Herrenkultur*. Ed. Luise Pusch. Frankfurt a. M.: Suhrkamp, 1983. 117–148.

Hewitt, Andrew . "A Feminine Dialectic of Enlightenment? Horkheimer and Adorno Revisited." *New German Critique* 56 (Spring 1992): 143–170.

Heym, Stefan. "Nach den Jahren der Dumpfheit." *TAZ. Journal zur Novemberrevolution* (1990): 74.

Hilzinger, Sonja. *"Als ganzer Mensch zu leben..." Emanzipatorische Tendenzen in der neueren Frauen-Literatur der DDR*. Frankfurt a. M.: Peter Lang, 1985.

————. *Christa Wolf*. Stuttgart: Metzler, 1986.

Hohendahl, Peter Uwe and Patricia Herminghouse, ed. *Literatur der DDR in den siebziger Jahren*. Frankfurt a. M.: Suhrkamp, 1983.

Höpke, Klaus. "Sicht auf Swantow—Überzeugendes und Bezweifelbares." *Sinn und Form* 36.1 (1984): 165–177.

Horkheimer, Max, *The Critique of Instrumental Reason*. Trans. Mathhew J. O'Connell et al. New York: Seabury, 1974. 51–62.

———. *Kritische Theorie*. 2 Vols. Ed. Alfred Schmidt. Frankfurt a. M.: Fischer, 1968.

Hörnigk, Therese. *Christa Wolf*. Göttingen: Steidel, 1989.

Huffzky, Karin. "'Irmtraud Morgner. Produktivkraft Sexualität souverän nutzen.' Ein Gespräch mit der DDR-Schriftstellerin." *Grundlagentexte zur Emanzipation der Frau*. Ed. Jutta Menschnik. 3rd ed. Köln: Pahl-Rugenstein, 1980. 328–335.

Hutcheon, Linda. *A Poetics of Postmodernism. History, Theory, Fiction*. London: Routledge, 1988.

Huyssen, Andreas. "After the Wall: The Failure of German Intellectuals." *New German Critique* 52 (Winter 1991): 109–143.

———. "Auf den Spuren Ernst Blochs. Nachdenken über Christa Wolf." *Basis: Jahrbuch für Literatur* 5 (1975): 100–116.

"Ist der Sozialismus am Ende?" *Die Zeit* 19. January 1990.

Jameson, Fredric. "Progress vs. Utopia; or, Can We Imagine the Future?" *Art after Modernism. Rethinking Representation*. Ed. Brian Wallis. New York: The New Museum of Contemporary Art, 1984. 239–252.

Jarmatz, Klaus et al. "40 Jahre DDR Literatur. Rundtischgespräch." *Weimarer Beiträge* 35.9 (1989): 1452–1484.

Jay, Martin. *The Dialectical Imagination*. Oxford: Little, Brown and Co., 1973.

Jens, Tilman. "Sand im Getriebe zweier Kulturen. M. Marons *Flugasche*—eine deutsch-deutsche Geschichte." *Deutsches Allgemeines Sonntagsblatt* 22. March 1981.

Jopke, Walter. "Grundlagen der Erkenntnis- und Gesellschaftstheorie Adornos und Horkheimers." *Die "Frankfurter Schule" im Lichte des Marxismus*. Ed. Heinrich von Heiseler et al. Frankfurt a. M.: Verlag Marxistische Blätter, 1974. 48–69.

Joppke, Christian. *Dissidents and the Revolution of 1989. Social Movement in a Leninist Regime*. New York: New York University Press, 1995.

Kane, Martin. "Culpabilities of the Imagination: The Novels of Monika Maron." *Literature on the Threshhold. The German Novel in the 1980s*. Ed. Arthur Williams, Stuart Parkes and Roland Smith. Oxford: Berg, 1990. 221–234.

Kant, Immanuel. "Beantwortung der Frage: Was ist Aufklärung?" *Was ist Aufkärung? Thesen und Definitionen*. Ed. Ehrhard Bahr. Stuttgart: Reclam, 1986. 8–17.

Kaufmann, Eva. "Haltung annehmen. Zu Helga Königsdorfs Erzählung *Respektloser Umgang*." *DDR Literatur '86 im Gespräch*. Ed. Siegfried Rönisch. Berlin/Weimar: Aufbau, 1987. 278–287.

———. "Irmtraud Morgner, Christa Wolf und andere. Feminismus in der DDR."

Text und Kritik. Literatur in der DDR. Rückblicke. München: text + kritik, 1991. 109–116.

———. "Neue Prosabücher von Frauen." *Die Literatur der DDR. 1976–1986. Akten der internationalen Konferenz. Pisa. Mai 1987.* Ed. Anna Chiarloni, Gemma Sartori and Fabrizio Cambi. Pisa: Giardini, 1988. 277–285.

———. "Spielarten des Komischen. Zur Schreibweise von Helga Königsdorf." *"Wen kümmert's, wer spricht": zur Literatur und Kulturgeschichte von Frauen aus Ost und West.* Ed. Inge Stefan. Köln: Böhlau, 1991. 177–184.

King, Ynestra. "Healing the Wounds: Feminism, Ecology, and the Nature/Culture Dualism." *Reweaving the world: the emergence of ecofeminism.* Ed. Irene Diamond and Gloria Feman Orenstein. San Francisco: Sierra Club Press, 1990. 106–121.

Klötzer, Silvia. "Patterns of Self-Destruction: Christa Wolf's *What Remains* and Monika Maron's *Flight of Ashes.*" *Other Germanies: Questioning Identity in Women's Literature and Art.* Ed. Karen Jankowsky and Carla Love. Albany: SUNY Press, 1997. 248–267.

———. "Perspektivenweschsel: Ich Verlust bei Monika Maron." *Zwischen gestern und morgen: Schriftstellerin der DDR aus amerikanischer Sicht.* Ed. Ute Brandes. Berlin: Peter Lang, 1992. 249–262.

Knabe, Hubertus. "'Der Mensch mordet sich selbst.' Ökologiekritik in der erzählenden DDR-Literatur." *Deutschland Archiv* 16 (1983): 954–973.

Königsdorf, Helga. "Diskussion nach der Lesung von Helga Königsdorf." *Die Literatur der DDR. 1976–1986. Akten der internationalen Konferenz. Pisa. Mai 1987.* Ed. Anna Chiarloni, Gemma Sartori and Fabrizio Cambi. Pisa: Giardini, 1988. 449–455.

———. *Ein sehr exakter Schein. Satiren und Geschichten aus dem Gebiet der Wissenschaften.* Frankfurt a. M.: Luchterhand, 1990.

———. *Der Lauf der Dinge.* Berlin/Weimar: Aufbau, 1982.

———. *Meine ungehörigen Träume.* Berlin/Weimar: Aufbau, 1990.

———. "Das Prinzip Menschenwürde. Thesen für einen Vortrag." *neue deutsche Literatur* 37.10 (1989): 5–10.

———. "Rede auf dem Meeting von Mitgliedern der SED vor dem Haus des ZK." *neue deutsche literatur* 38.3 (1990): 181–182.

———. "Rede auf dem X. Schriftstellerkongreß der DDR." *neue deutsche literatur* 36.3 (1988): 57–59.

———. *Respektoser Umgang.* Frankfurt a. M.: Luchterhand, 1988. First published Berlin: Aufbau, 1986.

———. "Der Schmerz über das eigene Versagen." *Die Zeit* 1 June 1990.

———. "Schreib-Auskunft: Helga Königsdorf." *neue deutsche literatur* 27.4 (1979): 9–12.

———. *Über die unverzügliche Rettung der Welt.* Berlin: Aufbau, 1994.

———. *Ungelegener Befund.* Frankfurt a. M.: Luchterhand, 1990. First published Berlin: Aufbau, 1989.

Kosorukow, Alexander. "Auf der Suche nach der Wahrheit. Über Christa Wolfs Erzählung *Störfall*." *Christa Wolf. Ein Arbeitsbuch. Studien—Dokumente— Bibliographie*. Ed. Angela Drescher. Berlin/Weimar: Aufbau, 1989. 292– 308.

Kristeva, Julia. "La femme, ce n'est jamais ca." *Tel Quel* 59 (Autumn 1974): 19–24.

———. "A New Type of Intellectual: The Dissident." *The Kristeva Reader*. Ed. Toril Moi. New York: Columbia University Press, 1986. 292–300.

———. "Julia Kristeva." *New French Feminisms. An Anthology*. Ed. Elaine Marks and Isabelle de Courtivron. New York: Schocken, 1981. 165–167.

Krüger, Ingrid, ed. *Mut zur Angst. Schriftsteller für den Frieden*. Darmstadt/Neuwied: Luchterhand, 1982.

Kuhn, Anna K. *Christa Wolf's Utopian Vision: From Marxism to Feminism*. Cambridge: Cambridge University Press, 1988.

———. "'Zweige vom selben Stamm'? Christa Wolf's *Was bleibt, Kein Ort. Nirgends*, and *Sommerstück*." *Christa Wolf in Perspective* (German Monitor No. 30). Ed. Ian Wallace. Amsterdam: Rodopi, 1994: 187–205.

Kulke, Christine. "Die Kritik der instrumentellen Rationalitäts—ein männlicher Mythos." *Die Aktualität der "Dialektik der Aufklärung*. Ed. Harry Kunneman and Hent de Vries. Frankfurt a. M.: Campus, 1989. 128–149.

Kurella, Alfred. "Begründung der Zuteilung des Heinrich-Mann-Preises Deutsche Akademie der Künste, Sektion Dichtkunst und Sprachpflege." *"Der geteilte Himmel" und seine Kritiker; Dokumentation mit einem Nachwort des Herausgebers*. Ed. Martin Reso. Halle: Mitteldeutscher Verlag, 1965. 26–30.

Kuschel, Karl-Josef. "Die Krise des Homo Faber. Aspekte der Technikkritik und der Verantwortung des Wissenschaftlers in der modernen Literatur." *Wissenschaft, Technik, Humanität: Beiträge zu einer konkreten Ethik*. Ed. Alois Buch and Jörg Splett. Frankfurt a. M.: Verlag Josef Knecht, 1982. 136–174.

Lewis, Alison. *Subverting Patriarchy: Feminism and Fantasy in the Works of Irmtraud Morgner.*Oxford: Berg, 1995.

Lloyd, Genevieve. *The Man of Reason. "Male" & "Female" in Western Philosophy*. 2nd. ed. Minneapolis: University of Minnesota Press, 1993.

Lorenz, Konrad. *On Aggression*. Trans. Marjorie Kerr Wilson. New York: Harcourt, Brace & World Inc., 1966.

Love, Myra N.. "'A Little Susceptible to the Supernatural?': On Christa Wolf." *Women in German Yearbook 7* (1991): 1–23.

———. "Christa Wolf and Feminism: Breaking the Patriarchal Connection." *New German Critique* (31–55).

———. *Christa Wolf: Literature and the Conscience of History*. New York,

Peter Lang, 1991.

———. "'To render the blind spot of this culture visible': Prose Beyond the 'Citadel of Reason.'" *Responses to Christa Wolf. Critical Essays*. Ed. Marilyn Sibley Fries. Detroit: Wayne State University Press, 1989. 186–195.

Luckmann, Thomas. "Constitution of Human Life in Time." *Chronotopes: The Construction of Time*. Ed. John Bender and David E. Wellbery. Stanford: Stanford University Press, 1991. 151–166.

Lunn, Eugene. *Marxism and Modernism*. Berkeley/Los Angeles: University of California Press, 1982.

Marcuse, Herbert. *One-Dimensional Man. Studies in the Ideology of Advanced Industrial Society*. Boston: Beacon Press, 1964.

Marcuse, Herbert, et al. "'Weiblichkeitsbilder.' Gesprächsteilnehmer: Herbert Marcuse, Silvia Bovenschen und Marianne Schuller." *Gespräche mit Herbert Marcuse*. Frankfurt a. M.: Suhrkamp, 1978. 65–90.

Maron, Monika. *Animale triste*. Frankfurt a. M.: Fischer, 1996.

———. *Flugasche*. Frankfurt a. M.: Fischer, 1981.

———. "Heuchelei und Niedertracht." *Frankfurter Allgemeine Zeitung* 14 October 1955.

———. *Nach Maßgabe meiner Begreifungskraft*. Frankfurt a. M.: Fischer, 1988.

———. "Das neue Elend der Intellektuellen." *TAZ . Journal No. 2: Die Wende der Wende* (1990): 96–98.

———. *Pawels Briefe*. Frankfurt a. M.: Fischer, 1999.

———. "Die Schriftsteller und das Volk." *Der Spiegel* 7 (12 February 1990): 68–70.

———. *Die Überläuferin*. Frankfurt a. M.: Fischer, 1986.

———. "'Zum Heulen—alles ist besser als bei uns,'" *Der Tagespiegel* 8 August 1995.

Maron, Monika and Joseph von Westphalen. *Trotzdem herzliche Grüße. Ein deutsch-deutscher Briefwechsel*. Frankfurt a. M.: Fischer, 1988.

McDonald, W.D. "Who's Afraid of Wolf's Cassandra—or Cassandra's Wolf?: Male Tradition and Women's Knowledge in *Cassandra*." *The Journal of Narrative Technique* 23:2 (1990): 267–283.

Meitner, Lise. "Otto Hahn zum 80. Geburtstag." *Naturwissenschaften* 46.5 (1959): 157–158.

Melchert, Rulo. "Erfindungen als Wahrheit." *Sinn und Form* 2 (1975): 439–446.

Merchant, Carol. "Ecofeminism and Feminist Theory." *Reweaving the world: the emergence of ecofeminism*. Ed. Irene Diamond and Gloria Feman Orenstein. San Francisco: Sierra Club Press, 1990. 100–105.

Meyer, Gerd. *Die DDR-Machtelite in der Ära Honecker*. Tübinger Mittel- und Osteuropastudien—Politik, Gesellschaft, Kultur, Vol. 3. Tübingen: Franke, 1991.

Moi, Toril. *Sexual/Textual Politics. Feminist Literary Theory*. London: Routledge, 1988.

Morgner, Irmtraud. *Amanda. Ein Hexenroman*. Darmstadt/Neuwied: Luchterhand, 1984.

Nagelschmidt, Ilse. "Sozialistische Frauenliteratur." *Weimarer Beiträge* 25.3 (1989): 450–471.

Naumann-Beyer, Waltraud. "Empfang einer Flaschenpost." *Sinn und Form* 6 (1989): 1207–1228.

Nägele, Rainer. "Trauer, Tropen und Phantasmen: Ver-rückte Geschichten aus der DDR." *Literatur der DDR in den siebziger Jahren*. Ed. Peter Uwe Hohendahl and Patricia Herminghouse. Frankfurt a. M.: Suhrkamp, 1983. 193–223.

Ortner, Sherry. "Is Female to Male as Nature Is to Culture?" *Woman, Culture & Society*. Ed. Michelle Rosaldo and Louise Lamphere. Stanford: Stanford University Press, 1974. 67–87.

Paul, Georgina. "'Ich meine nichts, was könnte gestrichen werden': Christa Wolf's 'Brief über die Bettine.'" *Christa Wolf in Perspective* (German Monitor 30). Ed. Ian Wallace. Amsterdam: Rodopi, 1994. 25–40.

Peterfreund, Stuart, ed. *Literature and Science*. Boston: Northeastern University Press, 1990.

Pischel, Joseph et al. "'Respektloser Umgang' von Helga Königsdorf. Für und Wider." *Weimarer Beiträge* 33.8 (1987): 1338–1357.

Probst, Lothar. "Die Revolution entläßt ihre Schriftsteller." *Deutschland Archiv* 23.6 (1990): 921–925.

Raimund Beyer, Wilhelm. *Die Sünden der Frankfurter Schule*. Frankfurt a. M.: Verlag Marxistische Blätter, 1971.

Reid, J. H.. *Writing without taboos: the new East German literature*. Oxford: Berg, 1990.

Reso, Martin. *"Der geteilte Himmel" und seine Kritiker; Dokumentation mit einem Nachwort des Herausgebers*. Halle: Mitteldeutscher Verlag, 1965.

Rose, Hilary. "Hand, Brain, and Heart: A Feminist Epistemology for the Natural Sciences." *Sex and Scientific Inquiry*. Ed. Sandra Harding and Jean F. O'Barr. Chicago: University of Chicago Press, 1987. 265–282.

Rossbacher, Brigitte. "Helga Königsdorf: *Über die unverzügliche Rettung der Welt*. Review." *GDR Bulletin* 23 (1996): 24–25.

———. "The Status of State and Subject: Reading Monika Maron from *Flugasche* to *Animal Triste*." *Wendezeiten/Zeitenwenden. Posistionsbestimmungen zur deutschsprachigen Literatur 1945–1995*. Ed. Robert Weninger and Brigitte Rossbacher. Tübingen: Stauffenburg, 1997. 193–214.

Ruddick, Sara. *Maternal Thinking. Toward a Politics of Peace*. Boston: Beacon Press, 1989.

Sagan, Carl. *The Dragons of Eden.* New York: Random House, 1977.

Samlowsky, Carola. "Sperrige Gedankenprosa. Helga Königsdorfs Abrechnung mit dem Antifaschismus." *Tagesspiegel* 11 March 1990.

Sauer, Klaus, ed. *Christa Wolf Materialienbuch.* Darmstadt/Neuwied: Luchterhand, 1979.

Sayre, Robert and Michael Löwy. "Romanticism as a Feminist Vision: The Quest for Christa Wolf." *New German Critique* 64 (Winter 1995): 105–134.

Schenk, Herrad. *Frauen kommen ohne Waffen. Feminismus und Pazifismus.* München: Beck, 1983.

Schenkel, Michael. *Fortschritts- und Modernitätskritik in der DDR-Literatur. Prosatexte der achtziger Jahre.* Tübingen: Stauffenburg Verlag, 1995.

Schiebinger, Londa. "The History and Philosophy of Women in Science: A Review Essay." *Sex and Scientific Inquiry.* Ed. Sandra Harding and Jean F. O'Barr. Chicago: University of Chicago Press, 1987. 7–34.

Schirrmacher, Frank. "'Dem Druck des härteren, strengeren Lebens standhalten'. Auch eine Studie über einen autoritären Charakter: Christa Wolfs Aufsätze, Reden, und ihre jüngste Erzählung *Was bleibt.*" *Frankfurter Allgemeine Zeitung* 2. June 1990.

Schmitt, James and James Miller. "Aspects of Technology in Marx and Rousseau." *The Technological Imagination.* Ed. Teresa De Lauretis, Andreas Huyssen and Kathleen M. Woodward. Milwaukee/Madison: University of Wisconsin Press, 1980. 85–94.

Schmitz-Köster, Dorothee. *Troubadora und Kassandra. Weibliches Schreiben in der DDR.* Köln: Pahl-Rugenstein, 1989.

Schoeller, Wilfried. "Literatur, das nicht gelebte Leben. Gespräch mit der Ostberliner Schriftstellerin Monika Maron." *Süddeutsche Zeitung,* 6. March 1987. 47.

Schregel, Friedrich. *Die Romanliteratur der DDR. Erzähltechniken, Leserlenkung, Kulturpolitik.* Opladen: Westdeutscher Verlag, 1991.

Schulz, Genia. "Kein Chorgesang. Neue Schreibweisen bei Autorinnen (aus) der DDR." *Bestandsaufnahme Gegenwartsliteratur. Text + Kritik Sonderband.* Ed. Heinz Ludwig Arnold. München: edition text + kritik, 1988.

Schultz, Gisela. "Ein überraschender Erstling." *Neue Deutsche Literatur* 9.7 (1961): 129.

Schwarzer, Alice. "Jetzt oder nie! Die Frauen sind die Hälfte des Volkes! Interview with Irmtraud Morgner." *Emma* 2 (1990): 32–38.

Scott, Joan W. "Deconstructing Equality-Versus-Difference: or, The Uses of Poststructuralist Theory for Feminism." *Feminist Studies* 14.1 (Spring 1988): 33–50.

Secci, Lia. "Helga Königsdorf: eine 'ungehörige' Schriftstellerin." *Die Literatur der DDR. 1976–1986. Akten der internationalen Konferenz. Pisa. Mai 1987.* Ed. Anna Chiarloni, Gemma Sartori, Fabrizio Cambi. Pisa: Giardini,

1988. 199–206.

Seghers, Anna. "Der japanishe Fischer." *Das Leben im Atomzeitalter: Schrift-steller und Dichter zum Thema unserer Zeit*. Ed. Walter Jens. Gräfelfing: Moos & Partner, 1987. 164–165.

Shattuck, Roger. *Forbidden Knowledge. From Prometheus to Pornography*. New York: St. Martin's Press, 1996.

"Sind Sie noch eine Leitfigur, Frau Wolf? Christa Wolf über Medea, Sündenbocke, Zerstörungslust, Wahrnehmungsblockaden, die Krise unserer Zivilisation." *Der Tagesspiegel* 29. April 1996.

Snow, C. P. "The Two Cultures and the Scientific Revolution." *Public Affairs*. New York: Charles Scribner's Sons, 1971.

——. "The Two Cultures: A Second Look." *Public Affairs*. New York: Charles Scribner's Sons, 1971.

Sorell, Walter. *The Story of the Human Hand*. Indianapolis: Bobb-Merrill Co., 1967.

"Stasi-Deckname 'Mitsu.'" *Der Spiegel* 32 (7 August 1995): 146–149.

Stephan, Alexander. "Die wissenschaftlich-technische Revolution in der Literatur der DDR." *Der Deutschunterricht* 2 (1978): 17–34.

Tarvis, Carol. *The Mismeasure of Woman*. New York: Simon & Schuster, 1992.

Thürmer-Rohr, Christina. "Einführung—Forschen heißt wühlen." *Mittäterschaft und Entdeckungslust*. Berlin: Orlanda Frauenverlag, 1989. 12–21.

——. *Vagabundinnen. Feministische Essays*. Berlin: Orlanda Frauenverlag, 1987.

Todorov, Tzvetan. *The Fantastic. A Structural Approach to a Literary Genre*. Trans. Richard Howard. Ithaca: Cornell University Press, 1975.

Torpey, John C. *Intellectuals, Socialism, and Dissent. The East German Opposition and its Legacy*. Minneapolis: University of Minnesota Press, 1995.

Träger, Claus. "Ursprünge und Stellung der Romantik." *Weimarer Beiträge* 21.2 (1975): 37–73.

Ueding, Gerd. "Wunschbilder Statt Erkenntnis: Warum die DDR-Revolution ohne Intellektuelle stattfand. Heimatlos im Supermarkt." *Die Welt* 28 July 1990.

Vinke, Hermann, ed. *Akteneinsicht Christa Wolf. Zerrspiegel und Dialog*. Hamburg: Luchterhand, 1993.

Walter, Joachim, ed. *Protokoll eines Tribunals. Die Ausschlüsse aus dem DDR-Schriftstellerverband 1979*. Reinbek bei Hamburg: Rowohlt, 1991.

Weigel, Sigrid. "Overcoming Absence: Contemporary German Women's Literature. Part Two." *New German Critique* 32 (Spring 1985): 3–22.

——. "Der schielende Blick. Thesen zur Geschichte weiblicher Schreib-praxis." *Die Verborgene Frau*. Ed. Sigrid Weigel and Inge Stefan. Berlin: Argument, 1983. 83–137.

————. "Das Schreiben des Mangels als Produktion von Utopie." *Women in German Yearbook 1* (1985): 29–38.

————. *Die Stimme der Medusa*. Reinbek bei Hamburg: Rowolt, 1989.

————. *Topographien der Geschlechter*. *Kulturgeschichtliche Studien zur Literatur*. Reinbek bei Hamburg: Rowolt, 1990.

————. "'Woman Begins Relating to Herself': Contemporary German Women's Literature. Part One." *New German Critique* 31 (Winter 1984): 53–94.

Weimann, Robert. "Kunst und Öffentlichkeit in der sozialistischen Gesellschaft. Zum Stand der Vergesellschaftung künstlerischer Verkehrsformen." *Sinn und Form* 31.2 (1979): 214–243.

Weimann, Robert et al. *Plädoyer für die Verantwortung. Technologie und Humanismus heute. Protokoll zu einer Diskussion*. Leipzig: Mitteldeutscher Verlag, 1988.

Wellmer, Albrecht. *Kritische Gesellschaftstheorie und Positivismus*. Frankfurt a. M.: Suhrkamp, 1969.

Werner, Hans Georg. "Zum Traditionsbezug der Erzählungen in Christa Wolfs 'Unter den Linden.'" *Weimarer Beiträge* 4 (1976): 36–64.

Wilke, Sabine. *Ausgraben und Erinnern. Zur Funktion von Geschichte, Subjekt und geschlechtlicher Identität in den Texten von Christa Wolf*. Würzburg: Königshausen und Neumann, 1993.

————. "Kreuz- und Wendepunkte unserer Zivilisation nach-denken: Christa Wolfs Stellung im Umfeld der zeitgenössischen Mythos-Diskussion." *German Quarterly* 61.2 (1988): 213–228.

Wilpert, Gero von. *Sachwörterbuch der Literatur*. Stuttgart: Kröner, 1969.

Wirth, Günter. "Den Blick zum klaren Horizont gewonnen." *"Der geteilte Himmel" und seine Kritiker; Dokumentation mit einem Nachwort des Herausgebers*. Ed. Martin Reso. Halle: Mitteldeutscher Verlag, 1965. 16–21.

Wittstock, Uwe. *Von der Stalinallee zum Prenzlauer Berg. Wege der DDR-Literatur 1949–1989*. München: Piper, 1989.

Wolf, Christa. *Ansprachen*. Darmstadt: Luchterhand, 1988.

————. *Auf dem Weg nach Tabou. Texte 1990–1994*. Köln: Kiepenheuer & Witsch, 1994.

————. "Befreite Sprache und Gefühlswörter." *TAZ: DDR Journal zur Novemberrevolution* (1990): 75.

————. *Die Dimension des Autors. Essays und Aufsätze, Reden und Gespräche 1959–1985. 2 Vols*. Darmstadt/Neuwied: Luchterhand, 1987.

————. "Documentation Christa Wolf. Ein Gespräch über *Kassandra*." *German Quarterly* 57.1 (1984): 105–115.

————. *Gesammelte Erzählungen*. Darmstadt/Neuwied: Luchterhand, 1980.

————. *Der geteilte Himmel*. Halle: Mitteldeutscher Verlag, 1963.

————. *Im Dialog*. Frankfurt a. M.: Luchterhand, 1990.

————. *Kassandra*. Darmstadt/Neuwied: Luchterhand, 1983.

————. *Kein Ort. Nirgends*. Frankfurt a. M.: Luchterhand, 1981.

————. *Lesen und Schreiben. Neue Sammlung. Essays, Aufsätze, Reden*. Darmstadt/Neuwied: Luchterhand, 1980.

————. *Medea. Stimmen*. Hamburg: Luchterhand, 1996.

————. "... mit der Jugend zu rechnen als mit einem Aktivposten. Gespräch mit Christa Wolf." *Christa Wolf. Ein Arbeitsbuch. Studien—Dokumente—Bibliographie*. Ed. Angela Drescher. Berlin/Weimar: Aufbau, 1989. 7–10.

————. *Moskauer Novelle*. Halle: Mitteldeutscher Verlag, 1961.

————. *Nachdenken über Christa T.*. Darmstadt/Neuwied: Luchterhand, 1969.

————. "Neue Lebensansichten eines Katers." *Gesammelte Erzählungen*. Darmstadt/Neuwied: Luchterhand, 1980. 118–151.

————. "Selbstversuch." *Gesammelte Erzählungen*. Darmstadt/Neuwied: Luchterhand, 1980. 192–226.

————. *Störfall. Nachrichten eines Tages*. Darmstadt/Neuwied: Luchterhand, 1987.

————. "Unter den Linden." *Gesammelte Erzählungen*. Darmstadt/Neuwied: Luchterhand, 1980. 65–117.

————. *Voraussetzungen einer Erzählung. Kassandra*. Darmstadt/Neuwied: Luchterhand, 1983.

————. *Was bleibt*. Frankfurt a. M.: Luchterhand, 1990.

Wolff, Charlotte. *The Human Hand*. New York: Alfred A. Knopf, 1943.

DDR-Studien/East German Studies

Richard Zipser   Karl-Heinz Schoeps
General Editor   *Associate Editor*

DDR-Studien/East German Studies series consists of scholarly monographs, in English or German, on topics in the humanities and social sciences pertaining to the (former) German Democratic Republic. This series is not restricted to literary topics, but—as the title suggests—is intended to focus on East German culture and society in the broadest sense. Original monographs in the following areas are especially welcome: literature, international relations, politics, philosophy, history, religion, education, music and musical life, the theater, art, architecture, and popular culture. Biographical studies of personalities who contributed substantially to the development of East German society and culture are also most welcome. The life, work, and times of important figures in GDR public life—including politicians, philosophers, social scientists, writers, musicians, artists, scientists, etc.—should be presented in context.

For additional information about this series or for the submission of manuscripts, please contact:

Peter Lang Publishing
Acquisitions Department
516 N. Charles Street, 2nd Floor
Baltimore, MD 21201

To order other books in this series, please contact our Customer Service Department:

(800) 770-LANG (within the U.S.)
(212) 647-7706 (outside the U.S.)
(212) 647-7707 FAX

Or browse online by series at:

www.peterlang.com